HIS FAMILY

THE MACMILLAN COMPANY
NEW YORK · BOSTON · CHICAGO · DALLAS
ATLANTA · SAN FRANCISCO

MACMILLAN & CO., LIMITED
LONDON · BOMBAY · CALCUTTA
MELBOURNE

THE MACMILLAN CO. OF CANADA, LTD.
TORONTO

HIS FAMILY

BY

ERNEST POOLE

AUTHOR OF "THE HARBOR"

New York

THE MACMILLAN COMPANY

1917

All rights reserved

To M. A.

HIS FAMILY

HIS FAMILY

CHAPTER I

HE was thinking of the town he had known. Not of
old New York—he had heard of that from old, old men
when he himself had still been young and had smiled at
their garrulity. He was thinking of a *young* New York,
the mighty throbbing city to which he had come long ago
as a lad from the New Hampshire mountains. A place
of turbulent thoroughfares, of shouting drivers, hurrying
crowds, the crack of whips and the clatter of wheels;
an uproarious, thrilling town of enterprise, adventure,
youth; a city of pulsing energies, the center of a boundless
land; a port of commerce with all the world, of stately
ships with snowy sails; a fascinating pleasure town, with
throngs of eager travellers hurrying from the ferry boats
and rolling off in hansom cabs to the huge hotels on Madison Square. A city where American faces were still to
be seen upon all its streets, a cleaner and a kindlier town,
with more courtesy in its life, less of the vulgar scramble.
A city of houses, separate homes, of quiet streets with
rustling trees, with people on the doorsteps upon warm
summer evenings and groups of youngsters singing as they
came trooping by in the dark. A place of music and romance. At the old opera house downtown, on those dazzling evenings when as a boy he had ushered there for the
sake of hearing the music, how the rich joy of being alive,
of being young, of being loved, had shone out of women's
eyes. Shimmering satins, dainty gloves and little jewelled
slippers, shapely arms and shoulders, vivacious move-
ments, nods and smiles, swift glances, ripples, bursts

1

of laughter, an exciting hum of voices. Then silence, sudden darkness—and music, and the curtain. The great wide curtain slowly rising. . . .

But all that had passed away.

Roger Gale was a rugged heavy man not quite sixty years of age. His broad, massive features were already deeply furrowed, and there were two big flecks of white in his close-curling, grayish hair. He lived in a narrow red brick house down on the lower west side of the town, in a neighborhood swiftly changing. His wife was dead. He had no sons, but three grown daughters, of whom the oldest, Edith, had been married many years. Laura and Deborah lived at home, but they were both out this evening. It was Friday, Edith's evening, and as was her habit she had come from her apartment uptown to dine with her father and play chess. In the living room, a cheerful place, with its lamp light and its shadows, its old-fashioned high-back chairs, its sofa, its book cases, its low marble mantel with the gilt mirror overhead, they sat at a small oval table in front of a quiet fire of coals. And through the smoke of his cigar Roger watched his daughter.

Edith had four children, and was soon to have another. A small demure woman of thirty-five, with light soft hair and clear blue eyes and limbs softly rounded, the contour of her features was full with approaching maternity, but there was a decided firmness in the lines about her little mouth. As he watched her now, her father's eyes, deep set and gray and with signs of long years of suffering in them, displayed a grave whimsical wistfulness. For by the way she was playing the game he saw how old she thought him. Her play was slow and absent-minded, and there came long periods when she did not make a move. Then she would recall herself and look up with a little affectionate smile that showed she looked upon him as too heavy with his age to have noticed her small lapses.

He was grimly amused at her attitude, for he did not feel old at all. With that whimsical hint of a smile which had grown to be a part of him, he tried various moves on the board to see how far he could go without interrupting her reveries. He checkmated her, re-lit his cigar and waited until she should notice it. And when she did not notice, gravely he moved back his queen and let the game continue. How many hundreds of games, he thought, Edith must have played with him in the long years when his spirit was dead, for her now to take such chances. Nearly every Friday evening for nearly sixteen years.

Before that, Judith his wife had been here. It was then that the city had been young, for to Roger it had always seemed as though he were just beginning life. Into its joys and sorrows too he had groped his way as most of us do, and had never penetrated deep. But he had meant to, later on. When in his busy city days distractions had arisen, always he had promised himself that sooner or later he would return to this interest or passion, for the world still lay before him with its enthralling interests, its beauties and its pleasures, its tasks and all its puzzles, intricate and baffling, all some day to be explored.

This deep zest in Roger Gale had been bred in his boyhood on a farm up in the New Hampshire mountains. There his family had lived for many generations. And from the old house, the huge shadowy barn and the crude little sawmill down the road; from animals, grown people and still more from other boys, from the meadows and the mountain above with its cliffs and caves and forests of pine, young Roger had discovered, even in those early years, that life was fresh, abundant, new, with countless glad beginnings.

At seventeen he had come to New York. There had followed hard struggles in lean years, but his rugged health had buoyed him up. And there had been genial friendships and dreams and explorations, a search for romance, the strange glory of love, a few furtive ventures that left him dismayed. But though love had seemed sordid at such times it had brought him crude exultations. And if his existence had grown more obscure, it had been somber only in patches, the main picture dazzling still. And still he had been just making starts.

He had ventured into the business world, clerking now at this, now at that, and always looking about him for some big opportunity. It had come and he had seized it, despite the warnings of his friends. What a wild adventure it had been—a bureau of news clippings, a business new and unheard of—but he had been sure that here was growth, he had worked at it day and night, and the business widening fast had revealed long ramifications which went winding and stretching away into every phase of American life. And this life was like a forest, boundless and impenetrable, up-springing, intertwining. How much could *he* ever know of it all?

Then had come his marriage. Judith's family had lived long in New York, but some had died and others had scattered until only she was left. This house had been hers, but she had been poor, so she had leased it to some friends. It was through them he had met her here, and within a few weeks he had fallen in love. He had felt profound disgust for the few wild oats he had sown, and in his swift reaction he had overworshipped the girl, her beauty and her purity, until in a delicate way of her own she had hinted that he was going too far, that she, too, was human and a passionate lover of living, in spite of her low quiet voice and her demure and sober eyes.

And what beginnings for Roger now, what a piling up of intimate joys, surprises, shocks of happiness. There had come disappointments, too, sudden severe little checks from his wife which had brought him occasional questionings. This love had not been quite *all* he had dreamed, this woman not so ardent. He had glimpsed couples here and there that set him to imagining more consuming passions. Here again he had not explored very deep. But he had dismissed regrets like these with only a slight reluctance. For if they had settled down a bit with the coming of their children, their love had grown rich in sympathies and silent understandings, in humorous enjoyment of their funny little daughters' chattering like magpies in the genial old house. And they had looked happily far ahead. What a woman she had been for plans. It had not been all smooth sailing. There had come reverses in business, and at home one baby, a boy, had died. But on they had gone and the years had swept by until he had reached his forties. Absorbed in his growing business and in his thriving family, it had seemed to Roger still as though he were just starting out.

But one day, quite suddenly, the house had become a strange place to him with a strange remote figure in it, his wife. For he had learned that she must die. There had followed terrible weeks. Then Judith had faced their disaster. Little by little she had won back the old intimacy with her husband; and through the slow but inexorable progress of her ailment, again they had come together in long talks and plans for their children. At this same chess-board, in this room, repeatedly she would stop the game and smiling she would look into the future. At one such time she had said to him,

"I wonder if it won't be the same with the children as it has been with us. No matter how long each one of them lives, won't their lives feel to them unfinished like ours, only just beginning? I wonder how far they will go. And then their children will grow up and it will be the same with them. Unfinished lives. Oh, dearie, what children all of us are."

He had put his arm around her then and had held her very tight. And feeling the violent trembling of her husband's fierce revolt, slowly bending back her head and looking up into his eyes she had continued steadily:

"And when you come after me, my dear, oh, how hungry I shall be for all you will tell me. For you will live on in our children's lives."

And she had asked him to promise her that.

But he had not kept his promise. For after Judith's dying he had felt himself terribly alone, with eternity around him, his wife slipping far away. And the universe had grown stark and hard, impersonal, relentless, cold. A storm of doubts had attacked his faith. And though he had resisted long, for his faith in God had been rooted deep in the mountains of New England, in the end it had been wrenched away, and with it he had lost all hope that either for Judith or himself was there any existence beyond the grave. So death had come to Roger's soul. He had been deaf and blind to his children. Nights by the thousand spent alone. Like a gray level road in his memory now was the story of his family.

When had his spirit begun to awaken? He could not tell, it had been so slow. His second daughter, Deborah, who had stayed at home with her father when Laura had gone away to school, had done little things continually to rouse his interest in life. Edith's winsome babies had attracted him when they came to the house. Laura had returned from school, a joyous creature, tall and slender, with snapping black eyes, and had soon made her presence felt. One day in the early afternoon, as he entered the house there had burst on his ears a perfect gale of laughter; and peering through the portières he had seen the dining-room full of young girls, a crew as wild as Laura herself. Hastily he had retreated upstairs. But he had enjoyed such glimpses. He had liked to see her fresh pretty gowns and to have her come in and kiss him good-night.

Then had come a sharp heavy jolt. His business had suffered from long neglect, and suddenly for two anxious weeks he had found himself facing bankruptcy. Edith's husband, a lawyer, had come to his aid and together they had pulled out of the hole. But he had been forced to mortgage the house. And this had brought to a climax all the feelings of guiltiness which had so long been stirring within him over his failure to live up to the promise he had made his wife.

And so Roger had looked at his children.

And at first to his profound surprise he had had it forced upon him that these were three grown women, each equipped with her own peculiar feminine traits and desires, the swift accumulations of lives which had expanded in a city that had reared to the skies in the many years of his long sleep. But very slowly, month by month, he had gained a second impression which seemed to him deeper and more real. To the eye they were grown women all, but inwardly they were children still, each groping for her happiness and each held back as he had been, either by checks within herself or by the gay distractions of the absorbing city. He saw each of his daughters, parts of himself. And he remembered what Judith had said: "You will live on in our children's lives." And he began to get glimmerings of a new immortality, made up of generations, an endless succession of other lives extending into the future.

Some of all this he remembered now, in scattered fragments here and there. Then from somewhere far away a great bell began booming the hour, and it roused him from his revery. He had often heard the bell of late. A calm deep-toned intruder, it had first struck in upon his attention something over two years ago. Vaguely he had wondered about it. Soon he had found it was on the top of a tower a little to the north, one of the highest pinnacles of this tumultuous modern town. But the bell was not tumultuous. And as he listened it seemed to say, "There is still time, but you have not long."

Edith, sitting opposite him, looked up at the sound with a stir of relief. Ten o'clock. It was time to go home.

"I wonder what's keeping Bruce," she said. Bruce was still in his office downtown. As a rule on Friday evenings he came with his wife to supper here, but this week he had some new business on hand. Edith was vague about it. As she tried to explain she knitted her brows and said that Bruce was working too hard. And her father grunted assent.

"Bruce ought to knock off every summer," he said, "for a good solid month, or better two. Can't you bring him up to the mountains this year?" He referred to the old New Hampshire home which he had kept as a summer place. But Edith smiled at the idea.

"Yes, I could bring him," she replied, "and in a week he'd be perfectly crazy to get back to his office again." She compressed her lips. "I know what he needs—and we'll do it some day, in spite of him."

"A suburb, eh," her father said, and his face took on a look of dislike. They had often talked of suburbs.

"Yes," his daughter answered, "I've picked out the very house." He threw at her a glance of impatience. He knew what had started her on this line. Edith's friend, Madge Deering, was living out in Morristown. All very well, he reflected, but her case was not at all the same. He had known Madge pretty well. Although the death of her husband had left her a widow at twenty-nine, with four small daughters to bring up, she had gone on determinedly. Naturally smart and able, Madge was always running to town, keeping up with all her friends and with every new fad and movement there, although she made fun of most of them. Twice she had taken her girls abroad. But Edith was quite different. In a suburb she would draw into her house and never grow another inch. And Bruce, poor devil, would commute and take work home from the office. But Roger couldn't tell her that.

"I'd be sorry to see you do it," he said. "I'd miss you up in the mountains."

"Oh, we'd come up in the summer," she answered. "I wouldn't miss the mountains for worlds!"

Then they talked of summer plans. And soon again Edith's smooth pretty brows were wrinkling absorbedly. It was hard in her planning not to be sure whether her new baby would come in May or early June. It was only the first of April now. While she talked her father watched her. He liked her quiet fearlessness in facing the ordeal ahead. Into the bewildering city he felt her searching anxiously to find good things for her small brood, to make every dollar count, to keep their little bodies strong, to guard their hungry little souls from many things she thought were bad. Of all his daughters, he told himself, she was the one most like his wife.

While she was talking Bruce came in. Of medium height and a wiry build, his quick kindly smile of greeting did not conceal the fine tight lines about his mouth and between his eyes. His small trim moustache was black, but his hair already showed streaks of gray although he was not quite thirty-eight, and as he lit a cigarette his right hand twitched perceptibly.

Bruce Cunningham had married just after he left law school. He had worked in a law office which took receiverships by the score, and through managing bankrupt concerns by slow degrees he had made himself a financial surgeon. He had set up an office of his own and was doing splendidly. But he worked under fearful tension. Bruce had to deal with bankrupts who had barely closed their eyes for weeks, men half out of their minds from the strain, the struggle to keep up their heads in those angry waters of finance which Roger vaguely pictured as a giant whirlpool. Though honest enough in his own affairs, Bruce showed a genial relish for all the tricks of the savage world which was as the breath to his nostrils. And at

times he appeared so wise and keen he made Roger
feel like a child. But again it was Bruce who seemed the
child. He seemed to be so naïve at times, and Edith
had him so under her thumb. Roger liked to hear Bruce's
stories of business, when Edith would let her husband talk.
But this she would not often do, for she said Bruce needed
rest at night.. She reproved him now for staying so late,
she wrung from him the fact that he'd had no supper.

"Well, Bruce," she exclaimed impatiently, "now isn't
that just like you? You're going straight home—that's
where you're going—"

"To be fed up and put to bed," her husband grumbled
good-naturedly. And while she made ready to bundle him
off he turned to his father-in-law.

"What do you think's my latest?" he asked, and he
gave a low chuckle which Roger liked. "Last week I was
a brewer, to-day I'm an engineer," he said. "Can you
beat it? A building contractor. Me." And as he smoked
his cigarette, in laconic phrases he explained how a huge
steel construction concern had gone to the wall, through
building skyscrapers "on spec" and outstripping even the
growth of New York. "They got into court last week,"
he said, "and the judge handed me the receivership. The
judge and I have been chums for years. He has hay
fever—so do I."

"Come, Bruce, I'm ready," said his wife.

"I've been in their office all day," he went on. "Their
general manager was stark mad. He hadn't been out of
the office since last Sunday night, he said. You had to ask
him a question and wait—while he looked at you and held
onto his chair. He broke down and blubbered—the poor
damn fool—he'll be in Matteawan in a week—"

"You'll be there yourself if you don't come home,"
broke in Edith's voice impatiently.

"And out of that poor devil, and out of the mess his
books are in, I've been learning engineering!"

He had followed his wife out on the steps. He turned
back with a quick appealing smile:

"Well, good-night—see you soon—"

"Good-night, my boy," said Roger. "Good luck to
the engineering."

"Oh, father dear," cried Edith, from the taxi down
below. "Remember supper Sunday night—"

"I won't forget," said Roger.

He watched them start off up the street. The night
was soft, refreshing, and the place was quiet and personal.
The house was one of a dozen others, some of red brick
and some of brown stone, that stood in an uneven row
on a street but a few rods in length, one side of a little
triangular park enclosed by a low iron fence, inside of
which were a few gnarled trees and three or four park
benches. On one of these benches his eye was caught by
the figure of an old woman there, and he stood a moment
watching her, some memory stirring in his mind.

Occasionally somebody passed. Otherwise it was silent
here. But even in the silence could be felt the throes of
change; the very atmosphere seemed charged with drastic
things impending. Already the opposite house line had
been broken near the center by a high apartment building,
and another still higher rose like a cliff just back of the
house in which Roger lived. Still others, and many factory
lofts, reared shadowy bulks on every hand. From the
top of one an enormous sign, a corset pictured forth in
lights, flashed out at regular intervals; and from farther
off, high up in the misty haze of the night, could be seen
the gleaming pinnacle where hour by hour that great bell
slowly boomed the time away. Yes, here the old was
passing. Already the tiny parklet was like the dark
bottom of a pit, with the hard sparkling modern town
towering on every side, slowly pressing, pressing in and
glaring down with yellow eyes.

But Roger noticed none of these things. He watched the old woman on the bench and groped for the memory she had stirred. Ah, now at last he had it. An April night long, long ago, when he had sat where she was now, while here in the house his wife's first baby, Edith, had begun her life. . . .

Slowly he turned and went inside.

CHAPTER II

ROGER'S hearing was extremely acute. Though the room where he was sitting, his study, was at the back of the house, he heard Deborah's key at the street door and he heard the door softly open and close.

"Are you there, dearie?" Her voice from the hallway was low; and his answer, "Yes, child," was in the same tone, as though she were with him in the room. This keen sense of hearing had long been a peculiar bond between them. To her father, Deborah's voice was the most distinctive part of her, for often as he listened the memory came of her voice as a girl, unpleasant, hurried and stammering. But she had overcome all that. "No grown woman," she had declared, when she was eighteen, "has any excuse for a voice like mine." That was eleven years ago; and the voice she had acquired since, with its sweet magnetic quality, its clear and easy articulation, was to him an expression of Deborah's growth. As she took off her coat and hat in the hall she said, in the same low tone as before,

"Edith has been here, I suppose—"

"Yes—"

"I'm so sorry I missed her. I tried to get home early, but it has been a busy night."

Her voice sounded tired, comfortably so, and she looked that way as she came in. Though only a little taller than Edith, she was of a sturdier build and more decided features. Her mouth was large with a humorous droop and her face rather broad with high cheekbones. As she put her soft black hair up over her high forehead, her father noticed her birthmark, a faint curving line of red running up from between her eyes. Imperceptible as a rule, it showed when she was tired. In the big school in the tenements where she had taught for many years, she gave herself hard without stint to her work, but she had such a good time through it all. She had a way, too, he reflected, of always putting things in their place. As now she came in and kissed him and sank back on his leather lounge with a tranquil breath of relief, she seemed to be dropping school out of her life.

Roger picked up his paper and continued his reading. Presently they would have a talk, but first he knew that she wanted to lie quite still for a little while. Vaguely he pictured her work that night, her class-room packed to bursting with small Jews and Italians, and Deborah at the blackboard with a long pointer in her hand. The fact that for the last two years she had been the principal of her school had made little impression upon him.

And meanwhile, as she lay back with eyes closed, her mind still taut from the evening called up no simple class-room but far different places—a mass meeting in Carnegie Hall where she had just been speaking, some schools which she had visited out in Indiana, a block of tenements far downtown and the private office of the mayor. For her school had long curious arms these days.

"Was Bruce here too this evening?" she asked her father presently. Roger finished what he was reading, then looked over to the lounge, which was in a shadowy corner.

"Yes, he came in late." And he went on to tell her of Bruce's "engineering." At once she was interested. Rising on one elbow she questioned him good-humoredly, for Deborah was fond of Bruce.

"Has he bought that automobile he wanted?"

"No," replied her father. "Edith said they couldn't afford it."

"Why not?"

"This time it's the dentist's bills. Young Betsy's teeth aren't straightened yet—and as soon as *she's* been beautified they're going to put the clamps on George."

"Poor Georgie," Deborah murmured. At the look of pain and disapproval on her father's heavy face, she smiled quietly to herself. George, who was Edith's oldest and the worry of her days, was Roger's favorite grandson. "Has he been bringing home any more sick dogs?"

"No, this time it was a rat—a white one," Roger answered. A glint of dry relish appeared in his eyes. "George brought it home the other night. He had on a pair of ragged old pants."

"What on earth—"

"He had traded his own breeches for the rat," said Roger placidly.

"No! Oh, father! Really!" And she sank back laughing on the lounge.

"His school report," said Roger, "was quite as bad as ever."

"Of course it was," said Deborah. And she spoke so sharply that her father glanced at her in surprise. She was up again on one elbow, and there was an eager expression on her bright attractive face. "Do you know what we're going to do some day? We're going to put the rat in the school," Deborah said impatiently. "We're going to take a boy like George and study him till we think we know just what interests him most. And if in his case it's animals, we'll have a regular zoo in school. And for other boys we'll have other things they really want to know about. And we'll keep them until five o'clock—when their mothers will have to drag them away." Her father looked bewildered.

"But arithmetic, my dear."

"You'll find they'll have learned their arithmetic without knowing it," Deborah answered.

"Sounds a bit wild," murmured Roger. Again to his

mind came the picture of hordes of little Italians and Jews.
"My dear, if I had *your children* to teach, I don't think
I'd add a zoo," he said. And with a breath of discomfort
he turned back to his reading. He knew that he ought
to question her, to show an interest in her work. But
he had a deep aversion for those millions of foreign tenement people, always shoving, shoving upward through
the filth of their surroundings. They had already spoiled
his neighborhood, they had flowed up like an ocean tide.
And so he read his paper, frowning guiltily down at the
page. He glanced up in a little while and saw Deborah
smiling across at him, reading his dislike of such talk.
The smile which he sent back at her was half apologetic,
half an appeal for mercy. And Deborah seemed to understand. She went into the living room, and there at the
piano she was soon playing softly. Listening from his
study, again the feeling came to him of her fresh and abundant vitality. He mused a little enviously on how it must
feel to be strong like that, never really tired.

And while her father thought in this wise, Deborah at
the piano, leaning back with eyes half closed, could feel
her tortured nerves relax, could feel her pulse stop throbbing so and the dull aching at her temples little by little
pass away. She played like this so many nights. Soon
she would be ready for sleep.

After she had gone to bed, Roger rose heavily from his
chair. By long habit he went about the house trying the
windows and turning out lights. Last he came to the
front door. There were double outer doors with a ponderous system of locks and bolts and a heavy chain. Mechanically he fastened them all; and putting out the light
in the hall, in the darkness he went up the stairs. He
could so easily feel his way. He put his hand lightly, first
on the foot of the banister, then on a curve in it halfway
up, again on the sharper curve at the top and last on the

knob of his bedroom door. And it was as though these
guiding objects came out to meet him like old friends.

In his bedroom, while he slowly undressed, his glance
was caught by the picture upon the wall opposite his bed,
a little landscape poster done in restful tones of blue, of
two herdsmen and their cattle far up on a mountainside
in the hour just before the dawn, tiny clear-cut silhouettes
against the awakening eastern sky. So immense and still,
this birth of the day—the picture always gave him the
feeling of life everlasting. Judith his wife had placed it
there.

From his bed through the window close beside him he
looked up at the cliff-like wall of the new apartment building, with tier upon tier of windows from which murmurous
voices dropped out of the dark: now soft, now suddenly
angry, loud; now droning, sullen, bitter, hard; now gay
with little screams of mirth; now low and amorous, drowsy
sounds. Tier upon tier of modern homes, all overhanging
Roger's house as though presently to crush it down.

But Roger was not thinking of that. He was thinking
of his children—of Edith's approaching confinement and
all her anxious hunting about to find what was best for her
family, of Bruce and the way he was driving himself in
the unnatural world downtown where men were at each
other's throats, of Deborah and that school of hers in the
heart of a vast foul region of tenement buildings swarming
with strange, dirty little urchins. And last he thought of
Laura, his youngest daughter, wild as a hawk, gadding
about the Lord knew where. She even danced in restau-
rants! Through his children he felt flowing into his house
the seething life of this new town. And drowsily he told
himself he must make a real effort, and make it soon, to
know his family better. For in spite of the storm of long
ago which had swept away his faith in God, the feeling
had come to him of late that somewhere, in some manner,
he was to meet his wife again. He rarely tried to think

this out, for as soon as he did it became a mere wish, a hungry longing, nothing more. So he had learned to let it lie, deep down inside of him. Sometimes he vividly saw her face. After all, who could tell? And she would want to hear of her children. Yes, he must know them better. Some day soon he must begin.

Suddenly he remembered that Laura had not yet come home. With a sigh of discomfort he got out of bed and went downstairs, relit the gas in the hallway, unfastened the locks and the chain at the door. He came back and was soon asleep. He must have dozed for an hour or two. He was roused by hearing the front door close and a big motor thundering. And then like a flash of light in the dark came Laura's rippling laughter.

CHAPTER III

On the next evening, Saturday, while Roger ate his dinner, Laura came to sit with him. She herself was dining out. That she should have dressed so early in order to keep him company had caused her father some surprise, and a faint suspicion entered his mind that she had overdrawn at the bank, as she had the last time she sat with him like this. Her manner certainly was a bit strange.

But Roger put the thought aside. Whatever she wanted, Laura was worth it. In a tingling fashion he felt what a glorious time she was having, what a gorgeous town she knew. It was difficult to realize she was his own daughter, this dashing stranger sitting here, playing idly with a knife and caressing him with her voice and her eyes. The blue evening gown she was wearing to-night (doubtless not yet paid for) made her figure even more supple and lithe, set off her splendid bosom, her slender neck, her creamy skin. Her hair, worn low over her temples, was brown with just a tinge of red. Her eyes were black, with gleaming lights; her lips were warm and rich, alive. He did not approve of her lips. Once when she had kissed him Roger had started slightly back. For his daughter's lips were rouged, and they had reminded him of his youth. He had asked her sister to speak to her. But Deborah had told him she did not care to speak to people in that way—"especially women—especially sisters," she had said, with a quiet smile. All very well, he reflected, but somebody ought to take Laura in hand.

She had been his favorite as a child, his pet, his tiny daughter. He remembered her on his lap like a kitten. How she had liked to cuddle there. And she had liked to bite his hand, a curious habit in a child. "I hurt daddy!" He could still recollect the gay little laugh with which she said that, looking up brightly into his face.

And here she was already grown, and like a light in the sober old house, fascinating while she disturbed him. He liked to hear her high pitched voice, gossiping in Deborah's room or in her own dainty chamber chatting with the adoring maid who was dressing her to go out. He loved her joyous thrilling laugh. And he would have missed her from the house as he would have missed Fifth Avenue if it had been dropped from the city. For the picture Roger had formed of this daughter was more of a symbol than of a girl, a symbol of the ardent town, spending, wasting, dancing mad. It was Laura who had kept him living right up to his income.

"Where are you dining to-night?" he asked.

"With the Raymonds." He wondered who they were. "Oh, Sarah," she added to the maid. "Call up Mrs. Raymond's apartment and ask what time is dinner to-night."

"Are you going to dance later on?" he inquired.

"Oh, I guess so," she replied. "On the Astor Roof, I think they said—"

Her father went on with his dinner. These hotel dances, he had heard, ran well into Sunday morning. How Judith would have disapproved. He hesitated uneasily.

"I don't especially care for this dancing into Sunday," he said. For a moment he did not look up from his plate. When he did he saw Laura regarding him.

"Oh, do you mind? I'm sorry. I won't, after this," she answered. And Roger colored angrily, for the glint of amusement in Laura's mischievous black eyes revealed quite unmistakably that she regarded both her father and his feeling for the Sabbath as very dear and quaint and old. Old? Of course he seemed old to *her*, Roger thought indignantly. For what was Laura but a child? Did she ever think of anything except having a good time? Had she ever stopped to think out her own morals, let alone anyone else's? Was she any judge of what was old—or of *who* was old? And he determined then and there to show her he was in his prime. Impatiently he strove to remember the names of her friends and ask her about them, to show a keen lively interest in this giddy gaddy life she led. And when that was rather a failure he tried his daughter next on books, books of the most modern kind. Stoutly he lied and said he was reading a certain Russian novel of which he had heard Deborah speak. But this valiant falsehood made no impression whatever, for Laura had never heard of the book.

"I get so little time for reading," she murmured. And meanwhile she was thinking, "As soon as he finishes talking, poor dear, I'll break the news."

Then Roger had an audacious thought. He would take her to a play, by George! Mustering his courage he led up to it by speaking of a play Deborah had seen, a full-fledged modern drama all centered upon the right of a woman "to lead her own life." And as he outlined the story, he saw he had caught his daughter's attention. With her pretty chin resting on one hand, watching him and listening, she appeared much older, and she seemed suddenly close to him.

"How would you like to go with me and see it some evening?" he inquired.

"See what, my love?" she asked him, her thoughts plainly far away; and he looked at her in astonishment:

"That play I've just been speaking of!"

"Why, daddy, I'd love to!" she exclaimed.

"When?" he asked. And he fixed a night. He was proud of himself Eagerly he began to talk of opening nights at Wallack's. Roger and Judith, when they were young, had been great first nighters there. And now it was Laura who drew him out, and as he talked on she

seemed to him to be smilingly trying to picture it all. . . .
"Now I'd better tell him," she thought.

"Do you remember Harold Sloane?" she asked a little
strangely.

"No," replied her father, a bit annoyed at the interruption.

"Why—you've met him two or three times—"

"Have I?" The queer note in her voice made him
look up. Laura had risen from her chair.

"I want you to know him—very soon." There was a
moment's silence. "I'm going to marry him, dad," she
said. And Roger looked at her blankly. He felt his limbs
beginning to tremble. "I've been waiting to tell you
when we were alone," she added in an awkward tone.
And still staring up at her he felt a rush of tenderness
and a pang of deep remorse. Laura in love and settled
for life! And what did he know of the affair? What had
he ever done for her? Too late! He had begun too late!
And this rush of emotion was so overpowering that while
he still looked at her blindly she was the first to recover
her poise. She came around the table and kissed him
softly on the cheek. And now more than ever Roger felt
how old his daughter thought him.

"Who is he?" he asked hoarsely. And she answered
smiling,

"A perfectly nice young man named Sloane."

"Don't, Laura—tell me! What does he do?"

"He's in a broker's office—junior member of the firm.
Oh, you needn't worry, dear, he can even afford to marry *me*."

They heard a ring at the front door.

"There he is now, I think," she said. "Will you see
him? Would you mind?"

"See him? No!" her father cried.

"But just to shake hands," she insisted. "You needn't
talk or say a word. We've only a moment, anyway."
And she went swiftly out of the room.

Roger rose in a panic and strode up and down. Before he could recover himself she was back with her man, or rather her boy—for the fellow, to her father's eyes, looked ridiculously young. Straight as an arrow, slender, his dress suit irreproachable, the chap nevertheless was more than a dandy. He looked hard, as though he trained, and his smooth and ruddy face had a look of shrewd self-reliance. So much of him Roger fathomed in the indignant cornered glance with which he welcomed him into the room.

"Why, good evening, Mr. Gale—glad to see you again, sir!" Young Sloane nervously held out his hand. Roger took it and muttered something. For several moments, his mind in a whirl, he heard their talk and laughter and his own voice joining in. Laura seemed enjoying herself, her eyes brimming with amusement over both her victims. But at last she had compassion, kissed her father gaily and took her suitor out of the room.

Soon Roger heard them leave the house. He went into his study, savagely bit off a cigar and gripped his evening paper as though he meant to choke it. The maid came in with coffee. "Coffee? No!" he snapped at her. A few moments later he came to his senses and found himself smoking fast and hard. He heartily damned this fellow Sloane for breaking into the family and asking poor Laura to risk her whole life—just for his own selfish pleasure, his whim! Yes, "whim" was the very word for it! Laura's attitude, too! Did she look at it seriously? Not at all! Quite plainly she saw her career as one long Highland fling and dance, with this Harry boy as her partner! Who had he danced with in his past? The fellow's past must be gone into, and at once, without delay!

Here indeed was a jolt for Roger Gale, a pretty shabby trick of fate. This was not what he had planned, this was a little way life had of jabbing a man with surprises. For months he had been slowly and comfortably feeling his way into the lives of his children, patiently, conscientiously. But now without a word of warning in popped this young whipper-snapper, turning the whole house upside down! Another young person to be known, another life to be dug into, and with pick and shovel too! The job was far from pleasant. Would Deborah help him? Not at all. She believed in letting people alone—a devilish easy philosophy! Still, he wanted to tell her at once, if only to stir her up a bit. He did not propose to bear this alone! But Deborah was out to-night. Why must she always be out, he asked, in that infernal zoo school? But no, it was not school to-night. She was dining out in some café with a tall lank doctor friend of hers. Probably she was to marry him!

"I'll have that news for breakfast!" Roger smote his paper savagely. Why couldn't Laura have waited a little? Restlessly he walked the room. Then he went into the hall, took his hat and a heavy stick which he used for his night rambles, and walked off through the neighborhood. It was the first Saturday evening of Spring, and on those quiet downtown streets he met couples strolling by. A tall thin lad and a buxom girl went into a cheap apartment building laughing gaily to themselves, and Roger thought of Laura. A group of young Italians passed, humming "Trovatore," and it put him in mind of the time when he had ushered at the opera. Would Laura's young man be willing to usher? More like him to *tango* down the aisle!

He reached Washington Square feeling tired but even more restless than before. He climbed to the top of a motor 'bus, and on the lurching ride uptown he darkly reflected that times had changed. He thought of the Avenue he had known, with its long lines of hansom cabs, its dashing broughams and coupés with jingling harness, liveried footmen, everything sprucely up-to-date. How the horses had added to the town. But they were gone,

and in their place were these great cats, these purring
motors, sliding softly by the 'bus. Roger had swift
glimpses down into lighted limousines. In one a big rich
looking chap with a beard had a dressy young woman in
his arms. Lord, how he was hugging her! Laura would
have a motor like that, kisses like that, a life like that!
She was the kind to go it hard! Ahead as far as he could
see was a dark rolling torrent of cars, lights gleaming by
the thousand. A hubbub of gay voices, cries and little
shrieks of laughter mingled with the blare of horns. He
looked at huge shop windows softly lighted with displays
of bedrooms richly furnished, of gorgeous women's apparel,
silks and lacy filmy stuffs. And to Roger, in his mood of
anxious premonition, these bedroom scenes said plainly,

"O come, all ye faithful wives! Come let us adore him,
and deck ourselves to please his eye, to catch his eye, to
hold his eye! For marriage is a game these days!"

Yes, Laura would be a spender, a spender and a speeder
too! How much money had he, that chap? And damn
him, what had he in his past? How Roger hated the very
thought of poking into another man's life! Poking where
nobody wanted him! He felt desperately alone. To-night
they were dancing, he recalled, not at a party in somebody's home, but in some flashy public place where girls
of her kind and fancy women gaily mixed together! How
mixed the whole city was getting, he thought, how mad
and strange, gone out of its mind, this city of his children's
lives crowding in upon him!

CHAPTER IV

HE breakfasted with Deborah late on Sunday morning. He had come down at the usual hour despite his long tramp of the previous night, for he wanted to tell her the news and talk it all out before Laura came down—because Deborah, he hadn't a doubt, with her woman's curiosity had probed deep into Laura's affairs in the many long talks they had had in her room. He had often heard them there. And so, as he waited and waited and still his daughter did not come, Roger grew distinctly annoyed; and when at last she did appear, his greeting was perfunctory:

"What kept you out so late last night?"

"Oh, I was having a very good time," said Deborah contentedly. She poured herself some coffee. "I've always wanted," she went on, "to see Laura really puzzled—downright flabbergasted. And I saw her just like that last night."

Roger looked up with a jerk of his head:

"You and Laura—together last night?"

"Exactly—on the Astor Roof." At her father's glare of astonishment a look of quiet relish came over her mobile features. Her wide lips twitched a little. "Well, why not?" she asked him. "I'm quite a dancer down at school. And last night with Allan Baird—we were dining together, you know—he proposed we go somewhere and dance. He's a perfectly awful dancer, and so I held out as long as I could. But he insisted and I gave in, though I much prefer the theater."

"Well!" breathed Roger softly. "So you hoof it with the rest!" His expression was startled and intent. Would

26

he ever get to know these girls? "Well," he added with
a sigh, "I suppose you know what you're about."

"Oh no, I don't," she answered. "I never know what
I'm about. If you always do, you miss so much—you get
into a solemn habit of trying nothing till you're sure. But
to return to Laura. As we came gaily down the room we
ran right into her, you see. That's how Allan dances.
And when we collided, I smiled at her sweetly and said,
'Why, hello, dearie—you here too?'" And Deborah sipped
her coffee. "I have never believed that the lower jaw of a
well-bred girl could actually drop open. But Laura's
did. With a good strong light, Allan told me, he could
have examined her tonsils for her. Rather a disgusting
thought. You see until she saw me there, poor Laura
had me so thoroughly placed—my school-marm job, my
tastes and habits, everything, all cut and dried. She has
never once come to my school, and in every talk we've
ever had there has always been some perfectly good and
absorbing reason why we should talk about Laura alone."

"There is now," said her father. He was in no mood
for tomfoolery. His daughter saw it and smiled a little.

"What is it?" she inquired. And then he let her have
it!

"Laura wants to get married," he snapped.

Deborah caught her breath at that, and an eager excited expression swept over her attractive face. She
had leaned forward suddenly.

"Father! No! Which one?" she asked. "Tell me!
Is it Harold Sloane?"

"It is."

"Oh, dad." She sank back in her chair. "Oh, dad,"
she repeated.

"What's the matter with Sloane?" he demanded.

"Oh, nothing, nothing—it's all right—"

"It is, eh? How do you know it is?" His anxious eyes
were still upon hers, and he saw she was thinking fast and

hard and shutting him completely out. And it irritated
him. "What do you know of this fellow Sloane?"

"Oh, nothing—nothing—"

"Nothing! Humph! Then why do you sit here and
say it's all right? Don't talk like a fool!" he exclaimed.
He waited, but she said no more, and Roger's exasperation
increased. "He has money enough apparently—and
they'll spend it like March hares!"

Deborah looked up at him:

"What did Laura tell you, dear?"

"Not very much. I'm only her father. She had a
dinner and dance on her mind."

But Deborah pressed her questions and he gave her
brief replies.

"Well, what shall we do about it?" he asked.

"Nothing—until we know something more." Roger
regarded her fiercely.

"Why don't you go up and talk to her, then?"

"She's asleep yet—"

"Never mind if she is! If she's going to marry a chap
like that and ruin her life it's high time she was up for her
breakfast!"

While he scanned his Sunday paper he heard Deborah
in the pantry. She emerged with a breakfast tray and he
saw her start up to Laura's room. She was there for over
an hour. And when she returned to his study, he saw
her eyes were shining. How women's eyes will shine at
such times, he told himself in annoyance.

"Well?" he demanded.

"Better leave her alone to-day," she advised. "Harold
is coming some night soon."

"What for?"

"To have a talk with you."

Her father smote his paper. "What did she tell you
about him?" he asked.

"Not much more than she told you. His parents are

dead—but he has a rich widowed aunt in Bridgeport who adores him. They mean to be married the end of May. She wants a church wedding, bridesmaids, ushers—the wedding reception here, of course—"

"Oh, Lord," breathed Roger dismally.

"We won't bother you much, father dear—"

"You *will* bother me much," he retorted. "I propose to be bothered—bothered a lot! I'm going to look up this fellow Sloane—"

"But let's leave him alone for to-day." She bent over her father compassionately. "What a night you must have had, poor dear." Roger looked up in grim reproach.

"You like all this," he grunted. "You, a grown woman, a teacher too."

"I wonder if I do," she said. "I guess I'm a queer person, dad, a curious family mixture—of Laura and Edith and mother and you, with a good deal of myself thrown in. But it feels rather good to be mixed, don't you think? Let's stay mixed as long as we can—and keep together the family."

That afternoon, to distract him, Deborah took her father to a concert in Carnegie Hall. She had often urged him to go of late, but despite his liking for music Roger had refused before, simply because it was a change. But why balk at going anywhere now, when Laura was up to such antics at home?

"Do you mind climbing up to the gallery?" Deborah asked as they entered the hall.

"Not at all," he curtly answered. He did mind it very much!

"Then we'll go to the very top," she said. "It's a long climb but I want you to see it. It's so different up there."

"I don't doubt it," he replied. And as they made the slow ascent, pettishly he wondered why Deborah must always be so eager for queer places. Galleries, zoo schools, tenement slums—why not take a two dollar seat in life?

Deborah seated him far down in the front of the great gallery, over at the extreme right, and from here they could look back and up at a huge dim arena of faces.

"Now watch them close," she whispered. "See what the music does to them."

As the symphony began below the faces all grew motionless. And as the music cast its spell, the anxious ruffled feelings which had been with Roger all that day little by little were dispelled, and soon his imagination began to work upon this scene. He saw many familiar American types. He felt he knew what they had been doing on Sundays only a few years before. After church they had eaten large Sunday dinners. Then some had napped and some had walked and some had gone to Sunday school. At night they had had cold suppers, and afterwards some had gone back to church; while others, as in Roger's house in the days when Judith was alive, had gathered around the piano for hymns. Young men callers, friends of their daughters, had joined in the family singing. Yes, some of these people had been like that. To them, a few short years ago, a concert on the Sabbath would have seemed a sacrilege. He could almost hear from somewhere the echo of "Abide With Me."

But over this memory of a song rose now the surging music of Tschaikovsky's "Pathetique." And the yearnings and fierce hungers in this tumultuous music swept all the hymns from Roger's mind. Once more he watched the gallery, and this time he became aware that more than half were foreigners. Out of the mass from every side individual faces emerged, swarthy, weird, and staring hungrily into space. And to Roger the whole shadowy place, the very air, grew pregnant, charged with all these inner lives bound together in this mood, this mystery that had swept over them all, immense and

formless, baffling, this furious demanding and this blind
wistful groping which he himself had known so well,
ever since his wife had died and he had lost his faith in
God. What was the meaning of it all if life were nothing
but a start, and there were nothing but the grave?

"You will live on in our children's lives."

He glanced around at Deborah. Was *she* so certain, so
serene? "What do I know of her?" he asked. "Little
or nothing," he sadly replied. And he tried to piece together from things she had told him her life as it
had passed him by. Had there been no questionings, no
sharp disillusionments? There must have been. He recalled irritabilities, small acts and exclamations of impatience, boredom, "blues." And as he watched her he grew
sure that his daughter's existence had been like his own.
Despite its different setting, its other aims and visions, it
had been a mere beginning, a feeling for a foothold, a search
for light and happiness. And Deborah seemed to him
still a child. "How far will *you* go?" he wondered.

Although he was still watching her even after the music
had ceased, she did not notice him for a time. Then she
turned to him slowly with a smile.

"Well? What did you see?" she asked.

"I wasn't looking," he replied.

"Why, dearie," she retorted. "Where's that imagination of yours?"

"It was with you," he answered. "Tell me what you
were thinking."

And still under the spell of the music, Deborah said to
her father,

"I was thinking of hungry people—millions of them,
now, this minute—not only here but in so many places—
concerts, movies, libraries. Hungry, oh, for everything
—life, its beauty, all it means. And I was thinking this
is youth—no matter how old they happen to be—and
that to feed it we have schools. I was thinking how

little we've done as yet, and of all that we're so sure to do in the many, many years ahead. Do you see what I mean?" she squeezed his hand.

"Welcome back to school," she said, "back into the hungry army of youth! . . . Sh-h-h!"

Again the music had begun. And sitting by her side he wondered whether it was because she knew that Laura's affair had made him feel old that Deborah had brought him here.

They went to Edith's for supper.

The Cunninghams' apartment was on the west side, well uptown. It was not the neighborhood which Edith would have chosen, for nearly all the nice people she knew lived east of the park. But rents were somewhat lower here and there was at least an abundance of fresh air for her family. Edith had found that her days were full of these perplexing decisions. It was all very simple to resolve that her children be old-fashioned, normal, wholesome, nice. But then she looked into the city—into schools and kindergartens, clothes and friends and children's parties, books and plays. And through them all to her dismay she felt conflicting currents, clashes between old and new. She felt New York. And anxiously she asked herself, "What is old-fashioned? What is normal? What is wholesome? What is nice?" Cautiously she made her way, testing and comparing, trying small experiments. Often sharply she would draw in her horns. She had struck something "common!" And she knew all this was nothing compared to the puzzles that lay ahead. For from her friend, Madge Deering, whose girls were well along in their 'teens, she heard of deeper problems. The girls were so inquisitive. Dauntlessly Madge was facing each month the most disturbing questions. Thank Heaven, Edith had only one daughter. Sons were not quite so baffling.

So she had groped her way along.

When her father and Deborah arrived, placidly she asked them what they had been doing. And when she heard that they had been at a concert on the Sabbath, though this was far from old-fashioned and something she would not have done herself, it did not bother her half so much as the fact that Hannah, the Irish nurse, had slapped little Tad that afternoon. She had never known Hannah to do it before. Could it be that the girl was tired or sick? Perhaps she needed a few days off. "I must have a talk with her," Edith thought, "as soon as father and Deborah go."

Roger always liked to come here. Say what you would about Edith's habit of keeping too closely to her home, the children to whom she had devoted herself were a fine, clean, happy lot. Here were new lives in his family, glorious fresh beginnings. He sat on the floor with her three boys, watching the patient efforts of George to harness his perturbed white rat to Tad's small fire engine. George was a lank sprawling lad of fourteen, all legs and arms and elbows, with rumpled hair and freckled face, a quick bright smile and nice brown eyes—frank, simple, understandable eyes. All but one of Edith's children were boys, and boys were a blessed relief to a man who had three grown-up daughters.

And while Roger watched them, with a gentle glow of anticipation he waited for what should follow, when as had been already arranged Deborah should break to her sister the news of Laura's engagement. And he was not disappointed. The change in Edith was something tremendous. Until now so quietly self-absorbed, at the news that Laura was to be married instantly she was all alert. Sitting there in the midst of her children and facing a time of agony only a few weeks ahead which would add one more to her family, Edith's pretty florid face grew flushed and radiant as she exclaimed,

"What a perfectly wonderful thing for Laura! Now if only she can have a child!"

Her questions followed thick and fast, and with them her thoughts of what should be done. Bruce must look up this suitor at once. Bruce demurred stoutly but without avail. She eagerly questioned her sister as to Laura's plans for the wedding, but plainly she considered that Deborah was no woman to give her the full information she wanted. She must see Laura herself at once. For though she had thoroughly disapproved of the gay helter-skelter existence of her youngest sister, still Laura was now to be married, and this made all the difference.

Just before Roger and Deborah left, Edith drew her father aside, and with a curious concern and pity in her voice, she said,

"I'm so sorry I shan't be able to help you with the wedding, dear, and make it the sweet old-fashioned kind that mother would have wanted. Of course there's Deborah, she'll be there. But her head is so full of new ideas. I'm afraid she may find the house rather a burden after Laura has gone away." Edith gave a worried little sigh. "I'll be so glad," she added, "when we get that place in Morristown. We'll want you out there often, and for good long visits too. You may even find you'll care to try staying there with us for a while."

Roger scowled and thanked her. She had given him a shock of alarm.

"So she thinks that Deborah will find the housekeeping too hard," he reflected anxiously. And as he walked home with his daughter, he kept glancing at her face, which for all its look of quiet had so much tensity beneath. She had packed her life so full of school. What if she wanted to give up their home? "She'll try, of course, she'll try her best—but she'll find it too much of an added strain." And again he felt that sickening dread. Deborah said nothing.   He felt as though they had drifted apart.

And at night in his bed, as Roger stared up at the beetling cliff of apartment windows just outside, drearily he asked himself how it would feel to live like that.

CHAPTER V

ONE afternoon a few days later Roger was riding in the park. He rode "William," a large lazy cob who as he advanced in age had so subtly and insidiously slackened his pace from a trot to a jog that Roger barely noticed how slowly he was riding. As he rode along he liked to watch the broad winding bridle path with its bobbing procession of riders that kept appearing before him under the tall spreading trees. Though he knew scarcely anyone by name, he was a familiar figure here and he recognized scores of faces. To many men he nodded at passing, and to not a few alluring young dames, ardent creatures with bright eyes who gave him smiles of greeting, Roger gravely raised his hat. One was "The Silver Lady" in a Broadway musical show, but he thought she was "one of the Newport crowd." He liked to make shrewd guesses like that. There were so many kinds of people here. There were stout anxious ladies riding for figures and lean morose gentlemen riding for health. There were joyous care-free girls, chatting and laughing merrily. There were some gallant foreigners, and there were riding masters, and Roger could not tell them apart. There were mad boys from the Squadron who rode at a furious canter, and there were groups of children, eager and flushed, excited and gay, with stolid grooms behind them. The path in several places ran close beside the main road of the park, and with the coming of the dusk this road took on deep purple hues and glistened with reflections from countless yellow motor eyes. And from the polished limousines, sumptuous young women smiled out upon the riders.

At least so Roger saw this life. And after those bleak

lonely years confronted by eternity, it was good to come here and forget, to feel himself for the moment a part of the thoughtless gaiety, the ease and luxury of the town. Here he was just on the edge of it all. Often as a couple passed he would wonder what they were doing that night. In the riding school where he kept his horse, it was a lazy pleasure to have the English "valet" there pull off his boots and breeches—though if anyone had told him so, Roger would have denied it with indignation and surprise. For was he not an American?

It had been a wonderful tonic, a great idea of Laura's, this forcing him up here to ride. In one of her affectionate moods, just after a sick spell he had been through, his gay capricious daughter had insisted that he have his horse brought down from the mountains. She had promised to ride with him herself, and she had done so—for a week. Since then he had often met her here with one of her many smart young men. What a smile of greeting would flash on her face—when Laura happened to notice him.

He was thinking of Laura now, and there was an anxious gleam in his eyes. For young Sloane was coming to dinner to-night. What was he going to say to the fellow? Bruce had learned that Sloane played polo, owned and drove a racing car and was well liked in his several clubs. But what about women and his past? Edith had urged her father to go through the lad's life with a fine tooth comb, and if he should find anything there to kick up no end of a row for the honor of the family. All of which was nothing but words, reflected Roger pettishly. It all came to this, that he had a most ticklish evening ahead! On the path as a rider greeted him, his reply was a dismal frown.

Laura's suitor arrived at six o'clock. In his study Roger heard the bell, listened a moment with beating heart, then raised himself heavily from his chair and went into the hallway.

"Ah, yes! It's you!" he exclaimed, with a nervous cordiality. "Come in, my boy, come right in! Here, let me help you with your coat. I don't know just where Laura is. Ahem!" He violently cleared his throat. "Suppose while we're waiting we have a smoke." He kept it up back into his den. There the suitor refused a cigar and carefully lit a cigarette. Roger noticed again how young the chap was, and marriage seemed so ridiculous! All this feverish trouble was for something so unreal!

"Well, sir," the candidate blurted forth, "I guess I'd better come right to the point. Mr. Gale, I want to marry your daughter."

"Laura?"

"Yes." Roger cursed himself. Why had he asked, "Laura?" Of course it was Laura! Would this cub be wanting Deborah?

"Well, my boy," he said thickly. "I—I wish I knew you better."

"So do I, sir. Suppose we begin." The youth took a quick pull at his cigarette. He waited, stirred nervously in his seat. "You'll have some questions to ask, I suppose—"

"Yes, there are questions." Roger had risen mechanically and was slowly walking the room. He threw out short gruff phrases. "I'm not interested in your past—I don't care about digging into a man—I never have and I never will—except as it might affect my daughter. That's the main question, I suppose. Can you make her happy?"

"I think so," said Sloane, decidedly. Roger gave him a glance of displeasure.

"That's a large order, young man," he rejoined.

"Then let's take it in sections," the youngster replied. Confound his boyish assurance! "To begin with," he was saying, "I rather think I have money enough. We'd better go into that, hadn't we?"

"Yes," said Roger indifferently. "We might as well

go into it." Of course the chap had money enough. He was a money maker. You could hear it in his voice; you could see it in his jaw, in his small aggressive blonde moustache. Now he was telling briefly of his rich aunt in Bridgeport, of the generous start she had given him, his work downtown, his income.

"Twenty-two thousand this year," he said. "We can live on that all right, I guess."

"You won't starve," was the dry response. Roger walked for a moment in silence, then turned abruptly on young Sloane.

"Look here, young man, I don't want to dig," he continued very huskily. "But I know little or nothing of what may be behind you. I don't care to ask you about it now—unless it can make trouble."

"It can't make trouble." At this answer, low but sharp, Roger wheeled and shot a glance into those clear and twinkling eyes. And his own eyes gleamed with pain. Laura had been such a little thing in the days when she had been his pet, the days when he had known her well. What could he do about it? This was only the usual thing. But he felt suddenly sick of life.

"How soon do you want to get married?" he demanded harshly.

"Next month, if we can."

"Where are you going?"

"Abroad," said Sloane. Roger caught at this topic as at a straw. Soon they were talking of the trip, and the tension slackened rapidly. He had never been abroad himself but had always dreamed of going there. With maps and books of travel Judith and he had planned it out. In imagination they had lived in London and Paris, Munich and Rome, always in queer old lodgings looking on quaint crooked streets. He had dreamed of long delicious rambles, glimpses into queer old shops, vast, silent, dark cathedrals. For Laura how different it would be. This boy of hers knew Europe as a group of gorgeous new hotels.

The moment Laura joined them, her father's eye was caught and held by the ring upon her finger. Roger knew rings, they were his hobby, and this huge yellow solitaire in its new and brilliant setting at once awakened his dislike. It just fitted the life they were to lead! What life? As he listened to his daughter he kept wondering if she were so sure. Had she felt no uneasiness? She must have, he decided, for all her gay excitement. One Laura in that smiling face; another Laura deep inside, doubting and uncertain, reaching for her happiness, now elated, now dismayed, exclaiming, "Now at last I'm starting!" Oh, what an ignorant child she was. He wanted to cry out to her, "You'll *always* be just starting! You'll never be sure, you'll never be happy, you'll always be just beginning to be! And the happier you are, the more you will feel it is only a start! . . . And then—"

More and more his spirit withdrew from these two heedless children. Later on, when Deborah came, he barely noticed her meeting with Sloane. And through dinner, while they talked of plans for the wedding, the trip abroad, still Roger took no part at all. He felt dull and heavy. Deborah too, he noticed, after her first efforts to be welcoming and friendly, had gradually grown silent. He saw her watching Laura with a mingled look of affection and of whimsical dismay. Soon after dinner she left them, and Roger smoked with the boy for a while and learned that he was twenty-nine. Both had grown uneasy and rather dull with each other. It was a relief when again Laura joined them, dressed to go out. She and her lover left the house.

Roger sat motionless for some time. His cigar grew cold unheeded. One of the sorrows of his life had been that his only son had died. Bruce had been almost like a son. But this young man of Laura's? No.

Later he went for his evening walk. And as though drawn by invisible chains he strayed far down into the ghetto. Soon he was elbowing his way through a maze of uproarious tenement streets as one who had been there many times. But he noticed little around him. He went on, as he had always gone, seeing and hearing this seething life only as a background to his own adventure. He reached his destination. Pushing his way through a swarm of urchins playing in front of a pawnshop, he entered and was a long time inside, and when he came out again at last the whole expression of his face had undergone a striking change. As one who had found the solace he needed for the moment, his pace unconsciously quickened and he looked about him with brighter eyes.

Around the corner from his home, he went into a small jewelry shop, a remnant of the town of the past. There were no customers in the place, and the old Galician jeweler sat at the back playing solitaire. At sight of Roger he arose; and presently in a small back room, beneath the glare of a powerful lamp, the two were studying the ring which Roger had found in the ghetto that night. It was plain, just a thin worn band of gold with an emerald by no means large; but the setting was old and curious, and personal, distinctive. Somebody over in Europe had worked on it long and lovingly. Now as the Galician gently rubbed and polished and turned the ring this way and that, the light revealed crude tiny figures, a man and a woman under a tree. And was that a vine or a serpent? They studied it long and absorbedly.

At home, up in his bedroom, Roger opened a safe which stood in one corner, took out a large shallow tray and sat down with it by his lamp. A strange array of rings was there, small and delicate, huge, bizarre; great signet rings and poison rings, love tokens, charms and amulets, rings which had been worn by wives, by mistresses, by favorite slaves and by young girls in convents; rings with the Ma-

donna and rings with many other saints graven on large
heavy stones; rings French and Russian, Polish, Italian,
Spanish, Syrian. Some were many centuries old. In
nine shallow metal trays they filled the safe in Roger's
room. Although its money value was small, the Gale
collection was well known to a scattered public of con-
noisseurs, and Roger took pride in showing it. But what
had always appealed to him most was the romance, the
mystery, stored up in these old talismans that had lived
so many ages, travelled through so many lands, decked
so many fingers. Roger had found every one of them in
the pawnshops of New York. What new recruits to America had brought them here and pawned them? From what
old cities had they come? What passions of love and jealousy, of hatred, faith, devotion were in this glittering array? Roger's own love affair had been deep, but quiet
and even and happy. All the wild adventures, the might-
have-beens in his sex life, were gathered in these dusky
trays with their richly colored glints of light.

Of his daughters, Laura had been the one most interested in his rings, and so he thought of Laura now as he
placed in the tray the new ring he had bought, the one
he would have liked for her. But a vague uneasiness filled
his mind, for he knew she had the same craving as he for
what gleamed out of these somber trays. The old Galician
jeweler had long been quite a friend of hers, she had often
dropped in at his shop to ask him curious questions about
his women patrons. And it was just this side of him that
Roger did not care for. So many of those women were
from a dubious glittering world, and the old Galician took
a wierd vicarious joy in many of the gay careers into which
he sent his beloved rings, his brooches, earrings, neck-
laces, his clasps and diamond garters. And Laura loved
to make him talk. . . . Yes, she was her father's child,
a part of himself. He, too, had had his yearnings, his
burning curiosities, his youthful ventures into the town.

"You will live on in our children's lives." With her inheritance what would she do? Would she stop halfway as he had done, or would she throw all caution aside and let the flames within her rise?

He heard a step in the doorway, and Deborah stood there smiling.

"A new one?" she inquired. He nodded, and she bent over the tray. "Poor father," Deborah murmured. "I saw you eyeing Laura's engagement ring at dinner to-night. It wasn't like this one, was it?" He scowled:

"I don't like what I see ahead of her. Nor do you," he said. "Be honest." She looked at him perplexedly.

"We can't stop it, can we? And even if we could," she said, "I'm not quite sure I'd want to. It's her love affair, not yours or mine—grown out of a life she made for herself—curious, eager, thrilled by it all—and in the center of her soul the deep glad growing certainty, 'I'm going to be a beautiful woman—I myself, I, Laura Gale!' Oh, you don't know—nor do I. And so she felt her way along—eagerly, hungrily, making mistakes—and you and I left her to do it alone. I'm afraid we both rather neglected her, dad," Deborah ended sadly. "And all we can do now, I think, is to give her the kind of wedding she wants."

Roger started to speak but hesitated.

"What is it?" she inquired.

"Queer," he answered gruffly, "how a man can neglect his children—as I have done, as I do still—when the one thing he wants most in life is to see each one of 'em happy."

CHAPTER VI

ROGER soon grew accustomed to seeing young Sloane about the house. They could talk together more easily, and he began to call him Harold. Harold asked him with Laura to lunch at the Ritz to meet the aunt from Bridgeport, a lady excessively stout and profound. But that ended the formalities. It had all been so much easier than Roger had expected. So, in its calm sober fashion, the old house took into its life this new member, these new plans, and the old seemed stronger for the new—for Laura and Edith and Deborah drew together closer than they had been in many years. But only because they felt themselves on the eve of a still deeper and more lasting separation, as the family of Roger Gale divided and went different ways. At times he noticed it sadly. Laura, who had scarcely ever been home for dinner, now spent many evenings here. She needed her home for her wedding, he thought. Each daughter needed it now and then. But as the years wore slowly on, the seasons when they needed it grew steadily wider and wider apart. . . .

Early in May, when Roger came home from his office one night he found Edith's children in the house. From the hallway he could hear their gay excited voices, and going into the dining room he found them at their supper. Deborah was with them, and at once her father noticed how much younger she appeared—as she always did with these children who all idolized her so. She rose and followed him into the hall, and her quiet voice had a note of compassion.

"Edith's baby is coming," she said.

"Good Lord. Is anything wrong?" he asked.

44

"No, no, it's all right—"

"But I thought the child wasn't due for three weeks."

"I know, and poor Edith is fearfully worried. It has upset all her plans. I'd go up and see her if I were you. Your supper is ready; and if you like you can have it with the children."

There followed a happy boisterous meal, with much expectant chatter about the long summer so soon to begin at the farm up in the mountains. George, whose hair was down over his eyes, rumpled it back absorbedly as he told of a letter he had received from his friend Dave Royce, Roger's farmer, with whom George corresponded. One of the cows was to have a calf, and George was anxious to get there in time.

"I've never seen a real new calf, new absolutely," he explained. "And I want a look at this one the very minute that he's born. Gee, I hope we can get there in time—"

"Gee! So do I!" cried Bobby aged nine. And then Tad, the chubby three-year-old who had been intently watching his brothers, slowly took the spoon from his mouth and in his grave sweet baby voice said very softly, "Gee." At her end of the table, Elizabeth, blonde and short and rather plump, frowned and colored slightly. For she was eleven and she knew there was something dark and shameful about the way calves appear in barns. And so, with a quick conscious cough, she sweetly interrupted:

"Oh, Aunt Deborah! Won't you please tell us about—about—"

"About—about," jeered the ironical George. "About what, you little ninny?" Poor Elizabeth blushed desperately. She was neither quick nor resourceful.

"Now, George," said his aunt warningly.

"Wasn't I talking?" the boy rejoined. "And didn't Betsy butt right in—without even a thing to butt in about? About—about," he jeered again.

"About Paris!" cried his sister, successful at last in
her frantic search for a proper topic of conversation.
"Aunt Deborah's trip to Paris!"

"How many times has she told it already?" her brother
replied with withering scorn. "And anyhow, I was talking of cows!"

"Very well," said his aunt, "we'll talk about cows, some
cows I saw on a lovely old farm in a little village over in
France."

"There!" cried his young sister. "Did she ever tell
of *that* part of her trip?" And she made a little face at
her brother.

"I don't care," he answered doggedly. "She has told
about Paris lots of times—and that was what *you* wanted.
Yes, you did. You said, 'About Paris.' Didn't she, Bob?"

"You bet she did," young Bob agreed.

"Now, children, children, what does it matter?"

"All right, go ahead with your barn in France," said
George with patient tolerance. "Did they have any
Holsteins?"

Soon the questions were popping from every side, while
little Tad beamed from one to the other. To Tad it was
all so wonderful, to be having supper away from home,
to be here, to go to bed upstairs, to take part perhaps in a
pillow fight. . . . And glancing at the glowing face and
the parted lips of his small grandson Roger felt a current
of warm new life pour into his soul.

Early in the evening he went up to Edith's apartment.
He found his daughter in her room, looking flushed and
very tense. He took her arm and they walked for a time.
A trained nurse was soaping the windows. Roger asked
the reason for this and was told that in case the baby did
not come till morning the doctor wanted to pull up the
shades in order to work by daylight. "And neighbors in
New York are such cats! You've no idea!" said Edith.
She looked out at the numberless windows crowding close

about her home, and she fairly bristled with scorn. "Oh, how I loathe apartments!"

"They seem to have come to stay, my dear. In a few years more New York will be a city without a house," he said. "Only a palace here and there." The thought flashed in his mind, "But I shall be gone."

"Then we'll move out to the country!" she cried. Still walking the floor with her father, she talked of the perplexities which in her feverish state of mind had loomed suddenly enormous. She had planned everything so nicely for the baby to come the first of June, but now her plans were all upset. She did not want the children here, it would make too much confusion. They had much better go up to the mountains, even though George and Elizabeth lost their last few weeks at school. But who could she find to take them? Bruce was simply rushed to death with his new receivership. Laura was getting her trousseau. Deborah, said Edith, had time for nothing on earth but school.

"Suppose I take them," Roger ventured. But she only smiled at this. "My dear," he urged, "your nurse will be with me, and when we arrive there's the farmer's wife." But Edith impatiently shook her head. Her warm bright eyes seemed to picture it all, hour by hour, day and night, her children there without her.

"You poor dear," she told him, "you haven't the slightest idea what it means. The summer train is not on yet, and you have to change three times on the way—with all the children—luggage, too. And there are their naps, and all their meals. You don't arrive till late at night. No," she decided firmly, "Bruce will simply have to go." She drew a breath of discomfort. "You go and talk to him," she said.

"I will, my dear." Roger looked at his daughter in deep concern. Awkwardly his heavy hand touched her small plump shoulder, and he felt the constant quivering there. "Now, now," he muttered, uneasily, "it's going to be all right, you know—" And at that she gave him a rapid glance out of those warm hunted eyes, as though to ask, "What do you know of this?" And Roger flinched and turned to the door.

Bruce was working at his desk, with an old briar pipe in his teeth. He looked up with a quick nervous smile which showed his dread of the coming ordeal, but his voice had a carefully casual tone.

"Does she want me now?" he asked.

"No," said Roger. And he told of her plan for the children. "I volunteered myself," he added, "but she wouldn't hear to it."

"Oh, my God, man, you wouldn't do," said Bruce, in droll disparagement. "You with forty-nine bottles of pasteurized milk? Suppose you smashed one? Where'd you be? Moving our family isn't a job; it's a science, and I've got my degree." He rose and his face softened. "Poor girl, she mustn't worry like that. I'll run in and tell her I'll do it myself—just to get it off her mind."

He went to his wife. And when he came back his dark features appeared a little more drawn.

"Poor devil," thought Roger, "he's scared to death—just as I used to be myself."

"Pretty tough on a woman, isn't it?" Bruce muttered, smiling constrainedly.

"Did Baird say everything's going well?" Baird was Edith's physician.

"Yes. He was here this afternoon, and he said he'd be back this evening." Bruce stopped with a queer little scowl of suspense. "I told her I'd see to the trip with the kiddies, and it seemed to relieve her a lot." His eye went to a pile of documents that lay on the desk before him. "It'll play the very devil with business, taking three days off just now. But I guess I can manage it some-how—"

A muscle began to twitch on his face. He re-lit his pipe with elaborate care and looked over at Roger confidingly:

"Do you know what's the matter with kids these days? It's the twentieth century," he said. "It's a disease. It starts in their teeth. No modern girl can get married unless she has had her teeth straightened for years. Our dentist's bill, this year alone, was over eight hundred dollars. But that isn't all. It gets into their young intestines, God bless 'em, and makes you pasteurize all they eat. It gets into their nerves and tears 'em up, and your only chance to save 'em is school—not a common school but a 'simple' school, tuition four hundred dollars a year. And you hire a dancing teacher besides—I mean a rhythm teacher—and let 'em shake it out of their feet. And after that you buy 'em clothes—not fluffy clothes, but 'simple' clothes, the kind which always cost the most. And then you build a simple home, in a simple place like Morristown. The whole idea is simplicity. If you can't make enough to buy it, you're lost. If you can make enough, just barely enough, you get so excited you lose your head—and do what I did Monday."

The two men smiled at each other. Roger was very fond of Bruce.

"What did you do Monday?" he asked.

"I bought that car I told you about."

"Splendid! Best thing in the world for you! Tell me all about it!"

And while Bruce rapidly grew engrossed in telling of the car's fine points, Roger pictured his son-in-law upon hot summer evenings (for Bruce spent his summers in town) forgetting his business for a time and speeding out into the country. Then he thought of Edith and the tyranny of her motherhood, always draining her husband's purse and keeping Edith so wrapt up in her children and their daily needs that she had lost all interest in anything outside her home. What was there wrong about it? He knew that Edith prided herself on being like her mother. But Judith had always found time for her friends. He himself had been more as Edith was now. How quickly after Judith died he had dropped all friends, all interests. "That's it," he ruefully told himself, "Edith takes after her father." And the same curious feeling which he had had with Laura, came back to him with her sister. This daughter, too, was a part of himself. His deep instinctive craving to keep to himself and his family was living on in Edith, was already dominating her home. What a queer mysterious business it was, this tie between a man and his child.

He was thinking of this when Baird arrived. Allan Baird was not only the doctor who had brought Edith's children into the world, he was besides an intimate friend, he had been Bruce's room-mate at college. As he came strolling into the room with his easy greeting of "Well, folks—" his low gruff voice, his muscular frame, over six feet two, and the kindly calm assurance in his lean strong visage, gave to Bruce and Roger the feeling of safety they needed. For this kind of work was his life. He had specialized on women, and after over fifteen years of toilsome uphill labor he had become at thirty-seven one of the big gynecologists. He was taking his success with the quiet relish of a man who had had to work for it hard. And yet he had not been spoiled by success. He worked even harder than before—so hard, in fact, that Deborah, with whom through Bruce and Edith he had long ago struck up an easy bantering friendship, had sturdily set herself the task of prying open his eyes a bit. She had taken him to her school at night and to queer little foreign cafés. And Baird, with a humor of his own, had retaliated by dragging her to the Astor Roof and to musical plays.

"If my eyes are to be opened," he had doggedly declared, "I propose to have some diamonds in the scenery,

and a little cheery ragtime, too. You've got a good heart,
Deborah Gale, but your head is full of tenements."

To-night to divert Bruce's thoughts from his wife, Baird
started him talking of his work. In six weeks Bruce had
crammed his mind with the details of skyscraper building,
and his talk was bewildering now, bristling with technical
terms, permeated through and through with the feeling
of strain and fierce competition. As Roger listened he
had again that sharp and oppressive sensation of a savage
modern town unrelentingly pressing, pressing in. Restlessly he glanced at Baird who sat listening quietly.
And Roger thought of the likeness between their two
professions. For Bruce, too, was a surgeon. His patients
were the husbands in their distracting offices. Baird's
were the wives and mothers in their equally distracting
homes. Which were more tense, the husbands or wives?
And, good Lord, what was it all about, this feverish strain
of getting and spending? What were they spending?
Their very life's blood. And what were they getting?
Happiness? What did most of them know of real happiness? How little they knew, how blind they were, and
yet how they laughed and chattered along, how engrossed
in their little games. What children, oh, what children!

"And am I any better than the rest? Do I know what
I'm after—what I'm about?"

He left them soon, for he felt very tired. He went to
his daughter to say good-night. And in her room the talk
he had heard became to him suddenly remote, that restless
world of small account. For in Edith, in the one brief
hour since her father had seen her last, there had come a
great transformation, into her face an eager light. She
was slipping down into a weird small world which for a
brief but fearful season was to be utterly her own, with
agony and bloody sweat, and joy and a deep mystery.
Clumsily he took her hand. It was moist and he felt it
clutch his own. He heard her breathing rapidly.

"Good-night," he said in a husky tone. "I'll be so glad, my dear, so glad."

For answer she gave him a hurried smile, a glance from her bright restless eyes. Then he went heavily from the room.

At home he found Deborah sitting alone, with a pile of school papers in her lap. As he entered she slowly turned her head.

"How is Edith?" she asked him. Roger told of his visit uptown, and spoke of Edith's anxiety over getting the children up to the farm.

"I'll take them myself," said Deborah.

"But how can you get away from school?"

"Oh, I think I can manage it. We'll leave on Friday morning and I can be back by Sunday night. I'll love it," Deborah answered.

"It'll be a great relief to her," said Roger, lighting a cigar. Deborah resumed her work, and there was silence for a time.

"I let George sit up with me till an hour after his bedtime," she told her father presently. "We started talking about white rats—you see it's still white rats with George —and that started us wondering about God. George wonders if God really knows about rats. 'Has he ever stuck his face right down and had a good close look at one? Has God ever watched a rat stand up and brush his whiskers with both paws? Has he ever really laughed at rats? And that's another thing, Aunt Deborah—does God ever laugh at all? Does he know how to take a joke? If he don't, we might as well quit right now!'"

Roger laughed with relish, and his daughter smiled at him:

"Then the talk turned from rats and God to a big dam out in the Rockies. George has been reading about it, he's thinking of being an engineer. And there was so much he wanted to know that he was soon upon the verge of discovering my ignorance—when all of a sudden a dreamy look, oh, a very dreamy look, came into his eyes—and he asked me this." And over her bright expressive face came a scowl of boyish intensity: "'Suppose I *was* an engineer—and I was working on a dam, or may be a bridge, in the Rockies. And say it was pretty far down south—say around the Grand Canyon. I should think they'd need a dam down there, or anyhow a bridge,' said George. And he eyed me in a cautious way which said as plain as the nose on your face, 'Good Lord, she's only a woman, and she won't understand.' But I showed him I was serious, and he asked me huskily, 'Suppose it was winter, Aunt Deborah, and the Giants were in Texas. Do you think I could get a few days off?' And then before he could tell me the Giants were a baseball nine, I said I was sure he could manage it. You should have seen his face light up. And he added very fervently, 'Gee, it must be wonderful to be an engineer out there!'"

Roger chuckled delightedly and Deborah went on with her work. "How good she is with young uns," he thought. "What a knack she has of drawing 'em out. What a pity she hasn't some of her own."

He slept until late the next morning, and awoke to find Deborah by his bed.

"It's another boy," she told him. Roger sat up excitedly. "Bruce has just telephoned the news. The children and I have breakfasted, and they're going out with their nurse. Suppose you and I go up and see Bruce and settle this trip to the mountains."

About an hour later, arriving at Edith's apartment, they found Bruce downstairs with Allan Baird who was just taking his departure. Bruce's dark eyes shone with relief, but his hand was hot and nervous. Allan, on the contrary, held out to Edith's father a hand as steady and relaxed as was the bantering tone of his voice.

"Bruce," he said, "has for once in his life decided to do something sensible. He's going to drop his wretched job and take a week off with his children."

"And worry every minute he's gone," Deborah retorted, "and come back and work day and night to catch up. But he isn't going to do it. I've decided to take the children myself."

"You have?" cried Bruce delightedly.

"You'll do no such thing," said Allan, indignant.

"Oh, you go to thunder," Bruce put in. "Haven't you any delicacy? Can't you see this is no business of yours?"

"It isn't, eh," Allan sternly rejoined. And of Deborah he demanded, "Didn't you say you'd go with me to 'Pinafore' this Saturday night?"

"Ah," sneered Bruce. "So that's your game. And for one little night of your pleasure you'd do me out of a week of my life!"

"Like that," said Baird, with a snap of his fingers.

"I'm going, though," said Deborah.

"Quite right, little woman," Bruce admonished her earnestly. "Don't let him rob you of your happiness."

"Come here," growled Baird to Deborah. She followed him into the living room, and Roger went upstairs with Bruce.

"If he ever hopes to marry that girl," said Bruce, with an anxious backward glance, "he's got to learn to treat her with a little consideration."

"Quit your quarreling," Roger said. "What's a week in the mountains to you? Hasn't your wife just risked her life?"

"Sure she has," said Bruce feelingly. "And I propose to stick by her, too."

"Can I see her?"

"No, you can't—another of Baird's fool notions."

"Then where's the baby?"

" Right in here."

Silently in front of the cradle Bruce and Roger stood looking down with the content which comes to men on such occasions when there is no woman by their side expecting them to say things.

"I made it a rule in my family," Roger spoke up presently, "to have my first look at each child alone."

"Same here," said Bruce. And they continued their silent communion. A few moments later, as they were leaving, Deborah came into the room and went softly to the cradle. Downstairs they found that Allan had gone, and when Deborah rejoined them she said she was going to stick to her plan. It was soon arranged that she and the youngsters should start on their journey the following day.

Back at home she threw herself into the packing and was busy till late that night. At daybreak she was up again, for they were to make an early start. Bruce came with his new automobile, the children were all bundled in, together with Deborah and their nurse, and a half hour later at the train Bruce and Roger left them—Deborah flushed and happy, surrounded by luggage, wraps, small boys, an ice box, toys and picture books. The small red hat upon her head had already been jerked in a scrimmage, far down over one of her ears.

"Don't worry about us, Bruce," she said. "We're going to have the time of our lives!" Bruce fairly beamed his gratitude.

"If she don't marry," he declared, as he watched the train move slowly out, "there'll be a great mother wasted."

CHAPTER VII

In the weeks which followed, Roger found the peace of his home so interrupted and disturbed by wedding preparations that often retreating into his den he earnestly told himself he was through, that a man with three grown daughters was a fool to show any sympathy with the utter folly of their lives. Yield an inch and they took a mile! It began one night when Deborah said,

"Now, dearie, I think you had better make up your mind to give Laura just the kind of wedding she likes."

And Roger weakly agreed to this, but as time wore on he discovered that the kind of wedding Laura liked was a thing that made his blood run cold. There seemed to be no end whatever to the young bride's blithe demands. The trousseau part of it he didn't mind. To the gowns and hats and gloves and shoes and trunks and jaunty travelling bags which came pouring into the house, he made no objection. All that, he considered, was fair play. But what got on Roger's nerves was this frantic fuss and change! The faded hall carpet had to come up, his favorite lounge was whisked away, the piano was re-tuned while he was trying to take a nap, rugs were beaten, crates and barrels filled the halls, and one whole bed-room stripped and bare was transformed into a shop where the wedding presents were displayed. In the shuffle his box of cigars disappeared. In short, there was the devil to pay!

And Deborah was as bad as the bride. At times it appeared to Roger as though her fingers fairly itched to jab and tug at his poor old house, which wore an air of

56

mute reproach. She revealed a part of her nature that he viewed with dark amazement. Every hour she could spare from school, she was changing something or other at home —with an eager glitter in her eyes. Doing it all for Laura, she said. Fiddlesticks and rubbish! She did it because she liked it!

In gloomy wrath one afternoon he went up to see Edith and quiet down. She was well on the way to recovery, but instead of receiving solace here he only found fresh troubles. For sitting up in her old-fashioned bed, with an old-fashioned cap of lace upon her shapely little head, Edith made her father feel she had washed her hands of the whole affair.

"I'm sorry," she said in an injured tone, "that Laura doesn't care enough about her oldest sister to put off the wedding two or three weeks so I could be there. It seems rather undignified, I think, for a girl to hurry her wedding so. I should have loved to make it the dear simple kind of wedding which mother would have wanted. But so long as she doesn't care for that—and in fact has only found ten minutes—once—to run in and see the baby—"

In dismay her father found himself defending the very daughter of whom he had come to complain. It was not such a short engagement, he said, he had learned they had been engaged some time before they told him.

"Do you approve of that?" she rejoined. "When I was engaged, I made Bruce go to you before I even let him—" here Edith broke off primly. "Of course that was some time ago. An engagement, Laura tells me, is 'a mere experiment' nowadays. They 'experiment' till they feel quite sure—then notify their parents and get married in a week."

"She is rushing it, I admit," Roger soothingly replied. "But she has her mind set on Paris in June."

"Paris in June," said Edith, "sums up in three words

Laura's whole conception of marriage. You really ought
to talk to her, father. It's your duty, it seems to me."

"What do you mean?"

"I'd rather not tell you." Edith's glance went sternly
to the cradle by her bed. "Laura pities me," she said,
"for having had five children."

"Oh, now, my dear girl!"

"She does, though—she said as much. When she
dropped in the other day and I tried to be sympathetic
and give her a little sound advice, she said I had had
the wedding I liked and the kind of married life I liked,
and she was going to have hers. And she made it quite
plain that her kind is to include no children. It's to be
simply an effort to find by 'experiment' whether or not
she loves Hal Sloane. If she doesn't—" Edith gave a
slight but emphatic wave of dismissal.

"Do you mean to say Laura told you that?" her father
asked with an angry frown.

"I mean she made me feel it—as plainly as I'm telling
it! What I can't understand," his daughter went on, "is
Deborah's attitude in the affair."

"What's the matter with Deborah?" inquired Roger
dismally.

"Oh, nothing's the matter with Deborah. She's quite
self-sufficient. She at least can play with modern ideas
and keep her head while she's doing it. But when poor
Laura—a mere child with the mind of a chicken—catches
vaguely at such ideas, applies them to her own little self
and risks her whole future happiness, it seems to me
perfectly criminal for Deborah not to interfere! Not even
a word of warning!"

"Deborah believes," said her father, "in everyone's
leading his own life."

"That's rot," was Edith's curt reply. "Do I lead my
own life? Does Bruce? Do you?"

"No," growled Roger feelingly.

"Do my children?" Edith demanded. "I know Deborah would like them to. That's her latest and most modern fad, to run a school where every child shall sit with a rat in its lap or a goat, and do just what he pleases— follow his natural bent, she says. I hope she won't come up to the mountains and practice on my children. I should hate to break with Deborah," Edith ended thoughtfully.

Roger rose and walked the room. The comforting idea entered his mind that when the wedding was over he would take out his collection of rings and carefully polish every one. But even this hope did not stay with him long.

"With Laura at home," he heard Edith continue, "you at least had a daughter to run your house. If Deborah tries to move you out—"

"She won't!" cried Roger in alarm.

"If she does," persisted Edith, "or if she begins any talk of the kind—you come to me and *I'll* talk to her!"

Her father walked in silence, his head down, frowning at the floor.

"It seems funny," Edith continued, "that women like me who give children their lives, and men like Bruce who are building New York—actually doing it all the time— have so little to say in these modern ideas. I suppose it's because we're a little too real."

"To come back to the wedding," Roger suggested.

"To come back to the wedding, father dear," his daughter said compassionately. "I'm afraid it's going to be a 'mere form' which will make you rather wretched. When you get so you can't endure it, come in and see me and the baby."

As he started for home, her words of warning recurred to his mind. Yes, here was the thing that disturbed him most, the ghost lurking under all this confusion, the part which had to do with himself. It was bad enough to know that his daughter, his own flesh and blood, was about to settle her fate at one throw. But to be moved out of his house bag and baggage! Roger strode wrathfully up the street.

"It's your duty to talk to her," Edith had said. And he meditated darkly on this: "Maybe I will and maybe I won't. I know my duties without being told. How does Edith know what her mother liked? We had our own likings, her mother and I, and our own ideas, long after she was tucked into bed. And yet she's always harping on 'what mother would have wanted.' What I should like to know—right now—is what Judith would want if she were here!"

With a pang of utter loneliness amid these vexing problems, Roger felt it crowding in, this city of his children's lives. As he strode on down Broadway, an old hag selling papers thrust one in his face and he caught a glimpse of a headline. Some bigwig woman re-divorced. How about Laura's "experiment"? A mob of street urchins nearly upset him. How about Deborah? How about children? How about schools, education, the country? How about God? Was anyone thinking? Had anyone time? What a racket it made, slam-banging along. The taxis and motor trucks thundered and brayed, dark masses of people swept endlessly by, as though their very souls depended on their dinners or their jobs, their movies, roaring farces, thrills, their harum scarum dances, clothes. A plump little fool of a woman, her skirt so tight she could barely walk, tripped by on high-heeled slippers. That was it, he told himself, the whole city was high-heeled! No solid footing anywhere! And, good Lord, how they chattered!

He turned into a less noisy street. What would Judith want if she were here? It became disturbingly clear to him that she would undoubtedly wish him to have a talk with Laura now, find out if she'd really made up her mind not to have any children, and if so to tell her plainly that she was not only going against her God but risking her own happiness. For though Judith had been liberal about any number of smaller things, she had been decidedly clear on this. Yes, he must talk to Laura.

"And she'll tell me," he reflected, "that Edith put me up to it!"

If only his oldest daughter would leave the other girls alone! Here she was planning a row with Deborah over whether poor young George should be allowed to play with rats! It was all so silly! . . . Yes, his three children were drifting apart, each one of them going her separate way. And he rather took comfort in the thought, for at least it would stop their wrangling. But again he pulled himself up with a jerk. No, certainly Judith would not have liked this. If she'd ever stood for anything, it was for keeping the family together. It had been the heart and center of their last talks before she died.

His face relaxed as he walked on, but in his eyes was a deeper pain. If only Judith could be here.

Before he reached home he had made up his mind to talk with Laura that very night. He drew out his latch-key, opened his door, shut it firmly and strode into his house. In the hall they were putting down the new carpet. Cautiously picking his way upstairs, he inquired for Laura and was told she was dressing for dinner. He knocked at her door.

"Yes?" came her voice.

"It's I," he said, "your father."

"Oh, hello, dad," came the answer gaily, in that high sweet voice of hers. "I'm frightfully rushed. It's a dinner dance to-night for the bridesmaids and the ushers." Roger felt a glow of relief. "Come in a moment. won't you?"

What a resplendent young creature she was, seated at her dresser. Behind her the maid with needle and thread was swiftly mending a little tear in the fluffy blue tulle she was wearing. The shaded light just over her head brought a shimmer of red in her sleek brown hair. What lips she had, what a bosom. She drew a deep breath and smiled at him.

"What are you doing to-morrow night?" her father asked her.

"Oh, dad, my love, we have every evening filled and crammed right up to the wedding," she replied. "No—the last evening I'll be here. Hal's giving his ushers a dinner that night."

"Good. I want to talk to you, my dear." He felt his voice solemn, a great mistake. He saw the quick glance from her luminous eyes.

"All right, father—whenever you like."

Much embarrassed Roger left the room.

The few days which remained were a crowding confusion of dressmakers, gowns and chattering friends and gifts arriving at all hours. As a part of his resolve to do what he could for his daughter, Roger stayed home from his office that week. But all he could do was to unpack boxes, take out presents and keep the cards, and say, "Yes, my dear, it's very nice. Where shall I put this one?" As the array of presents grew, from time to time unconsciously he glanced at the engagement ring upon Laura's finger. And all the presents seemed like that. They would suit her apartment beautifully. He'd be glad when they were out of the house.

The only gift that appealed to his fancy was a brooch, neither rich nor new, a genuine bit of old jewelry. But rather to his annoyance he learned that it had been sent to Laura by the old Galician Jew in the shop around the corner. It recalled to his mind the curious friendship which had existed for so long between the old man and his daughter. And as she turned the brooch to the light Roger thought he saw in her eyes anticipations which made him uneasy. Yes, she was a child of his. "June in Paris—"

other Junes—"experiments"—no children. Again he felt he must have that talk. But, good Lord, how he dreaded it.

The house was almost ready now, dismantled and made new and strange. It was the night before the wedding. Laura was taking her supper in bed. What was he going to say to her? He ate his dinner silently. At last he rose with grim resolution.

"I think I'll go up and see her," he said. Deborah quickly glanced at him.

"What for?" she asked.

"Oh, I just want to talk to her—"

"Don't stay long," she admonished him. "I've a masseuse coming at nine o'clock to get the child in condition to rest. Her nerves are rather tense, you know."

"How about mine?" he said to himself as he started upstairs. "Never mind, I've got to tackle it."

Laura saw what he meant to say the moment that he entered the room, and the tightening of her features made it all the harder for Roger to think clearly, to remember the grave, kind, fatherly things which he had intended to tell her.

"I don't want to talk of the wedding, child, but of what's coming after that—between you and this man— all your life." He stopped short, with his heart in his mouth, for although he did not look at her he had a quick sensation as though he had struck her in the face.

"Isn't this rather late to speak about that? Just now? When I'm nervous enough as it is?"

"I know, I know." He spoke hurriedly, humbly. "I should have talked to you long ago, I should have known you better, child. I've been slack and selfish. But it's better late than never."

"But you needn't!" the girl exclaimed. "You needn't tell me anything! I know more than you think—I know enough!" Roger looked at her, then at the wall. She went on in a voice rather breathless: "I know what I'm doing—exactly—just what I'm getting into. It's not as it was when you were young—it's different—we talk of these things. Harold and I have talked it all out." In the brief and dangerous pause which followed Roger kept looking at the wall.

"Have you talked—about having children?"

"Yes," came the answer sharply, and then he felt the hot clutch of her hand. "Hadn't you better go now, dad?" He hesitated.

"No," he said. His voice was low. "Do you mean to have children, Laura?"

"I don't know."

"I think you do know. Do you mean to have children?" Her big black eyes, dilating, were fixed defiantly on his own.

"Well then, no, I don't!" she replied. He made a desperate effort to think what he could say to her. Good God, how he was bungling! Where were all his arguments?

"How about your religion?" he blurted out.

"I haven't any—which makes me do that—I've a right to be happy!"

"You haven't!" His voice had suddenly changed. In accent and in quality it was like a voice from the heart of New England where he had been born and bred. "I mean you won't be happy—not unless you have a child! It's what you need—it'll fill your life! It'll settle you—deepen you—tone you down!"

"Suppose I don't want to be toned down!" The girl was almost hysterical. "I'm no Puritan—I want to live! I tell you we are different now! We're not all like Edith—and we're not like our mothers! We want to live! And we have a right to! Why don't you go? Can't you see I'm nearly crazy? It's my last night, my very last! I don't want to talk to you—I don't even know what I'm saying! And you come and try to frighten me!" Her voice caught and broke into sobs. "You know nothing about me! You never did! Leave me alone, can't you— leave me alone!"

"Father?" He heard Deborah's voice, abrupt and stern, outside the door.

"I'm sorry," he said hoarsely. He went in blind fashion out of the room and down to his study. He lit a cigar and smoked wretchedly there. When presently Deborah appeared he saw that her face was set and hard; but as she caught the baffled look, the angry tortured light in his eyes, her own expression softened.

"Poor father," she said, in a pitying way. "If Edith had only let you alone."

"I certainly didn't do much good."

"Of course you didn't—you did harm—oh, so much more harm than you know." Into the quiet voice of his daughter crept a note of keen regret. "I wanted to make her last days in this house a time she could look back on, so that she'd want to come home for help if ever she's in trouble. She has so little—don't you see?—of what a woman needs these days. She has grown up so badly. Oh, if you'd only let her alone. It was such a bad, bad time to choose." She went to her father and kissed him. "Well, it's over now," she said, "and we'll make the best we can of it. I'll tell her you're sorry and quiet her down. And to-morrow we'll try to forget it has happened."

For Roger the morrow went by in a whirl. The wedding, a large church affair, was to take place at twelve o'clock. He arose early, put on his Prince Albert, went down and ate his breakfast alone. The waitress was flustered, the coffee was burnt. He finished and anxiously wandered about. The maids were bustling in and out, with Deborah giving orders pellmell. The caterers came trooping in. The bridesmaids were arriving and hurrying up to Roger's room. That place was soon a chaos of voices, giggles,

peals of laughter. Laura's trunks were brought downstairs, and Roger tagged them for the ship, one for the
cabin and three for the hold, and saw them into the wagon.
Then he strode distractedly everywhere, till at last he was
hustled by Deborah into a taxi waiting outside.

"It's all going so smoothly," Deborah said, and a faint
sardonic glimmer came into her father's hunted eyes.
Deborah was funny!

Soon he found himself in the church. He heard whispers, eager voices, heard one usher say to another, "God,
what a terrible head I've got!" And Roger glared at him
for that. Plainly these youngsters, all mere boys, had
been up with the groom a good part of the night. . . .
But here was Laura, pale and tense. She smiled at him
and squeezed his hand. There was silence, then the organ,
and now he was taking her up the aisle. Strange faces
stared. His jaw set hard. At last they reached the altar.
An usher quickly touched his arm and he stepped back
where he belonged. He listened but understood nothing.
Just words, words and motions.

"If any man can show just cause why they may not be
lawfully joined together, let him now speak or else here-
after forever hold his peace."

"No," thought Roger, "I won't speak."

Just then he caught sight of Deborah's face, and at the
look in her steady gray eyes all at once he could feel the
hot tears in his own.

At the wedding breakfast he was gay to a boisterous
degree. He talked to strange women and brought them
food, took punch with men he had never laid eyes on,
went off on a feverish hunt for cigars, came back distractedly, joked with young girls and even started some
of them dancing. The whole affair was over in no time.
The bride and the groom came rushing downstairs; and
as they escaped from the shower of rice, Roger ran after
them down the steps. He gripped Sloane's hand.

"Remember, boy, it's her whole life!" entreated Roger hoarsely.

"Yes, sir! I'll look out! No fear!"

"Good-bye, daddy!"

"God bless you, dear!"

They were speeding away. And with the best man, who looked weary and spent, Roger went slowly back up the steps. It was an effort now to talk. Thank Heaven these people soon were gone. Last of all went the ponderous aunt of the groom. How the taxi groaned as he helped her inside and started her off to Bridgeport. Back in his study he found his cigars and smoked one dismally with Bruce. Bruce was a decent sort of chap. He knew when to be silent.

"Well," he spoke finally, rising, "I guess I'll have to get back to the office." He smiled a little and put his hand on Roger's weary shoulder. "We're glad it's over— eh?" he asked.

"Bruce," said Roger heavily, "you've got a girl of your own growing up. Don't let her grow to feel you're old. Live on with her. She'll need you." His massive blunt face darkened. "The world's so damnably new," he muttered, "so choked up with fool ideas." Bruce still smiled affectionately.

"Go up and see Edith," he said, "and forget 'em. She never lets one into the flat. She said you were to be sure to come and tell her about the wedding."

"All right, I'll go," said Roger. He hunted about for his hat and coat. What a devilish mess they had made of the house. A half hour later he was with Edith; but there, despite his efforts to answer all her questions, he grew heavier and heavier, till at last he barely spoke. He sat watching Edith's baby.

"Did you talk to Laura?" he heard her ask.

"Yes," he replied. "It did no good." He knew that Edith was waiting for more, but he kept doggedly silent.

"Well, dear," she said presently, "at least you did what you could for her."

"I've never done what I could," he rejoined. "Not with any one of you." He glanced at her with a twinge of pain. "I don't know as it would have helped much if I had. This town is running away with itself. I want a rest now, Edith, I want things quiet for a while." He felt her anxious, pitying look.

"Where's Deborah?" she asked him. "Gone back to school already?"

"I don't know where she is," he replied. And then he rose forlornly. "I guess I'll be going back home," he said.

On his way, as his thoughts slowly cleared, the old uneasiness rose in his mind. Would Deborah want to keep the house? Suppose she suggested moving to some titty-tatty little flat. No, he would not stand in her way. But, Lord, what an end to make of his life.

His home was almost dark inside, but he noticed rather to his surprise that the rooms had already been put in order. He sank down on the living room sofa and lay motionless for a while. How tired he was. From time to time he drearily sighed. Yes, Deborah would find him old and life here dull and lonely. Where was she to-night, he wondered. Couldn't she quit her zoo school for one single afternoon? At last, when the room had grown pitch dark, he heard the maid lighting the gas in the hall. Roger loudly cleared his throat, and at the sound the startled girl ejaculated, "Oh, my Gawd!"

"It's I," said Roger sternly. "Did Miss Deborah say when she'd be back?"

"She didn't go out, sir. She's up in her room."

Roger went up and found her there. All afternoon with both the maids she had been setting the house to rights, and now she ached in every limb. She was lying on her bed, and she looked as though she had been crying.

"Where have you been?" she inquired.

"At Edith's," her father answered. She reached up and took his hand, and held it slowly tighter.

"You aren't going to find it too lonely here, with Laura gone?" she asked him. And the wistfulness in her deep sweet voice made something thrill in Roger.

"Why should I?" he retorted. Deborah gave a queer little laugh.

"Oh, I'm just silly, that's all," she said. "I've been having a fit of blues. I've been feeling so old this afternoon—a regular old woman. I wanted you, dearie, and I was afraid that you—" she broke off.

"Look here," said Roger sharply. "Do you really want to keep this house?"

"Keep this house? Why, father!"

"You think you can stand it here alone, just the two of us?" he demanded.

"I can," cried Deborah happily. Her father walked to the window. There as he looked blindly out, his eyes were assaulted by the lights of all those titty-tatty flats. And a look of vicious triumph appeared for a moment on his face.

"Very well," he said quietly, turning back. "Then we're both suited." He went to the door. "I'll go and wash up for supper," he said.

CHAPTER VIII

It was a relief to him to find how smoothly he and Deborah dropped back into their old relations. It was good to get home those evenings; for in this new stage of its existence, with its family of two, the house appeared to have filled itself with a deep reposeful feeling. Laura had gone out of its life. He glanced into her room one night, and it looked like a guest room now. The sight of it brought him a pang of regret. But the big ship which was bearing her swiftly away to "Paris in June" seemed bearing off Roger's uneasiness too. He could smile at his former fears, for Laura was safely married and wildly in love with her husband. Time, he thought, would take care of the rest. Occasionally he missed her here—her voice, high-pitched but musical, chatting and laughing at the 'phone, her bustle of dressing to go out, glimpses of her extravagances, of her smart suits and evening gowns, of all the joyous color and dash that she had given to his home. But these regrets soon died away. The old house shed them easily, as though glad to enter this long rest.

For the story of his family, from Roger's point of view at least, was a long uneven narrative, with prolonged periods of peace and again with events piling one on the other. And now there came one of those peaceful times, and Roger liked the quiet. The old routine was re-established—his dinner, his paper, his cigar and then his book for the evening, some good old-fashioned novel or some pleasant book of travel which he and Judith had read aloud when they were planning out their lives. They had meant to go abroad so often when the children had grown up. And

70

he liked to read about it still. Life was so quiet over the sea, things were so old and mellow there. He resumed, too, his horseback rides, and on the way home he would stop in for a visit with Edith and her baby. The wee boy grew funnier every day, with his sudden kicks and sneezes, his waving fists and mighty yawns. And Roger felt drawn to his daughter here, for in these grateful seasons of rest that followed the birth of each of her children, Edith loved to lie very still and make new plans for her small brood.

Only once she spoke of Laura, and then it was to suggest to him that he gather together all the bills his daughter had doubtless left behind.

"If you don't settle them," Edith said, "they'll go to her husband. And you wouldn't like that, would you?"

Roger said he would see to it, and one evening after dinner he started in on Laura's bills. It was rather an appalling time. He looked into his bank account and found that Laura's wedding would take about all his surplus. But this did not dismay him much, for money matters never did. It simply meant more work in the office.

The next day he rose early and was in his office by nine o'clock. He had not been so prompt in months, and many of his employees came in late that morning. But nobody seemed very much perturbed, for Roger was an easy employer. Still, he sternly told himself, he had been letting things get altogether too slack. He had been neglecting his business again. The work had become so cut and dried, there was nothing creative left to do. It had not been so in years gone by. Those years had fairly bristled with ideas and hopes and schemes. But even those old memories were no longer here to hearten him. They had all been swept away when Bruce had made him move out of his office in a dark creaky edifice down close under Brooklyn Bridge, and come up to this new building, this

steel-ribbed caravansary for all kinds of business ventures, this place of varnished woodwork, floods of daylight, concrete floors, this building fireproof throughout.
That expressed it exactly, Roger thought. Nothing
could take fire here, not even a man's imagination, even
though he did not feel old. Now and then in the elevator,
as some youngster with eager eyes pushed nervously
against him, Roger would frown and wonder, "What are
you so excited about?"

But again the business was running down, and this
time he must jerk it back before it got beyond him. He
set himself doggedly to the task, calling in his assistants
one by one, going through the work in those outer
rooms, where at tables long rows of busy young girls,
with colored pencils, scissors and paste, were demolish-
ing enormous piles of newspapers and magazines. And
vaguely, little by little, he came to a realization of how
while he had slumbered the life of the country had swept
on. For as he studied the lists and the letters of his patrons, Roger felt confusedly that a new America was here.

Clippings, clippings, clippings. Business men and business firms, gigantic corporations, kept sending here for
clippings, news of themselves or their rivals, keeping keen
watch on each other's affairs for signs of strength or weak-
ness. How savage was the fight these days. Here was
news of mines and mills and factories all over the land,
clippings sent each morning by special messengers downtown to reach the brokers' offices before the market
opened. One broker wrote, "Please quote your terms for
the following. From nine to two o'clock each day our
messenger will call at your office every hour for clippings
giving information of the companies named below."
The long list appended carried Roger's fancy out all over
the continent. And then came this injunction: "Remember that our messenger must leave your office every hour.
In information of this kind every minute counts."

Clippings, clippings, clippings. As Roger turned over his morning mail, in spite of himself he grew absorbed. What a change in the world of literature. What a host of names of scribblers, not authors but just writers, not only men but women too, novelists and dramatists, poets and muckrakers all jumbled in together, each one of them straining for a place. And the actors and the actresses, the musicians and the lecturers, each with his press agent and avid for publicity, "fame!" And here were society women, from New York and other cities, all eager for press notices of social affairs they had given or managed, charity work they had conducted, suffrage speeches they had made. Half the women in the land were fairly talking their heads off, it seemed. Some had been on his lists for years. They married and wanted to hear what was said in the papers about their weddings, they quarreled and got divorces and still sent here for clippings, they died and still their relatives wrote in for the funeral notices. And even death was commercialized. A maker of monuments wanted news "of all people of large means, dead or dangerously ill, in the State of Pennsylvania." Here were demands from charity bodies, hospitals and colleges, from clergymen with an anxious eye on the Monday morning papers. And here was an anarchist millionaire! And here was an insane asylum wanting to see itself in print!

With a grim smile on his heavy visage, Roger stared out of his window. Slowly the smile faded, a wistful look came on his face.

"Who'll take my business when I'm gone?"

If his small son had only lived, with what new zest and vigor it might have been made to grow and expand. If only his son had been here by his side. . . .

CHAPTER IX

DEBORAH needed rest, he thought, for the bright attractive face of his daughter was looking rather pale of late, and the birthmark on her forehead showed a faint thin line of red. One night at dinner, watching her, he wondered what was on her mind. She had come in late, and though several times she had made an effort to keep up the conversation, her cheeks were almost colorless and more than once in her deepset eyes came a flash of pain that startled him.

"Look here. What's the matter with you?" he asked. Deborah looked up quickly.

"I'd rather not talk about it, dad—"

"Very well," he answered. And with a slight hesitation, "But I think I know the trouble," he said. "And perhaps some other time—when you do feel like talking—" He stopped, for on her wide sensitive lips he saw a twitch of amusement.

"What do you think is the trouble?" she asked. And Roger looked at her squarely.

"Loneliness," he answered.

"Why?" she asked him.

"Well, there's Edith's baby—and Laura getting married—"

"I see—and so I'm lonely for a family of my own. But you're forgetting my school," she said.

"Yes, yes, I know," he retorted. "But that's not at all the same. Interesting work, no doubt, but—well, it isn't personal."

"Oh, isn't it?" she answered, and she drew a quivering breath. Rising from the table she went into the living

74

room, and there a few moments later he found her walking up and down. "I think I *will* tell you now," she said. "I'm afraid of being alone to-night, of keeping this matter to myself." He looked at her apprehensively.

"Very well, my dear," he said.

"This is the trouble," she began. "Down in my school we've a family of about three thousand children. A few I get to know so well I try to follow them when they leave. And one of these, an Italian boy—his name is Joe Bolini—was one of the best I ever had, and one of the most appealing. But Joe took to drinking and got in with a gang of boys who blackmailed small shopkeepers. He used to come to me at times in occasional moods of re-pentance. He was a splendid physical type and he'd been a leader in our athletics, so I took him back into the school to manage our teams in basket-ball. He left the gang and stopped drinking, and we had long talks to-gether about his great ambition. He wanted to enter the Fire Department as soon as he was twenty-one. And I promised to use my influence." She stopped, still frown-ing slightly.

"What happened?" Roger asked her.

"His girl took up with another man, and Joe has hot Italian blood. He got drunk one night and—shot them both." There was another silence. "I did what I could," she said harshly, "but he had a bad record behind him, and the young assistant district attorney had his own record to think of, too. So Joe got a death sentence. We appealed the case but it did no good. He was sent up the river and is in the death house now—and he sent for me to come to-day. His letter hinted he was scared, he wrote that his priest was no good to him. So I went up this afternoon. Joe goes to the chair to-morrow at six."

Deborah went to the sofa and sat down inertly. Roger remained motionless, and a dull chill crept over him.

"So you see my work is personal," he heard her mutter

presently. All at once she seemed so far away, such a stranger to him in this life of hers.

"By George, it's horrible!" he said. "I'm sorry you went to see the boy!"

"I'm glad," was his daughter's quick retort. "I've been getting much too sure of myself—of my school, I mean, and what it can do. I needed this to bring me back to the kind of world we live in!"

"What do you mean?" he roughly asked.

"I mean there are schools and prisons! And gallows and electric chairs! And I'm for schools! They've tried their jails and gallows for whole black hideous centuries! What good have they done? If they'd given Joe back to the school and me, I'd have had him a fireman in a year! I know, because I studied him hard! He'd have *grown* fighting fires, he would have *saved* lives!"

Again she stopped, with a catch of her breath. In suspense he watched her angry struggle to regain control of herself. She sat bolt upright, rigid; her birthmark showed a fiery red. In a few moments he saw her relax.

"But of course," she added wearily, "it's much more complex than that. A school is nothing nowadays—just by itself alone, I mean—it's only a part of a city's life —which for most tenement children is either very dull and hard, or cheap and false and overexciting. And behind all that lie the reasons for that. And there are so many reasons." She stared straight past her father as though at something far away. Then she seemed to recall herself: "But I'm talking too much of my family."

Roger carefully lit a cigar:

"I don't think you are, my dear. I'd like to hear more about it." She smiled:

"To keep my mind off Joe, you mean."

"And mine, too," he answered.

They had a long talk that evening about her hope of making her school what Roger visaged confusedly as a

kind of mammoth home, the center of a neighborhood,
of one prodigious family. At times when the clock on the
mantle struck the hour loud and clear, there would fall
a sudden silence, as both thought of what was to happen
at dawn. But quickly Roger would question again and
Deborah would talk steadily on. It was after midnight
when she stopped.

"You've been good to me to-night, dearie," she said.
"Let's go to bed now, shall we?"

"Very well," he answered. He looked at his daughter
anxiously. She no longer seemed to him mature. He
could feel what heavy discouragements, what problems
she was facing in the dark mysterious tenement world
which she had chosen to make her own. And compared
to these she seemed a mere girl, a child groping its way,
just making a start. And so he added wistfully, "I wish
I could be of more help to you." She looked up at him
for a moment.

"Do you know why you *are* such a help?" she said.
"It's because you have never grown old—because you've
never allowed yourself to grow absolutely certain about
anything in life." A smile half sad and half perplexed
came on her father's heavy face.

"You consider that a strong point?" he asked.

"I do," she replied, "compared to being a bundle of
creeds and prejudices."

"Oh, I've got prejudices enough."

"Yes," she said. "And so have I. But we're not even
sure of *them*, these days."

"The world has a habit of crowding in," her father
muttered vaguely.

Roger did not sleep that night. He could not keep his
thoughts away from what was going to happen at dawn.
Yes, the city was crowding in upon this quiet house of his.
Dimly he could recollect, in the genial years of long ago,

just glancing casually now and then at some small and
unobtrusive notice in his evening paper: "Execution at
Sing Sing." It had been so remote to him. But here it
was smashing into his house, through the life his own
daughter was leading day and night among the poor!
Each time he thought of that lad in a cell, again a chill
crept over him! But savagely he shook it off, and by a
strong effort of his will he turned his thoughts to the things
she had told him about her school. Yes, in her main idea
she was right. He had no use for wild reforms, but here
was something solid, a good education for every child.
More than once, while she had talked, something very
deep in Roger had leaped up in swift response.

For Deborah, too, was a part of himself. He, too, had
had his feeling for humanity in the large. For years he
had run a boys' club at a little mission school in which
his wife had been interested, and on Christmas Eve he
had formed the habit of gathering up a dozen small urchins
right off the street and taking them 'round and fitting
them out with good warm winter clothing, after which
he had gone home to help Judith trim the Christmas tree
and fill their children's stockings. And later, when she
had gone to bed, invariably he had taken "The Christmas
Carol" from its shelf and had settled down with a glow
of almost luxurious brotherhood. There was sentiment
in Roger Gale, and as he read of "Tiny Tim" his deepset
eyes would glisten with tears.

And now here was Deborah fulfilling a part of him in
herself. "You will live on in our children's lives." But
this was going much too far! She was letting herself be
swallowed up completely by this work of hers! It was all
very well for the past ten years, but she was getting on
in age! High time to marry and settle down!

Again angrily he shook off the thought of that boy Joe
alone in a cell, eyes fixed in animal terror upon the steel
door which would open so soon.

The day was slowly breaking. It was the early part of June. How fresh and lovely it must be up there in the big mountains with Edith's happy little lads. Here it was raw and garish, weird. Some sparrows began quarreling just outside his window. Roger rose and walked the room. Restlessly he went into the hall. The old house appeared so strange in this light—as though stripped bare—there was something gone. Softly he came to Deborah's door. It was open wide, for the night had been warm, and she lay awake upon her bed with her gaze fixed on the ceiling. She turned her head and saw him there. He came in and sat down by her window. For a long time neither made a sound. Then the great clock on the distant tower, which had been silent through the night, resumed its deep and measured boom. It struck six times. There was silence again. More and more taut grew his muscles, and suddenly it felt to him as though Deborah's fierce agony were pounding into his very soul. The slow, slow minutes throbbed away. At last he rose and left her. There was a cold sweat on his brow.

"I'll go down and make her some coffee," he thought.

Down in the kitchen it was a relief to bang about hunting for the utensils. On picnics up in the mountains his coffee had been famous. He made some now and boiled some eggs, and they breakfasted in Deborah's room. She seemed almost herself again. Later, while he was dressing, he saw her in the doorway. She was looking at her father with bright and grateful, affectionate eyes.

"Will you come to school with me to-day? I'd like you to see it," Deborah said.

"Very well," he answered gruffly.

CHAPTER X

Out of the subway they emerged into a noisy tenement street. Roger had known such streets as this, but only in the night-time, as picturesque and adventurous ways in an underground world he had explored in search of strange old glittering rings. It was different now. Gone were the Rembrandt shadows, the leaping flare of torches, the dark surging masses of weird uncouth humanity. Here in garish daylight were poverty and ugliness, here were heaps of refuse and heavy smells and clamor. It disgusted and repelled him, and he was tempted to turn back. But glancing at Deborah by his side he thought of the night she had been through. No, he decided, he would go on and see what she was up to here.

They turned into a narrower street between tall dirty tenements, and in a twinkling all was changed. For the street, as far as he could see, was gay with flaunting colors, torrents of bobbing hats and ribbons, frocks and blouses, shirts and breeches, vivid reds and yellows and blues. It was deafening with joyous cries, a shrill incessant chatter, chatter, piercing yells and shrieks of laughter. Children, swarms of children, children of all sizes passed him, clean and dirty, smiling, scowling, hurrying, running, pummeling, grabbing, whirling each other 'round and 'round—till the very air seemed quivering with wild spirits and new life!

He heard Deborah laughing. Five hilarious small boys had hold of her hands and were marching in triumph waving their caps. "Heigh there—heigh there! Heigh—heigh—heigh!"

The school was close in front of them. An enormous

80

building of brick and tile wedged into a disordered mass
of tenements, shops and factories, it had been built around
a court shut out from the street by a high steel fence.
They squeezed into the gateway, through which a shouting
punching mob of urchins were now pushing in; and soon
from a balcony above Roger looked down into the court,
where out of a wild chaos order was appearing. Boys to
the right and girls to the left were forming in long sinuous
lines, and three thousand faces were turned toward the
building. In front appeared the Stars and Stripes. Then
suddenly he heard a crash from underneath the balcony,
and looking down he saw a band made up of some thirty
or forty boys. Their leader, a dark Italian lad, made a
flourish, a pass with his baton, and the band broke into
a blaring storm, an uproarious, booming march. The mob
below fell into step, and line after line in single file the
children marched into their school.

"Look up! Look all around you!" He heard Deborah's
eager voice in his ear. And as he looked up from the
court below he gave a low cry of amazement. In hundreds
of windows all around, of sweatshops, tenements, factories,
on tier upon tier of fire escapes and even upon the roofs
above, silent watchers had appeared. For this one moment in the day the whole congested neighborhood had
stopped its feverish labor and become an amphitheater
with all eyes upon the school. And the thought flashed
into Roger's mind: "Deborah's big family!"

He had a strange confusing time. In her office, in a
daze, he sat and heard his daughter with her two assistant
principals, her clerk and her stenographer, plunge into the
routine work of the day. What kind of school teacher
was this? She seemed more like the manager of some
buzzing factory. Messages kept coming constantly from
class-rooms, children came for punishment, and on each
small human problem she was passing judgment quickly.
Meanwhile a score of mothers, most of them Italians with

colored shawls upon their heads, had straggled in and
taken seats, and one by one they came to her desk. For
these women who had been children in peasant huts in
Italy now had children of their own in the great city of
New York, and they found it very baffling. How to keep
them in at night? How to make them go to the priest?
How to feed and clothe them? How to live in these tenement homes, in this wild din and chaos? They wanted
help and they wanted advice. Deborah spoke in Italian,
but turning to her father she would translate from time to
time.

A tired scowling woman said, "My boy won't obey me.
His father is dead. When I slap him he only jumps away.
I lock him in and he steals the key, he keeps it in his pocket.
He steals the money that I earn. He says I'm from the
country." And a flabby anxious woman said, "My girl
runs out to dance halls. Sometimes she comes back at
two in the morning. She is fifteen and she ought to get
married. But what can I do? A nice steady man who
never dances comes sometimes to see her—but she makes
faces and calls him a fatty, she dances before him and
pushes him out and slams the door. What can I do?"

"Please come and see our janitor and make him fix our
kitchen sink!" an angry little woman cried. "When I
try to wash the dishes the water spouts all over me!"
And then a plump rosy mother said in a soft coaxing voice,
"I have eight little children, all nice and clean. When
you tell them to do anything they always do it quickly.
They smile at you, they are like saints. So could the kind
beautiful teacher fix it up with a newspaper to send them
to the country—this summer when it is so hot? The
newspaper could send a man and he could take our pictures."

"Most of us girls used to be in this school," said a bright
looking Jewess of eighteen. "And you taught us how we
should live nice. But how can we live nice when our shop

is so rotten? Our boss is trying to kiss the girls, he is trying to hug them on the stairs. And what he pays us is a joke, and we must work till nine o'clock. So will you help us, teacher, and give us a room for our meetings here? We want to have a union."

A truant officer brought in two ragged, frightened little chaps. Found on the street during school hours, they had to give an account of themselves. Sullenly one of them gave an address far up in the Bronx, ten miles away. They had not been home for a week, he said. Was he lying? What was to be done? Somewhere in the city their homes must be discovered. And the talk of the truant officer made Roger feel ramifications here which wound out through the police and the courts to reformatories, distant cells. He thought of that electric chair, and suddenly he felt oppressed by the heavy complexity of it all.

And this was part and parcel of his daughter's daily work in school! Still dazed, disturbed but curious, he sat and watched and listened, while the bewildering demands of Deborah's big family kept crowding in upon her. He went to a few of the class-rooms and found that reading and writing, arithmetic and spelling were being taught in ways which he had never dreamed of. He found a kindergarten class, a carpenter shop and a printing shop, a sewing class and a cooking class in a large model kitchen. He watched the nurse in her hospital room, he went into the dental clinic where a squad of fifty urchins were having their teeth examined, and out upon a small side roof he found a score of small invalids in steamer chairs, all fast asleep. It was a strange astounding school! He heard Deborah speak of a mothers' club and a neighborhood association; and he learned of other ventures here, the school doctor, the nurse and the visitor endlessly making experiments, delving into the neighborhood for ways to meet its problems. And by the way Deborah talked

to them he felt she had gone before, that years ago
by day and night she had been over the ground alone.
And she'd done all this while she lived in his house!

Scattered memories out of the past, mere fragments
she had told him, here flashed back into his mind: humorous little incidents of daily battles she had waged in
rotten old tenement buildings with rags and filth and gar-
bage, with vermin, darkness and disease. Mingled with
these had been accounts of dances, weddings and christen-
ings and of curious funeral rites. And struggling with
such dim memories of Deborah in her twenties, called
forth in his mind by the picture of the woman of thirty
here, Roger grew still more confused. What was to be the
end of it? She was still but a pioneer in a jungle, endlessly groping and trying new things.

"How many children are there in the public schools?"
he asked.

"About eight hundred thousand," Deborah said.

"Good Lord!" he groaned, and he felt within him a
glow of indignation rise against these immigrant women
for breeding so inconsiderately. With the mad city growing so fast, and the people of the tenements breeding,
breeding, breeding, and packing the schools to bursting,
what could any teacher be but a mere cog in a machine,
ponderous, impersonal, blind, grinding out future New
Yorkers?

He reached home limp and battered from the storm of
new impressions coming on top of his sleepless night.
He had thought of a school as a simple place, filled with
little children, mischievous at times perhaps and some
with dirty faces, but still with minds and spirits clean,
unsoiled as yet by contact with the grim spirit of the
town. He had thought of childhood as something intimate and pure, inside his home, his family. Instead of
that, in Deborah's school he had been disturbed and
thrilled by the presence all around him of something

wild, barbaric, dark, compounded of the city streets, of surging crowds, of rushing feet, of turmoil, filth, disease and death, of poverty and vice and crime. But Roger could still hear that band. And behind its blaring crash and din he had felt the vital throbbing of a tremendous joyousness, of gaiety, fresh hopes and dreams, of leaping young emotions like deep buried bubbling springs bursting up resistlessly to renew the fevered life of the town! Deborah's big family! Everybody's children!

"You will live on in our children's lives." The vision hidden in those words now opened wide before his eyes.

CHAPTER XI

She told him the next morning her night school closed for the summer that week.

"I think I should like to see it," her father said determinedly. She gave him an affectionate smile:

"Oh, dearie. Haven't you had enough?"

"I guess I can stand it if you can," was his gruff rejoinder, "though if I ran a school like yours I think by night I'd have schooled enough. Do most principals run night schools too?"

"A good many of them do."

"Isn't it taxing your strength?" he asked.

"Don't you have to tax your strength," his daughter replied good humoredly, "to really accomplish anything? Don't you have to risk yourself in order to really live these days? Suppose you come down to-morrow night. We won't go to the school, for I doubt if the clubs and classes would interest you very much. I'll take you through the neighborhood."

They went down the following evening. The night was warm and humid, and through the narrow tenement streets there poured a teeming mass of life. People by the thousands passed, bareheaded, men in shirt sleeves, their faces glistening with sweat. Animal odors filled the air. The torches on the pushcarts threw flaring lights and shadows, the peddlers shouted hoarsely, the tradesmen in the booths and stalls joined in with cries, shrill peals of mirth. The mass swept onward, talking, talking, and its voice was a guttural roar. Small boys and girls with piercing yells kept darting under elbows, old women dozed on door-

steps, babies screamed on every side. Mothers leaned out
of windows, and by their faces you could see that they were
screaming angrily for children to come up to bed. But you
could not hear their cries. Here around a hurdy-gurdy
gravely danced some little girls. A tense young Jew, dark
faced and thin, was shouting from a wagon that all men
and women must be free and own the factories and mills.
A mob of small boys, clustered 'round a "camp fire"
they had made on the street, were leaping wildly through
the flames. It was a mammoth cauldron here, seething,
bubbling over with a million foreign lives. Deborah's
big family.

She turned into a doorway, went down a long dark passage and came into a court-yard enclosed by greasy tenement walls that reared to a spot of dark blue sky where a
few quiet stars were twinkling down. With a feeling of
repugnance Roger followed his daughter into a tall rear
building and up a rickety flight of stairs. On the fourth
landing she knocked at a door, and presently it was opened
by a stout young Irish woman with flushed haggard features
and disheveled hair.

"Oh. Good evening, Mrs. Berry."

"Good evening. Come in," was the curt reply. They
entered a small stifling room where were a stove, two kitch-
en chairs and three frowzled beds in corners. On one
of the beds lay a baby asleep, on another two small restless boys sat up and watched the visitors. A sick man lay
upon the third. And a cripple boy, a boarder here, stood
on his crutches watching them. Roger was struck at
once by his face. Over the broad cheek bones the sallow
skin was tightly drawn, but there was a determined set
to the jaws that matched the boy's shrewd grayish eyes,
and his face lit up in a wonderful smile.

"Hello, Miss Deborah," he said. His voice had a
cheery quality.

"Hello, Johnny. How are you?"

"Fine, thank you."

"That's good. I've brought my father with me."

"Howdado, sir, glad to meet you."

"It's some time since you've been to see me, John," Deborah continued.

"I know it is," he answered. And then with a quick jerk of his head, "He's been pretty bad," he said. Roger looked at the man on the bed. With his thin waxen features drawn, the man was gasping for each breath.

"What's the matter?" Roger whispered.

"Lungs," said the young woman harshly. "You needn't bother to speak so low. He can't hear you anyhow. He's dying. He's been dying weeks."

"Why didn't you let me know of this?" Deborah asked gently.

"Because I knew what you'd want to do—take him off to a hospital! And I ain't going to have it! I promised him he could die at home!"

"I'm sorry," Deborah answered. There was a moment's silence, and the baby whimpered in its sleep. One child had gone to his father's bed and was frowning at his agony as though it were a tiresome sight.

"Are any of them coughing?" Deborah inquired.

"No," said the woman sharply.

"Yes, they are, two of 'em," John cheerfully corrected her.

"You shut up!" she said to him, and she turned back to Deborah. "It's my home, I guess, and my family, too. So what do you think that *you* can do?" Deborah looked at her steadily.

"Yes, it's your family," she agreed. "And it's none of my business, I know—except that John is one of my boys —and if things are to go on like this I can't let him board here any more. If he had let me know before I'd have taken him from you sooner. You'll miss the four dollars a week he pays."

The woman swallowed fiercely. The flush on her face had deepened. She scowled to keep back the tears.

"We can all die for all I care! I've about got to the end of my rope!"

"I see you have." Deborah's voice was low. "You've made a hard plucky fight, Mrs. Berry. Are there any empty rooms left in this building?"

"Yes, two upstairs. What do you want to know for?"

"I'm going to rent them for you. I'll arrange it to-night with the janitor, on condition that you promise to move your children to-morrow upstairs and keep them there until this is over. Will you?"

"Yes."

"That's sensible. And I'll have one of the visiting nurses here within an hour."

"Thanks."

"And later on we'll have a talk."

"All right—"

"Good-night, Mrs. Berry."

"Good-night, Miss Gale, I'm much obliged. . . . Say, wait a minute! Will you?" The wife had followed them out on the landing and she was clutching Deborah's arm. "Why can't the nurse give him something," she whispered, "to put him to sleep for good and all? It ain't right to let a man suffer like that! I can't stand it! I'm —I'm—" she broke off with a sob. Deborah put one arm around her and held her steadily for a moment.

"The nurse will see that he sleeps," she said. "Now, John," she added, presently, when the woman had gone into the room, "I want you to get your things together. I'll have the janitor move them upstairs. You sleep there to-night, and to-morrow morning come to see me at the school."

"All right, Miss Deborah, much obliged. I'll be all right. Good-night, sir—"

"Good-night, my boy," said Roger, and suddenly he

cleared his throat. He followed his daughter down the stairs. A few minutes she talked with the janitor, then joined her father in the court.

"I'm sorry I took you up there," she said. "I didn't know the man was sick."

"Who are they?" he asked.

"Poor people," she said. And Roger flinched.

"Who is this boy?"

"A neighbor of theirs. His mother, who was a widow, died about two years ago. He was left alone and scared to death lest he should be 'put away' in some big institution. He got Mrs. Berry to take him in, and to earn his board he began selling papers instead of coming to our school. So our school visitor looked him up. Since then I have been paying his board from a fund I have from friends uptown, and so he has finished his schooling. He's to graduate next week. He means to be a stenographer."

"How old is he?"

"Seventeen," she replied.

"How was he crippled? Born that way?"

"No. When he was a baby his mother dropped him one Saturday night when she was drunk. He has never been able to sit down. He can lie down or he can stand. He's always in pain, it never stops. I learned that from the doctor I took him to see. But whenever you ask him how he feels you get the same answer always: 'Fine, thank you.' He's a fighter, is John."

"He looks it. I'd like to help that boy—"

"All right—you can help him," Deborah said. "You'll find him quite a tonic."

"A what?"

"A tonic," she repeated. And with a sudden tightening of her wide and sensitive mouth, Deborah added slowly, "Because, though I've known many hungry boys, Johnny Geer is the hungriest of them all—hungry to get on in life, to grow and learn and get good things, get friends, love, happiness, everything!" As she spoke of this child in her family, over her strong quiet face there swept a fierce, intent expression which struck Roger rather cold. What a fight she was making, this daughter of his, against what overwhelming odds. But all he said to her was this:

"Now let's look at something more cheerful, my dear."

"Very well," she answered with a smile. "We'll go and see Isadore Freedom."

"Who's he?"

"Isadore Freedom," said Deborah, "is the beginning of something tremendous. He came from Russian Poland—and the first American word he learned over there was 'freedom.' So in New York he changed his name to that—very solemnly, by due process of law. It cost him seven dollars. He had nine dollars at the time. Isadore is a flame, a kind of a torch in the wilderness."

"How does the flame earn his living?"

"At first in a sweatshop," she replied. "But he came to my school five nights a week, and at ten o'clock when school was out he went to a little basement café, where he sat at a corner table, drank one glass of Russian tea and studied till they closed at one. Then he went to his room, he told me, and used to read himself to sleep. He slept as a rule four hours. He said he felt he needed it. Now he's a librarian earning fifteen dollars a week, and having all the money he needs he has put the thought of it out of his life and is living for education—education in freedom. For Isadore has studied his name until he thinks he knows what it means."

They found him in a small public library on an ill-smelling ghetto street. The place had been packed with people, but the clock had just struck ten and the readers were leaving reluctantly, many with books under their arms. At sight of Deborah and her father, Isadore leaped up from his desk and came quickly to meet them with outstretched hands.

"Oh, this is splendid! Good evening!" he cried. Hardly more than a boy, perhaps twenty-one, he was short of frame but large of limb. He had wide stooping shoulders and reddish hollows in his dark cheeks. Yet there was a springiness in his step, vigor and warmth in the grip of his hand, in the very curl of his thick black hair, in his voice, in his enormous smile.

"Come," he said to Roger, when the greetings were over. "You shall see my library, sir. But I want that you shall not see it alone. While you look you must close for me your eyes and see other libraries, many, many, all over the world. You must see them in big cities and in very little towns to-night. You must see people, millions there, hungry, hungry people. Now I shall show you their food and their drink." As he spoke he was leading them proudly around. In the stacks along the walls he pointed out fiction, poetry, history, books of all the sciences.

"They read all, all!" cried Isadore. "Look at this Darwin on my desk. In a year so many have read this book it is a case for the board of health. And look at this shelf of economics. I place it next to astronomy. And I say to these people, 'Yes, read about jobs and your hours and wages. Yes, you must strike, you must have better lives. But you must read also about the stars— and about the big spaces—silent—not one single little sound for many, many million years. To be free you must grow as big as that—inside of your head, inside of your soul. It is not enough to be free of a czar, a kaiser or a sweatshop boss. What will you do when they are gone? My fine people, how will you run the world? You are deaf and blind, you must be free to open your own ears and eyes, to look into the books and see what is there— great thoughts and feelings, great ideas! And when you have seen, then you must think—you must think it all out every time! That is freedom!'" He stopped abruptly. Again on his dark features came a huge and winning smile, and with an apologetic shrug, "But I talk too much of my books," he said. "Come. Shall we go to my café?"

On a neighboring street, a few minutes later, down a flight of steep wooden stairs they descended into a little café, shaped like a tunnel, the ceiling low, the bare walls soiled by rubbing elbows, dirty hands, the air blue and hot with smoke. Young men and girls packed in at small tables bent over tall glasses of Russian tea, and gesturing with their cigarettes declaimed and argued excitedly. Quick joyous cries of greeting met Isadore from every side.

"You see?" he said gaily. "This is my club. Here we are like a family." He ordered tea of a waiter who seemed more like a bosom friend. And leaning eagerly forward, he began to speak in glowing terms of the men and girls from sweatshops who spent their nights in these feasts of the soul, talking, listening, grappling, "for the power to think with minds as clear as the sun when it rises," he ardently cried. "There is not a night in this city, not one, when hundreds do not talk like this until the breaking of the day! And then they sleep! A little joke! For at six o'clock they must rise to their work! And that is a force," he added, "not only for those people but a force for you and me. Do you see? When you feel tired, when all your hopes are sinking low, you think of those people and you say, 'I will go to their places.' And you go. You listen and you watch their faces, and such fire makes you burn! You go home, you are happy, you have a new life!

"And perhaps at last you will have a religion," he continued, in fervent tones. "You see, with us Jews—and with Christians, too—the old religion, it is gone. And in its place there is nothing strong. And so the young people go all to pieces. They dance and they drink. If you go to those dance halls you say, 'They are crazy!' For dancing alone is not enough. And you say, 'These people must have a religion.' You ask, 'Where can I find a new

God?' And you reply, 'There is no God.' And then you must be very sad. You know how it is? You feel too free. And you feel scared and lonely. You look up at the stars. There are millions. You are only a speck of dust—on one.

"But then you come to my library. And you see those hungry people—more hungry than men have ever been. And you see those books upon the shelves. And you know when they come together at last, when that power to think as clear as the sun comes into the souls of those people so hungry, then we shall have a new god for the world. For there is no end to what they shall do," Isadore ended huskily.

Roger felt a lump in his throat. He glanced into his daughter's eyes and saw a suspicious brightness there. Isadore looked at her happily.

"You see?" he said to Roger. "When she came here to-night she was tired, half sick. But now she is all filled with life!"

Later, on the street outside when Isadore had left them, Deborah turned to her father:

"Before we go home, there's one place more."

And they went to a building not far away, a new structure twelve floors high which rose out of the neighboring tenements. It had been built, she told him, by a socialist daily paper. A dull night watchman half asleep took them in the elevator up to the top floor of the building, where in a bustling, clanking loft the paper was just going to press. Deborah seemed to know one of the foremen. He smiled and nodded and led the way through the noise and bustle to a large glass door at one end. This she opened and stepped out upon a fire escape so broad it was more like a balcony. And with the noise of the presses subdued, from their high perch they looked silently down.

All around them for miles, it seemed, stretched dark uneven fields of roofs, with the narrow East River winding its way through the midst of them to the harbor below, silvery, dim and cool and serene, opening to the distant sea. From the bridges rearing high over the river, lights by thousands sparkled down. But directly below the spot where they stood was only a dull hazy glow, rising out of dark tenement streets where dimly they could just make out numberless moving shadowy forms, restless crowds too hot to sleep. The roofs were covered everywhere with men and women and children—families, families, families, all merged together in the dark. And from them rose into the night a ceaseless murmur of voices, laughing and joking, quarreling, loving and hating, demanding, complaining, and fighting and slaving and scheming for bread and the means of stark existence. But among these struggling multitudes confusedly did Roger feel the brighter presence here and there of more aspiring figures, small groups in glaring, stifling rooms down there beneath the murky dark, young people fiercely arguing, groping blindly for new gods. And all these voices, to his ears, merged into one deep thrilling hum, these lights into one quivering glow, that went up toward the silent stars.

And there came to him a feeling which he had often had before in many different places—that he himself was a part of all this, the great, blind, wistful soul of mankind, which had been here before he was born and would be here when he was dead—still groping, yearning, struggling upward, on and on—to something distant as the sun. And still would he be a part of it all, through the eager lives of his children. He turned and looked at Deborah and caught the light that was in her eyes.

CHAPTER XII

ROGER awoke the next morning feeling sore and weary, and later in his office it was hard to keep his mind on his work. He thought of young Isadore Freedom. He was glad he had met that boy, and so he felt toward Deborah's whole terrific family. Confused and deafening as it was, there was something inspiring in it all. But God save him from many such evenings! For half his life Roger had been a collector, not only of rings but of people, too, of curious personalities. These human bits, these memories, he had picked up as he lived along and had taken them with him and made them his own, had trimmed and polished every one until its rough unpleasant edges were all nicely smoothed away and it glittered and shone like the gem that it was. For Roger was an idealist. And so he would have liked to do here. What a gem could be made of Isadore with a little careful polishing.

But Deborah's way was different. She stayed in life, lived in it close, with its sharp edges bristling. In this there was something splendid, but there was something tragic, too. It was all very well for that young Jew to burn himself up with his talk about freedom, his feverish searching for new gods. "In five years," Roger told himself, "Mr. Isadore Freedom will either tone down or go stark mad." But quite probably he would tone down, for he was only a youngster, these were Isadore's wild oats. But this was no longer Deborah's youth, she had been at this job ten years. And she hadn't gone mad, she had kept herself sane, she had many sides her father knew. He knew her in the mountains, or bustling about at home getting

96

ready for Laura's wedding, or packing Edith's children off for their summer up at the farm. But did that make it any easier? No. To let yourself go was easy, but to keep hold of yourself was hard. It meant wear and tear on a woman, this constant straining effort to keep her balance and see life whole.

"Well, it will break her down, that's all, and I don't propose to allow it," he thought. "She's got to rest this summer and go easier next fall."

But how could he accomplish it? As he thought about her school, with its long and generous arms reaching upon every side out into the tenements, the prospect was bewildering. He searched for something definite. What could he do to prove to his daughter his real interest in her work? Presently he remembered Johnny Geer, the cripple boy whom he had liked, and at once he began to feel himself back again upon known ground. Instead of millions here was one, one plucky lad who needed help. All right, by George, he should have it! And Roger told his daughter he would be glad to pay the expense of sending John away for the summer, and that in the autumn perhaps he would take the lad into his office.

"That's good of you, dearie," Deborah said. It was her only comment, but from the look she gave him Roger felt he was getting on.

One evening not long afterwards, as they sat together at dinner, she rose unsteadily to her feet and said in a breathless voice,

"It's rather close in here, isn't it? I think I'll go outside for a while." Roger jumped up.

"Look here, my child, you're faint!" he cried.

"No, no, it's nothing! Just the heat!" She swayed and reeled, pitched suddenly forward. "Father! Quick!" And Roger caught her in his arms. He called to the maid, and with her help he carried Deborah up to her bed. There she shuddered violently and beads of sweat broke out on her brow. Her breath came hard through chattering teeth.

"It's so silly!" she said fiercely.

But as moments passed the chill grew worse. Her whole body seemed to be shaking, and as Roger was rubbing one of her arms she said something to him sharply, in a voice so thick he could not understand.

"What is it?" he asked.

"I can't feel anything."

"What do you mean?"

"In my arm where you're rubbing—I can't feel your hand."

"You'd better have a doctor!"

"Telephone Allan—Allan Baird. He knows about this," she muttered. And Roger ran down to the telephone. He was thoroughly frightened.

"All right, Mr. Gale," came Baird's gruff bass, steady and slow, "I think I know what the trouble is—and I wouldn't worry if I were you. I'll be there in about ten minutes." And it was hardly more than that when he came into Deborah's room. A moment he looked down at her.

"Again?" he said. She glanced up at him and nodded, and smiled quickly through set teeth. Baird carefully examined her and then turned to Roger: "Now I guess you'd better go out. You stay," he added to Sarah, the maid. "I may need you here awhile."

About an hour later he came down to Roger's study.

"She's safe enough now, I guess," he said. "I've telephoned for a nurse for her, and she'll have to stay in bed a few days."

"What's the trouble?"

"Acute indigestion."

"You don't say!" exclaimed Roger brightly, with a

rush of deep relief. Baird gave him a dry quizzical smile.

"People have died of that," he remarked, "in less than an hour. We caught your daughter just in time. May I stay a few moments?"

"Glad to have you! Smoke a cigar!"

"Thanks—I will." As Baird reached out for the proffered cigar, Roger suddenly noticed his hand. Long and muscular, finely shaped, it seemed to speak of strength and skill and an immense vitality. Baird settled himself in his chair. "I want to talk about her," he said. "This little attack is only a symptom—it comes from nerves. She's just about ready for a smash. She's had slighter attacks of this kind before."

"I never knew it," Roger said.

"No—I don't suppose you did. Your daughter has a habit of keeping things like this to herself. She came to me and I warned her, but she wanted to finish out her year. Do you know anything about her school work?"

"Yes, I was with her there this week."

"What did she show you?" Baird inquired. Roger tried to tell him. "No, that's not what I'm after," he said. "That's just one of her *usual* evenings." For a moment he smoked in silence. "I'm hunting now for something else, for some unusual nervous shock which she appears to me to have had."

"She has!" And Roger told him of her visit up to Sing Sing. Baird's lean muscular right hand slowly tightened on his chair.

"That's a tough family of hers," he remarked.

"Yes," said Roger determinedly, "and she's got to give it up."

"You mean she ought to. But she won't."

"She's got to be made to," Roger growled. "This summer at least." Baird shook his head.

"You forget her fresh air work," he replied. "She has

three thousand children on her mind. The city will be like a furnace, of course, and the children must be sent to camps. If you don't see the necessity, go and talk to her, and then you will."

"But you can forbid it, can't you?"

"No. Can you?"

"I can try," snapped Roger.

"Let's try what's possible," said Baird. "Let's try to keep her in bed three days."

"Sounds modest," Roger grunted. And a glimmer of amusement came into Baird's impassive eyes.

"Try it," he drawled. "By to-morrow night she'll ask for her stenographer. She'll make you think she is out of the woods. But she won't be, please remember that. A few years more," he added, "and she'll have used up her vitality. She'll be an old woman at thirty-five."

"It's got to be stopped!" cried Roger.

"But how?" came the low sharp retort. "You've got to know her trouble first. And her trouble is deep, it's motherhood—on a scale which has never been tried before— for thousands of children, all of whom are living in a kind of hell. I know your daughter pretty well. Don't make the mistake of mixing her up with the old-fashioned teacher. It isn't what those children learn, it's how they live that interests her, and how they are all growing up. I say she's a mother—in spirit—but her body has never borne a child. And that makes it worse—because it makes her more intense. It isn't natural, you see."

A little later he rose to go.

"By the way," he said, at the door, "there's something I meant to tell her upstairs—about a poor devil she has on her mind. A chap named Berry—dying—lungs. She asked me to go and see him."

"Yes?"

"I found it was only a matter of days." The tragic pity in Baird's quiet voice was so deep as barely to be heard.

"So I shot him full of morphine. He won't wake up. Please tell her that."

Tall, ungainly, motionless, he loomed there in the doorway. With a little shrug and a smile he turned and went slowly out of the house.

CHAPTER XIII

DEBORAH'S recovery was rapid and determined. The next night she was sitting up and making light of her illness. On the third day she dismissed her nurse, and when her father came home from his office he found gathered about her bed not only her stenographer but both her assistant principals. He frowned severely and went to his room, and a few minutes later he heard them leave. Presently she called to him, and he came to her bedside. She was lying back on the pillow with rather a guilty expression.

"Up to your old antics, eh?" he remarked.

"Exactly. It couldn't be helped, you see. It's the last week of our school year, and there are so many little things that have to be attended to. It's simply now or never."

"Humph!" was Roger's comment. "It's now or never with you," he thought. He went down to his dinner, and when he came back he found her exhausted. In the dim soft light of her room her face looked flushed and feverish, and vaguely he felt she was in a mood where she might listen to reason. He felt her hot dry hand on his. Her eyes were closed, she was smiling.

"Tell me the news from the mountains," she said. And he gave her the gossip of the farm in a letter he had had from George. It told of a picnic supper, the first one of the season. They had had it in the usual place, down by the dam on the river, "with a bonfire—a perfect peach —down by the big yellow rock—the one you call the Elephant." As Roger read the letter he could feel his daughter listening, vividly picturing to herself the great dark boulders by the creek, the shadowy firs, the stars above and the cool fresh tang of the mountain night.

"After this little sickness of yours—and that harum scarum wedding," he said, "I feel we're both entitled to a good long rest in mountain air."

"We'll have it, too," she murmured.

"With Edith's little youngsters. They're all the medicine you need." He paused for a moment, hesitating. But it was now or never. "The only trouble with you," he said, "is that you've let yourself be caught by the same disease which has its grip upon this whole infernal town. You're like everyone else, you're tackling about forty times what you can do. You're actually trying not only to teach but to bring 'em all up as your own, three thousand tenement children. And this is where it gets you." Again he halted, frowning. What next?

"Go on, dear, please," said Deborah, in demure and even tones. "This is very interesting."

"Now then," he continued, "in this matter of your school. I wouldn't ask you to give it up, I've already seen too much of it. But so long as you've got it nicely started, why not give somebody else a chance? One of those assistants of yours, for example—capable young women, both. You could stand right behind 'em with help and advice—"

"Not yet," was Deborah's soft reply. She had turned her head on her pillow and was looking at him affectionately. "Why not?" he demanded.

"Because it's not nicely started at all. There's nothing brilliant about me, dear—I'm a plodder, feeling my way along. And what I have done in the last ten years is just coming to a stage at last where I can really see a chance to make it count for something. When I feel I've done that, say in five years more—"

"Those five years," said her father, "may cost you a very heavy price." As Deborah faced his troubled regard, her own grew quickly serious.

"I'd be willing to pay the price," she replied.

"But why?" he asked with impatience. "Why pay when you don't have to? Why not by taking one year off get strength for twenty years' work later on? You'd be a different woman!"

"Yes, I think I should be. I'd never be the same again. You don't quite understand, you see. This work of mine with children—well, it's like Edith's having a baby. You have to do it while you're young."

"That works both ways," her father growled.

"What do you mean?" He hesitated:

"Don't you want any children of your own?"

Again she turned her eyes toward his, then closed them and lay perfectly still. "Now I've done it," he thought anxiously. She reached over and took his hand.

"Let's talk of our summer's vacation," she said.

A little while later she fell asleep.

Downstairs he soon grew restless and after a time he went out for a walk. But he felt tired and oppressed, and as he had often done of late he entered a little "movie" nearby, where gradually the pictures, continually flashing out of the dark, drove the worries from his mind. For a half an hour they held his gaze. Then he fell into a doze. He was roused by a roar of laughter, and straightening up in his seat with a jerk he looked angrily around. Something broadly comic had been flashed upon the screen; and men and women and children, Italians, Jews and Irish, jammed in close about him, a dirty and perspiring mass, had burst into a terrific guffaw. Now they were suddenly tense again and watching the screen in absorbed suspense, while the crude passions within themselves were played upon in the glamorous dark. And Roger scanned their faces—one moment smiling, all together, as though some god had pulled a string; then mawkish, sentimental, soft; then suddenly scowling, twitching, with long rows of animal eyes. But eager—eager all the time! Hungry people—yes, indeed! Hungry for all the good things in the town, and for as many bad things, too! On one who tried to feed this mob there was no end to their demands! What was one woman's life to them? Deborah's big family!

Edith came to the house one afternoon, and she was in Deborah's room when her father returned from his office. Her convalescence over at last, she was leaving for the mountains.

"Do learn your lesson, Deborah dear," she urged upon her sister. "Let Sarah pack your trunk at once and come up with me on Saturday night."

"I can't get off for two weeks yet."

"Why can't you?" Edith demanded. And when Deborah spoke of fresh air camps and baby farms and other work, Edith's impatience only grew. "You'll have to leave it to somebody else! You're simply in no condition!" she cried.

"Impossible," said Deborah. Edith gave a quick sigh of exasperation.

"Isn't it enough," she asked, "to have worked your nerves to a frazzle already? Why can't you be sensible? You've got to think of yourself a little!"

"You'd like me to marry, wouldn't you, dear?" her sister put in wearily.

"Yes, I should, while there is still time! Just now you look far from it! It's exactly as Allan was saying! If you keep on as you're going you'll be an old woman at thirty-five!"

"Thank you!" said Deborah sharply. Two spots of color leaped in her checks. "You'd better leave me, Edith! I'll come up to the mountains as soon as I can!

And I'll try not to look any more like a hag than I have to!
Good-night!"

Roger followed Edith out of the room.

"That last shot of mine struck home," she declared to
him in triumph.

"I wouldn't have done it," her father said. "I gave
you that remark of Baird's in strict confidence, Edith—"

"Now father," was her good-humored retort, "suppose
you leave this matter to me. I know just what I'm doing."

"Well," he reflected uneasily, after she had left him,
"here's more trouble in the family. If Edith isn't careful
she'll make a fine mess of this whole affair."

After dinner he went up to Deborah's room, but through
the open doorway he caught a glimpse of his daughter
which made him instinctively draw back. Sitting bolt
upright in her bed, sternly she was eyeing herself in a small
mirror in her hand. Her father chuckled noiselessly. A
moment later, when he went in, the glass had disappeared
from view. Soon afterwards Baird himself arrived, and
as they heard him coming upstairs Roger saw his daughter
frown, but she continued talking.

"Hello, Allan," she said with indifference. "I'm feeling
much better this evening."

"Are you? Good," he answered, and he started to pull
up an easy chair. "I was hoping I could stay awhile—
I've been having one of those long mean days—"

"I'd a little rather you wouldn't," Deborah put in
softly. Allan turned to her in surprise. "I didn't sleep
last night," she murmured, "and I feel so drowsy." There
was a little silence. "And I really don't think there's any
need of your dropping in to-morrow," she added. "I'm so
much better—honestly."

Baird looked at her a moment.

"Right—O," he answered slowly. "I'll call up to-morrow night."

Roger followed him downstairs.

"Come into my den and smoke a cigar!" he proposed in hearty ringing tones. Allan thanked him and came in, but the puzzled expression was still on his face, and through the first moments of their talk he was very absent-minded. Roger's feeling of guilt increased, and he cursed himself for a meddlesome fool.

"Look here, Baird," he blurted out, "there's something I think you ought to know." Allan slightly turned his head, and Roger reddened a little. "The worst thing about living in a house chock full of meddling women is that you get to be one yourself," he growled. "And the fact is—" he cleared his throat—"I've put my foot in it, Baird," he said. "I was fool enough the other day to quote you to Edith."

"To what effect?"

"That if Deborah keeps on like this she'll be an old woman at thirty-five."

Allan sat up in his chair:

"Was Edith here this afternoon?"

"She was," said Roger.

"Say no more."

Baird had a wide, likable, generous mouth which wrinkled easily into a smile. He leaned back now and enjoyed himself. He puffed a little cloud of smoke, looked over at Roger and chuckled aloud. And Roger chuckled with relief. "What a decent chap he is," he thought.

"I'm sorry, of course," he said to Baird. "I thought of trying to explain—"

"Don't," said Allan. "Leave it alone. It won't do Deborah any harm—may even do her a little good. After all, I'm her physician—"

"Are you?" Roger asked with a twinkle. "I thought upstairs you were dismissed."

"Oh no, I'm not," was the calm reply. And the two men went on smoking. Roger's liking for Baird was growing fast. They had had several little talks during Deborah's illness, and Roger was learning more of the man. Raised on a big cattle ranch that his father had owned in New Mexico, riding broncos on the plains had given him his abounding health of body, nerve and spirit, his steadiness and sanity in all this feverish city life.

"Are you riding these days?" he inquired.

"No," said Roger, "the park is too hot—and they don't sprinkle the path as they should. I've had my cob sent up to the mountains. By the way," he added cordially, "you must come up there and ride with me."

"Thanks, I'd like to," Allan said, and with a little inner smile he added dryly to himself, "He's getting ready to meddle again." But whatever amusement Baird had in this thought was concealed behind his sober gray eyes. Soon after that he took his leave.

"Now then," Roger reflected, with a little glow of expectancy, "if Edith will only leave me alone, she may find I'm smarter than she thinks!"

One evening in the following week, after Edith had left town, Roger had Bruce to dine at his club, a pleasant old building on Madison Square, where comfortably all by themselves they could discuss Baird's chances.

"A. Baird and I have been chums," said Bruce, "ever since we were in college. Take it from me I know his brand. And he isn't the kind to be pushed."

"Who wants to push him?" Roger demanded, with a sudden guilty twinge.

"Edith does," Bruce answered. "And I tell you that won't do with A. Baird. He has his mind set on Deborah sure. He's been setting it harder and harder for months— and he knows it—and so does she. But they're both the kind of people who don't like interference, they've got to get to it by themselves. Edith must keep out of the way. She mustn't take it on herself to ask him up to the mountains." Roger gave a little start. "If she does, there'll be trouble with Deborah."

Roger smoked for a moment in silence and then sagely nodded his head.

"That's so," he murmured thoughtfully. "Yes, my boy, I guess you're right."

Bruce lifted his mint julep:

"God, but it's hot in here to-night. How about taking a spin up the river?"

"Delighted," replied his father-in-law.

And a half hour later in Bruce's new car, which was the pride and joy of his life, they were far up the river. On a long level stretch of road Bruce "let her out to show what she could do." And Roger with his heart in his mouth and his eye upon the speedometer, saw it creep to sixty-three.

"Almost as good as a horse," remarked Bruce, when the car had slowed a little.

"Almost," said Roger, "but not quite. It's—well, it's dissipation."

"And a horse?"

"Is life," was the grave reply. "You'll have a crash some day, my boy, if you go on at your present speed. It gets me worried sometimes. You see you're a family man."

"I am and I'm glad of it. Edith and the kiddies suit me right down to the ground. I'm crazy about 'em—you know that. But a chap with a job like mine," Bruce continued pleadingly, as he drove his car rushing around a curve, "needs a little dissipation, too. I can't tell you what it means to me, when I'm kept late at the office, to have this car for the run up home. Lower Broadway's empty then, and I know the cops. I swing around through Washington Square, and the Avenue looks clear for miles, nothing but two long rows of lights to the big hump at Murray Hill. It's the time between crowds—say about ten. And I know the cops."

"That's all right," said Roger. "No one was more delighted than I when you got this car. You deserve it. It's the *work* that I was speaking of. You've got it going at such a speed—"

"Only way on earth to get on—to get what I want for my family—"

"Yes, yes, I know," muttered Roger vaguely. Bruce began talking of his work for the steel construction concern downtown.

"Take it from me," he declared at the end, "this town has only just begun!"

"Has, eh," Roger grunted. "Aren't the buildings high enough?"

"My God, I wish they were twenty times higher," Bruce rejoined good-humoredly. "But they won't be—we've stopped going up. We've done pretty well in the air, and now we're going underground. And when we get through, this old rock of Manhattan will be such a network of tunnels there'll be a hole waiting at every corner to take you wherever you want to go. Speed? We don't even know what it means!"

And again Bruce "let her out" a bit. It was *quite* a bit. Roger grabbed his hat with one hand and the side of the car with the other.

"They'll look back on a mile a minute," said Bruce, "as we look back on stage coach days! And in the rush hour there'll be a rush that'll make you think of pneumatic tubes! Not a sound nor a quiver—*just pure speed!* Shooting people home at night at a couple of hundred miles an hour! The city will be as big as that! And there won't be any accidents and there won't be any smoke. Instead of coal they'll use the sun! And, my God, man, the boulevards—and parks and places for the kids! The way they'll use the River—and the ocean and the Sound! The Catskills will be Central Park! Sounds funny, don't it—but it's true. I've studied it out from A to Z. This town is choking itself to death simply because we're so damn slow! We don't know how to spread ourselves! All this city needs is speed!"

"Bruce," said Roger anxiously, "just go a bit easy on that gas. The fact is, it was a great mistake for me to eat those crabs to-night."

Bruce slowed down compassionately, and soon they turned and started home. And as they drew near the glow of the town, other streets and boulevards poured more motors into the line, until at last they were rushing along amid a perfect bedlam made up of honks and shrieks of horns. The air grew hot and acrid, and looking back through the bluish haze of smoke and dust behind him Roger could see hundreds of huge angry motor eyes. Crowding and jamming closer, pell mell, at a pace which barely slackened, they sped on, a wild uproarious crew, and swept into the city.

Roger barely slept that night. He felt the city clamoring down into his very soul. "Speed!" he muttered viciously. "Speed—speed! We need more speed!" The words beat in like a savage refrain. At last with a sigh of impatience he got up in his nightshirt and walked about. It was good to feel his way in the dark in this cool silent house which he knew so well. Soon his nerves felt quieter. He went back to his bed and lay there inert. How good it would be to get up to the farm.

The next Saturday evening, with Deborah, he started for the mountains. And Bruce came down to see them off.

"Remember, son," said Roger, as the two walked on the platform. "Come up this year for a month, my boy. You need it." The train was about to start.

"Oh, I'll be all right," was the answer. "My friend the Judge, who has hay fever, tells me he has found a cure."

"Damn his cure! You come to us!"

"Hold on a minute, live and learn. The Judge is quite

excited about it. You drink little bugs, he says, a billion after every meal. They come in tall blue bottles. We're going to dine together next week and drink 'em till we're all lit up. Oh, we're going to have a hell of a time. *His* wife left town on Tuesday."

"Bruce," said Roger sternly, as the train began to move, "leave bugs alone and come up and breathe! And quit smoking so many cigarettes!" He stepped on the car. "Remember, son, a solid month!" Bruce nodded as the train moved out.

"Good luck—good-bye—fine summer—my love to the wife and the kiddies—" and Bruce's dark, tense, smiling face was left behind. Roger went back into the smoker.

"Now for the mountains," he thought. "Thank God!"

CHAPTER XIV

A FEW hours later Roger awakened. His lower berth was still pitch dark. The train had stopped, and he had been roused by a voice outside his window. Rough and slow and nasal, the leisurely drawl of a mountaineer, it came like balm to Roger's ears. He raised the curtain and looked out. A train hand with a lantern was listening to a dairy man, a tall young giant in top boots. High overhead loomed a shadowy mountain and over its rim came the glow of the dawn. With a violent lurch the train moved on. And Roger, lying back on his pillow, looked up at the misty mountain sides all mottled in the strange blue light with patches of firs and birches and pines. In the narrow valley up which the train was thundering, were small herds of grazing cattle, a lonely farmhouse here and there. From one a light was twinkling. And the city with its heat and noise, its nervous throb, its bedlam nights, all dropped like a fever from his soul.

Now, close by the railroad track, through a shallow rocky gorge a small river roared and foamed. Its cool breath came up to his nostrils and gratefully he breathed it in. For this was the Gale River, named after one of his forefathers, and in his mind's eye he followed the stream back up its course to the little station where he and Deborah were to get off. There the narrowing river bed turned and wound up through a cleft in the hills to the homestead several miles away. On the dark forest road beside it he pictured George, his grandson, at this moment driving down to meet them in a mountain wagon with one of the two hired men, a lantern swinging under the wheels. What an adventure for young George.

113

Presently he heard Deborah stirring in the berth next
to his own.

At the station George was there, and from a thermos
bottle which Edith had filled the night before he poured
coffee piping hot, which steamed in the keen, frosty
air.

"Oh, how good!" cried Deborah. "How thoughtful
of your mother, George. How is she, dear?"

"Oh, she's all right, Aunt Deborah." His blunt freckled
features flushed from his drive, George stood beaming on
them both. He appeared, if anything, tougher and
scrawnier than before. "Everything's all right," he said.
"There ain't a sick animal on the whole farm."

As Roger sipped his coffee he was having a look at the
horses. One of them was William, his cob.

"Do you see it?" inquired his grandson.

"What?"

"The boil," George answered proudly, "on William's
rump. There it is—on the nigh side. Gee, but you ought
to have seen it last week. It was a whale of a boil," said
George, "but we poulticed him, me and Dave did—and
now the swelling's nearly gone. You can ride him to-
morrow if you like."

Luxuriously Roger lit a cigar and climbed to the front
seat with George. Up the steep and crooked road the
stout horses tugged their way, and the wagon creaked,
and the Gale River, here only a brook, came gurgling,
dashing to meet them—down from the mountains, from
the farm, from Roger's youth to welcome him home. And
the sun was flashing through the pines. As they drew
near the farmhouse through a grove of sugar maples, he
heard shrill cries of, "There they come!" And he glimpsed
the flying figures of George's brothers, Bob and Tad.
George whipped up the horses, the wagon gained upon the
boys and reached the house but a few rods behind the little
runners. Edith was waiting by the door, fresh and smiling,

blooming with health. How well this suited her, Roger thought. Amid a gay chorus of greetings he climbed down heavily out of the wagon, looked about him and drew a deep breath. The long lazy days on the farm had begun.

From the mountain side the farm looked down on a wide sweeping valley of woods and fields. The old house straggled along the road, with addition after addition built on through generations by many men and women. Here lay the history, unread, of the family of Roger Gale. Inside there were steps up and down from one part to another, queer crooks in narrow passageways. The lower end was attached to the woodshed, and the woodshed to the barn. Above the house a pasture dotted with gray boulders extended up to a wood of firs, and out of this wood the small river which bore the name of the family came rushing down the field in a gully, went under the road, swept around to the right and along the edge of a birch copse just below the house. The little stream grew quieter there and widened into a mill pond. At the lower end was a broken dam and beside it a dismantled mill.

Here was peace for Roger's soul. The next day at dawn he awakened, and through the window close by his bed he saw no tall confining walls; his eye was carried as on wings out over a billowy blanket of mist, soft and white and cool and still, reaching over the valley. From underneath to his sensitive ears came the numberless voices of the awakening sleepers there, cheeps and tremulous warbles from the birch copse just below, cocks crowing in the valley, and ducks and geese, dogs, sheep and cattle faintly heard from distant farms. Just so it had been when he was a boy. How unchanged and yet how new were these fresh hungry cries of life. From the other end of the house he heard Edith's tiny son lustily demanding his breakfast, as other wee boys before him had done for over a hundred years, as other babies still unborn would

do in the many years to come. Soon the cry of the child
was hushed. Quiet fell upon the house. And Roger sank
again into deep happy slumber.

Here was nothing new and disturbing. Edith's children? Yes, they were new, but they were not disturbing.
Their growth each summer was a joy, a renewal of life in
the battered old house. Here was no huge tenement
family crowding in with dirty faces, clamorous demands for
aid, but only five delightful youngsters, clean and fresh,
of his own blood. He loved the small excitements, the
plans and plots and discoveries, the many adventures that
filled their days. He spent hours with their mother, listening while she talked of them. Edith did so love this place
and she ran the house so beautifully. It was so cool and
fragrant, so clean and so old-fashioned.

Deborah, too, came under the spell. She grew as lazy
as a cat and day by day renewed her strength from the hills
and from Edith's little brood. Roger had feared trouble
there, for he knew how Edith disapproved of her sister's new ideas. But although much with the children,
Deborah apparently had no new ideas at all. She seemed
to be only listening. One balmy day at sunset, Roger saw
her lying on the grass with George sprawled by her side.
Her head upon one arm, she appeared to be watching
the cattle in the sloping pasture above. Slowly, as though
each one of them was drawn by mysterious unseen chains,
they were drifting down toward the barn where it was
almost milking time. George was talking earnestly. She
threw a glance at him from time to time, and Roger could
see how intent were her eyes. Yes, Deborah knew how
to study a boy.

Only once during the summer did she talk about her
work. On a walk with her father one day she took him
into a small forlorn building, a mere cabin of one room.
The white paint had long been worn away, the windows
were all broken, half the old shingles had dropped from

the roof and on the flagpole was no flag. It was the district schoolhouse where for nearly half his life Deborah's grandfather had taught a score of pupils. Inside were a blackboard, a rusty stove, a teacher's desk and a dozen forms, grown mouldy and worm-eaten now. A torn and faded picture of Lincoln was upon one wall, half hidden by a spider's web and by a few old dangling rags which once had been red, white and blue. Below, still clinging to the wall, was an old scrap of paper, on which in a large rugged hand there had been written long ago a speech, but it had been worn away until but three words were legible—"conceived and dedicated—"

"Tell me about your school," she said. "All you can remember." Seated at her grandfather's desk she asked Roger many questions. And his recollections, at first dim and hazy, began to clear a little.

"By George!" he exclaimed. "Here are my initials!" He stooped over one of the benches.

"Oh, dearie! Where?" He pointed them out, and then while he sat on the rude old bench for some time more she questioned him.

"But your school was not all here," she said musingly at last, "it was up on the farm, besides, where you learned to plough and sow and reap and take care of the animals in the barn, and mend things that were broken, and—oh, turn your hand to anything. But millions of children nowadays are growing up in cities, you see."

Half frowning and half smiling she began to talk of her work in town. "What is there about her," Roger asked, "that reminds me so of my mother?" His mind strayed back into the past while the low quiet voice of his daughter went on, and a wistful expression crept over his face. What would *she* do with the family name? What life would she lead in those many years? . . . "What a mother she would make." The words rose from within him, but in a voice which was not his own. It was Deb-

orah's grandmother speaking, so clearly and distinctly
that he gave a start almost of alarm.

"And if you don't believe they'll do it," Deborah was
saying, "you don't know what's in children. Only we've
got to help bring it out." What had she been talking
about? He remembered the words "a new nation"—no
more. "We've got to grope around in the dark and hunt
for new ways and learn as we go. And when you've once
got into the work and really felt the thrill of it all—well,
then it seems rather foolish and small to bother about
your own little life."

Roger spent much of his time alone. He took long rides
on William along crooked, hilly roads. As the afternoon
drew to its end, the shadows would creep up the mountain
sides to their summits where glowed the last rays of the
sun, painting the slate and granite crags in lovely pink
and purple hues. And sometimes mighty banks of clouds
would rear themselves high overhead, gigantic mountains
of the air with billowy, misty caverns, cliffs and jagged
peaks, all shifting there before his eyes. And he would
think of Judith his wife. And the old haunting certainty,
that her soul had died with her body, was gone. There
came to him the feeling that he and his wife would meet
again. Why did this hope come back to him? Was it all
from the glory of the sun? Or was it from the presence,
silent and invisible, of those many other mortals, folk
of his own flesh and blood, who at their deaths had gone
to their graves to put on immortality? Or was this deepening faith in Roger simply a sign of his growing old age?
He frowned at the thought and shook it off, and again
stared up at the light on the hills. "You will live on in
our children's lives." Was there no other immortality?

He often thought of his boyhood here. On a ride one
day he stopped for a drink at a spring in a grove of maples
surrounding a desolate farmhouse not more than a mile

away from his own. And through the trees as he turned
to go he saw the stark figure of a woman, poorly clad and
gaunt and gray. She stood motionless watching him
with a look of sullen bitterness. She was the last of
"the Elkinses," a mountain family run to seed. As he
rode away he saw in the field a boy with a pitchfork in his
hands, a meager ragged little chap. He was staring into
the valley at a wriggling, blue smoke serpent made by the
night express to New York. And something leaped in
Roger, for he had once felt just like that! But the woman's
harsh voice cut in on his dream, as she shouted to her son
below, "Hey! Why the hell you standin' thar?" And the
boy with a jump of alarm turned back quickly to his work.

At home a few days later, George with a mysterious
air took his grandfather into the barn, and after a pledge
of secrecy he said in swift and thrilling tones,

"You know young Bill Elkins? Yes, you do—the boy
up on the Elkins place who lives alone with his mother.
Well, look here!" George swallowed hard. "Bill has
cleared out—he's run away! I was up at five this morning
and he came hiking down the road! He had a bundle on
his back and he told me he was off for good! And was he
scared? You bet he was scared! And I told him so and
it made him mad! 'Aw, you're scared!' I said. 'I ain't
neither!' he said. He could barely talk, but the kid had
his nerve! 'Where you going?' I asked. 'To New York,'
he said. 'Aw, what do you know of New York?' I said.
And then, by golly, he busted right down. 'Gee!' he said,
'Gee! Can't you lemme alone?' And then he beat it
down the road! You could hear the kid breathe, he was
hustling so! He's way off now, he's caught the train! He
wants to be a cabin boy on a big ocean liner!" For a
moment there was silence. "Well?" the boy demanded,
"What do you think of his chances?"

"I don't know," said Roger huskily. He felt a tightening at his throat. Abruptly he turned to his grandson.

"George," he asked, "what do *you* want to be?" The boy flushed under his freckles.

"I don't know as I know. I'm thinking," he answered very slowly.

"Talk it over with your mother, son."

"Yes, sir," came the prompt reply. "But he won't," reflected Roger.

"Or if you ever feel you want to, have a good long talk with me."

"Yes, sir," was the answer. Roger stood there waiting, then turned and walked slowly out of the barn. How these children grew up inside of themselves. Had boys always grown like that? Well, perhaps, but how strange it was. Always new lives, lives of their own, the old families scattering over the land. So the great life of the nation swept on. He kept noticing here deserted farms, and one afternoon in the deepening dusk he rode by a grave-yard high up on a bare hillside. A horse and buggy were outside, and within he spied a lean young woman neatly dressed in a plain dark suit. With a lawn mower brought from home she was cutting the grass on her family lot. And she seemed to fit into the landscape. New England had grown very old.

Late one night toward the end of July, there came a loud honk from down the hill, then another and another. And as George in his pajamas came rushing from his bed-room shouting radiantly, "Gee! It's dad!"—they heard the car thundering outside. Bruce had left New York at dawn and had made the run in a single day, three hundred and eleven miles. He was gray with dust all over and he was worn and hollow eyed, but his dark visage wore a look of solid satisfaction.

"I needed the trip to shake me down," he pleaded, when Edith scolded him well for this terrific manner of starting his vacation. "I had to have it to cut me off from the job I left behind me. Now watch me settle down on this farm."

But it appeared he could not settle down. For the first few days, in his motor, he was busy exploring the mountains. "We'll make 'em look foolish. Eh, son?" he said. And with George, who mutely adored him, he ran all about them in a day. Genially he gave everyone rides. When he'd finished with the family, he took Dave Royce the farmer and his wife and children, and even both the hired men, for Bruce was an hospitable soul. But more than anyone else he took George. They spent hours working on the car, and at times when they came into the house begreased and blackened from their work, Edith reproved them like bad boys—but Deborah smiled contentedly.

But at the end of another week Bruce grew plainly restless, and despite his wife's remonstrances made ready to return to town. When she spoke of his hay fever he bragged to her complacently of his newly discovered cure.

"Oh, bother your little blue bugs!" she cried.

"The *bugs* aren't blue," he explained to her, in a mild and patient voice that drove Edith nearly wild. "They're so little they have no color at all. Poor friendly little devils—"

"Bruce!" his wife exploded.

"They've been almighty good to *me*. You ought to have heard my friend the Judge, the last night I was with him. He patted his bottle and said to me, 'Bruce, my boy, with all these simple animals right here as our companions why be a damn fool and run off to the cows?' And there's a good deal in what he says. You ought to be mighty thankful, too, that my summer pleasures are so mild. If you could see what *some* chaps do—"

And Bruce started back for the city. George rode with him the first few miles, then left him and came trudging home. His spirits were exceedingly low.

As August drew toward a close, Deborah, too, showed signs of unrest. With ever growing frequency Roger felt her eagerness to return to her work in New York.

"You're as bad as Bruce," he growled at her. "You don't have to be back," he argued. "School doesn't begin for nearly three weeks."

"There's the suffrage campaign," she answered. He gave her a look of exasperation.

"Now what the devil has suffrage to do with your schools?" he demanded.

"When the women get the vote, we'll spend more money on the children."

"Suppose the money isn't there," was Roger's grim rejoinder.

"Then we'll act like old-fashioned wives, I suppose," his daughter answered cheerfully, "and keep nagging till it *is* there. We'll keep up such a nagging," she added, in sweet even tones, "that you'll get the money by hook or crook, to save yourselves from going insane."

After this he caught her reading in the New York papers the list of campaign meetings each night, meetings in hot stifling halls or out upon deafening corners. And as she read there came over her face a look like that of a man who has given up tobacco and suddenly sniffs it among his friends. She went down the last night of August.

Roger stayed on for another two weeks, on into the best time of the year. For now came the nights of the first snapping frosts when the dome of the heavens was steely blue, and clear sparkling mornings, the woods aflame with scarlet and gold. And across the small field below the house, at sunset Roger would go down to the copse of birches there and find it filled with glints of light that took his glance far in among the slender, creamy stems of the trees, all slowly swaying to and fro, the leafage rich with autumn hues, warm orange, yellow and pale green. Lovely and silent and serene. So it had been when he was a boy and so it would be when he was dead. Countless trees had been cut down but others had risen in their stead. Now and then he could hear a bird warbling.

Long ago this spot had been his mother's favorite refuge from her busy day in the house. She had almost always come alone, but sometimes Roger stealing down would watch her sitting motionless and staring in among the trees. Years later in his reading he had come upon the phrase, "sacred grove," and at once he had thought of the birches. And sitting here where she had been, he felt again that boundless faith in life resplendent, conquering death, and serenely sweeping him on—into what he did not fear. For this had been his mother's faith. Sometimes in the deepening dusk he could almost see her sitting here.

"This faith in you has come from me. This is my memory living on in you, my son, though you do not know. How many times have I held you back, how many times have I urged you on, roused you up or soothed you, made you hope or fear or dream, through memories of long ago. For you were once a part of me. I moulded you, my little son. And as I have been to you, so you will be to your children. In their lives, too, we shall be there— silent and invisible, the dim strong figures of the past. For this is the power of families, this is the mystery of birth."

Suddenly he started. What was it that had thrilled him so? Only a tall dark fir in the birches. But looming in there like a shadowy phantom it had recalled a memory of a dusk far back in his boyhood, when seeing a shadow just like this he had thought it a ghost in very truth and had run for the house like a rabbit! How terribly real that fright had been! The recollection suddenly became so vivid in his mind, that as though a veil had been lifted he felt the living presence here, close by his side, of a small barefoot mountain lad, clothed in sober homespun gray, but filled with warm desires, dreams and curiosities, exploring upon every hand, now marching boldly forward, now stealing up so cautiously, now galloping away like mad! "I was once a child." To most of us these are mere words. To few is it ever given to attain so much as even a glimpse into the warm and quivering soul of that little stranger of long ago. We do not know how we were made.

"I moulded you, my little son. And as I have been to you, so you will be to your children. In their lives, too, we shall be there."

Darker, darker grew the copse and the chill of the night descended. But to Roger's eyes there was no gloom. For he had seen a vision.

CHAPTER XV

On his return to the city, Roger found that Deborah's
school had apparently swept all other interests out of her
mind. Baird hardly ever came to the house, and she herself
was seldom there except for a hasty dinner at night. The
house had to run itself more or less; and though Annie the
cook was doing her best, things did not run so smoothly.
Roger missed little comforts, attentions, and he missed
Deborah most of all. When he came down to his breakfast she had already left the house, and often she did not
return until long after he was in bed. She felt the difference herself, and though she did not put it in words her
manner at times seemed to beg his forbearance. But there
were many evenings when her father found it difficult to
hold to the resolve he had made, to go slowly with his
daughter until he could be more sure of his ground. She
was growing so intense again. From the school authorities
she had secured a still wider range and freedom for her
new experiment, and she was working day and night to
put her ideas into effect.

"It's only too easy," she remarked, "to launch an idea
in this town. The town will put it in headlines at once,
and with it a picture of yourself in your best bib and
tucker, looking as though you loved the whole world.
And you can make a wonderful splurge, until they go on to
the next new thing. The real trouble comes in working it
out."

And this she had set out to do. Many nights in the
autumn Roger went down to the school, to try to get some
clear idea of this vision of hers for children, which in a

125

vague way he could feel was so much larger than his own, for he had seen its driving force in the grip it had upon her life. At first he could make nothing of it at all; everywhere chaos met his eyes. But he found something formless, huge, that made to him a strong appeal.

The big building fairly hummed at night with numberless activities. Fathers, mothers and children came pouring in together and went skurrying off to their places. They learned to speak English, to read and write; grown men and women scowled and toiled over their arithmetic. They worked at trades in the various shops; they hammered and sawed and set up type; they cooked and sewed and gossiped. "The Young Galician Socialist Girls" debated on the question: "Resolved that woman suffrage has worked in Colorado." "The Caruso Pleasure Club" gave a dance to "The Garibaldi Whirlwinds." An orchestra rehearsed like mad. They searched their memories for the songs and all the folk tales they had heard in peasant huts in Italy, in hamlets along rocky coasts, in the dark old ghettos of crowded towns in Poland and in Russia. And some of these songs were sung in school, and some of these tales were dramatized here. Children and parents all took part. And speakers emerged from the neighborhood. It was at times appalling, the number of young Italians and Jews who had ideas to give forth to their friends on socialism, poverty, marriage and religion, and all the other questions that rose among these immigrants jammed into this tenement hive. But when there were too many of these self-appointed guides, the neighborhood shut down on them.

"We don't want," declared one indignant old woman, "that every young loafer should shout in our face!"

Roger was slowly attracted into this enormous family life, and yielding to an impulse he took charge of a boys' club which met on Thursday evenings there. He knew well this job of fathering a small jovial group of lads; he had done it before, many years ago, in the mission school, to please his wife; he felt himself back on familiar ground. And from this point of vantage, with something definite he could do, he watched with an interest more clear the school form steadily closer ties with the tenements that hedged it 'round, gathering its big family. And this family by slow degrees began to make itself a part of the daily life of Roger's house. Committees held their meetings here, teachers dropped in frequently, and Roger invited the boys in his club to come up and see him whenever they liked.

His most frequent visitor was Johnny Geer, the cripple. He was working in Roger's office now and the two had soon become close friends. John kept himself so neat and clean, he displayed such a keen interest in all the details of office work, and he showed such a beaming appreciation of anything that was done for him.

"That boy is getting a hold on me lately almost like a boy of my own," Roger said one evening when Allan Baird was at the house. "He's the pluckiest young un I ever met. I've put him to work in my private office, where he can use the sofa to rest, and I've made him my own stenographer—partly because he's so quick at dictation and partly to try to make him slow down. He has the mind of a race horse. He runs at night to libraries until I should think he'd go insane. And his body can't stand it, he's breaking down—though whenever I ask him how he feels, he always says, 'Fine, thank you.'" Here Roger turned to Allan. "I wish you'd take the boy," he said, "to the finest specialist in town, and see what can be done for his spine. I'll pay any price."

"There won't be any price," said Allan, "but I'll see to it at once."

He had John examined the same week.

"Well?" asked Roger when next they met.

"Well," said Baird, "it isn't good news."

"You mean he's hopeless?" Allan nodded:

"It's Pott's disease, and it's gone too far. John is eighteen. He may live to be thirty."

"But I tell you, Baird, I'll do anything!"

"There's almost nothing you can do. If he had been taken when he was a baby, he might have been cured and given a chance. But the same mother who dropped him then, when she was full of liquor, just went to the druggist on her block, and after listening to his advice she bought some patent medicine, a steel jacket and some crutches, and thought she'd done her duty."

"But there must be something we can do!" retorted Roger angrily.

"Yes," said Baird, "we can make him a little more comfortable. And meanwhile we can help Deborah here to get hold of other boys like John and give 'em a chance before it's too late—keep them from being crippled for life because their mothers were too blind and ignorant to act in time." Baird's voice had a ring of bitterness.

"Most of 'em love their children," Roger said uneasily. Baird turned on him a steady look.

"Love isn't enough," he retorted. "The time is coming very soon when we'll have the right to guard the child not only when it's a baby but even before it has been born."

Roger drew closer to John after this. Often behind the beaming smile he would feel the pain and loneliness, and the angry grit which was fighting it down. And so he would ask John home to supper on nights when nobody else was there. One day late in the afternoon they were walking home together along the west side of Madison Square. The big open space was studded with lights sparkling up at the frosty stars, in a city, a world, a universe that seemed filled with the zest and the vigor of life. Out of these lights a mighty tower loomed high up into the sky. And stopping on his crutches, a grim small crooked figure in all this rushing turmoil, John set his jaws, and with his shrewd and twinkling eyes fixed on the top of the tower, he said,

"I meant to tell you, Mr. Gale. You was asking me once what I wanted to be. And I want to be an architect."

"Do, eh," grunted Roger. He, too, looked up at that thing in the stars, and there was a tightening at his throat. "All right," he added, presently, "why not start in and be one?"

"How?" asked John alertly.

"Well, my boy," said Roger, "I'd hate to lose you in the office—"

"Yes, sir, and I'd hate to go." Just then the big clock in the tower began to boom the hour, and a chill struck into Roger.

"You'd have to," he said gruffly. "You haven't any time to lose! I mean," he hastily added, "that for a job as big as that you'd need a lot of training. But if it's what you want to be, go right ahead. I'll back you. My son-in-law is a builder at present. I'll talk to him and get his advice. We may be able to arrange to have you go right into his office, begin at the bottom and work straight up." In silence for a moment John hobbled on by Roger's side.

"I'd hate to leave your place," he said.

"I know," was Roger's brusque reply, "and I'd hate to lose you. We'll have to think it over."

A few days later he talked with Bruce, who said he'd be glad to take the boy. And at dinner that night with Deborah, Roger asked abruptly,

"Why not let Johnny come here for a while and use one of our empty bedrooms?"

With a quick flush of pleased surprise, Deborah gave her father a look that embarrassed him tremendously.

"Well, why not?" he snapped at her. "Sensible, isn't it?"

" Perfectly."

And sensible it turned out to be. When John first
heard about it, he was apparently quite overcome, and
there followed a brief awkward pause while he rapidly
blinked the joy from his eyes. But then he said, "Fine,
thank you. That's mighty good of you, Mr. Gale," in
as matter of fact a tone as you please. And he entered
the household in much the same way, for John had a sense
of the fitness of things. He had always kept himself neat
and clean, but he became immaculate now. He dined
with Roger the first night, but early the next morning he
went down to the kitchen and breakfasted there; and
from this time on, unless he were especially urged to come
up to the dining room, John took all his meals downstairs.
The maids were Irish—so was John. They were good
Catholics—so was John. They loved the movies—so
did John. In short, it worked out wonderfully. In less
than a month John had made himself an unobtrusive and
natural part of the life of Roger's sober old house. It
had had to stretch just a little, no more.

CHAPTER XVI

BUT that winter there was more in the house than Deborah's big family. Though at times Roger felt it surging in with its crude, immense vitality, there were other times when it was not so, and the lives of his other two daughters attracted his attention, for both were back again in town.

Laura and her husband had returned from abroad in October, and in a small but expensive apartment in a huge new building facing on Park Avenue they had gaily started the career of their own little family, or "ménage," as Laura called it. This word had stuck in Roger's mind, for he had a suspicion that a "ménage" was no place for babies. Grimly, when he went there first to be shown the new home by its mistress, he looked about him for a room which might be made a nursery. But no such room was in evidence. "We decided to have no guest room," he heard Laura say to Deborah. And glancing at his daughter then, sleek and smiling and demure, in her tea-gown fresh from Paris, Roger darkly told himself that a child would be an unwelcome guest. The whole place was as compact and sparkling as a jewel box. The bed chamber was luxurious, with a gorgeous bath adjoining and a dressing-room for Harold.

"And look at this love of a closet!" said Laura to Deborah eagerly. "Isn't it simply enormous?" As Deborah looked, her father did, too, and his eye was met by an array of shimmering apparel which made him draw back almost with a start.

They found Harold in the pantry. Their Jap, it appeared, was a marvellous cook and did the catering as

well, so that Laura rarely troubled herself to order so
much as a single meal. But her husband had for many
years been famous for his cocktails, and although the Jap
did everything else Hal had kept this in his own hands.

"I thought this much of the house-keeping ought to
remain in the family," he said.

Roger did not like this joke. But later, when he had
imbibed the delicious concoction Harold had made, and
had eaten the dinner created by that Japanese artist of
theirs, his irritation subsided.

"They barely know we're here," he thought. "They're
both in love up to their ears."

Despite their genial attempts to be hospitable and
friendly, time and again he saw their glances meet in an
intimate gleaming manner which made him rather uncom-
fortable. But where was the harm, he asked himself.
They were married all right, weren't they? Still somehow
—somehow—no, by George, he didn't like it, he didn't
approve! The whole affair was decidedly mixing. Roger
went away vaguely uneasy, and he felt that Deborah was
even more disturbed than himself.

"Those two," she remarked to her father, "are so
fearfully wrapt up in each other it makes me afraid. Oh,
it's all right, I suppose, and I wouldn't for worlds try to
interfere. But I can't help feeling somehow that no two
people with such an abundance of youth and money and
happiness have the right to be so amazingly—selfish!"

"They ought to have children," Roger said.

"But look at Edith," his daughter rejoined. "She
hasn't a single interest that I can find outside her home.
It seems to have swallowed her, body and soul." A
frowning look of perplexity swept over Deborah's mobile
face, and with a whimsical sigh she exclaimed, "Oh, this
queer business of families!"

In December there came a little crash. Late one evening
Laura came bursting in upon them in a perfect tantrum,

every nerve in her lithe body tense, her full lips visibly quivering, her voice unsteady, and her big black eyes aflame with rage. She was jealous of her husband and "that nasty little cat!" Roger learned no more about it, for Deborah motioned him out of the room. He heard their two voices talk on and on, until Laura's slowly quieted down. Soon afterwards she left the house, and Deborah came in to him.

"She's gone home, eh?" asked Roger.

"Yes, she has, poor silly child—she said at first she had come here to stay."

"By George," he said. "As bad as that?"

"Of course it isn't as bad as that!" Deborah cried impatiently. "She just built and built on silly suspicions and let herself get all worked up! I don't see what they're coming to!" For a few moments nothing was said. "It's so unnatural!" she exclaimed. "Men and women weren't *made* to live like that!" Roger scowled into his paper.

"Better leave 'em alone," he admonished her. "You can't help—they're not your kind. Don't you mix into this affair."

But Deborah did. She remembered that her sister had once shown quite a talent for amateur theatricals; and to give Laura something to do, Deborah persuaded her to take a dramatic club in her school. And Laura, rather to Roger's surprise, became an enthusiast down there. She worked like a slave at rehearsals, and upon the costumes she spent money with a lavish hand. Moreover, instead of being annoyed, as Edith was, at Deborah's prominence in the press, Laura gloried in it, as though this "radical" sister of hers were a distinct social asset among her giddy friends uptown. For even Laura's friends, her father learned with astonishment, had acquired quite an appetite for men and women with ideas—the more "radical," the better. But the way Laura used this word at times made Roger's blood run cold. She was vivid in her approval of

her sister's whole idea, as a scheme of wholesale motherhood which would give "a perfectly glorious jolt" to the
old-fashioned home with its overworked mothers who let
their children absorb their days.

"As though having children and bringing them up,"
she disdainfully declared, "were something every woman
must do, whether she happens to like it or not, at the cost
of any real growth of her own!"

And smilingly she hinted at impending radical changes
in the whole relation of marriage, of which she was hearing
in detail at a series of lectures to young wives, delivered on
Thursday mornings in a hotel ball-room.

What the devil was getting into the town? Roger
frowned his deep dislike. Here was Laura with her
chicken's mind blithely taking her sister's thoughts and
turning them topsy-turvy, to make for herself a view of
life which fitted like a white kid glove her small and
elegant "ménage." And although her father had only
inklings of it all, he had quite enough to make him irate at
this uncanny interplay of influences in his family. Why
couldn't the girls leave each other alone?

Early in the winter, Edith, too, had entered in. It had
taken Edith just one glance into the bride's apartment to
grasp Laura's whole scheme of existence.

"Selfish, indulgent and abnormal," was the way she
described it. She and Bruce were dining with Roger that
night. "I wash my hands of the whole affair," continued
Edith curtly. "So long as she doesn't want my help, as
she has plainly made me feel, I certainly shan't stand in
her way."

"You're absolutely right," said her father.

"Stick to it," said Bruce approvingly.

But Edith did not stick to it. In her case too, as the
weeks wore on, those subtle family ties took hold and
made her feel the least she could do was "to keep up

appearances." So she and Bruce dined with the bride and groom, and in turn had them to dinner. And these dinners, as Bruce confided to Roger, were occasions no man could forget.

"They come only about once a month," he said in a tone of pathos, "but it seems as though barely a week had gone by when Edith says to me again, 'We're dining with Laura and Hal to-night.' Well, and we dine. Young Sloane is not a bad sort of a chap—works hard downtown and worships his wife. The way he lives—well, it isn't mine—and mine isn't his—and we both let it go at that. But the women can't, they haven't it in 'em. Each sits with her way of life in her lap. You can't see it over the tablecloth, but, my God, how you feel it! The worst of it is," he ended, "that after one of these terrible meals each woman is more set than before in her own way of living. Not that I don't like Edith's way," her husband added hastily.

Edith also disapproved of the fast increasing publicity which Deborah was getting.

"I may be very old-fashioned," she remarked to her father, "but I can't get used to this idea that a woman's place is in headlines. And I think it's rather hard on you—the use she's making of your house."

One Friday night when she came to play chess, she found her father in the midst of a boisterous special meeting of his club of Italian boys. It had been postponed from the evening before. And though Roger, overcome with dismay at having forgotten Edith's night, apologized profusely, the time-honored weekly game took place no more from that day on.

"Edith's pretty sore," said Bruce, who dropped in soon afterwards. "She says Deborah has made your house into an annex to her school."

Roger smoked in silence. His whole family was about his ears.

"My boy," he muttered earnestly, "you and I must stick together."

"We sure must," agreed his son-in-law. "And what's more, if we're to keep the peace, we've got to try to put some punch into Deborah's so-called love affair. She ought to get married and settle down."

"Yes," said Roger, dubiously. "Only let's keep it to ourselves."

"No chance of that," was the cheerful reply. "You can't keep Edith out of it. It would only make trouble in *my* family." Roger gave him a pitying look and said, "Then, for the Lord's sake, let her in!"

So they took Edith into their councils, and she gave them an indulgent smile.

"Suppose you leave this to me," she commanded. "Don't you think I've been using my eyes? There's no earthly use in stepping in now, for Deborah has lost her head. She sees herself a great new woman with a career. But wait till the present flare-up subsides, till the newspapers all drop her and she is thoroughly tired out. Until then, remember, we keep our hands off."

"Do you think you can?" asked Roger, with a little glimmer of hope.

"I?" she retorted. "Most certainly! I mean to leave her alone absolutely—until she comes to me herself. When she does, we'll know it's time to begin."

"I'm afraid Edith is hurt about something," said Deborah to her father, about a month after this little talk. "She hasn't been near us for over three weeks."

"Let her be!" said Roger, in alarm. "I mean," he hastily added, "why can't you let Edith come when she likes? There's nothing the matter. It's simply her children—they take up her time."

"No," said Deborah calmly, "it's I. She as good as told me so last month. She thinks I've become a perfect fanatic—without a spare moment or thought for my family."

"Oh, my family!" Roger groaned. "I tell you, Deborah, you're wrong! Edith's children are probably sick in bed!"

"Then I'll go and see," she answered.

"Something has happened to Deborah," Edith informed him blithely, over the telephone the next night.

"Has, eh," grunted Roger.

"Yes, she was here to see me to-day. And something has happened—she's changing fast. I felt it in all kinds of ways. She was just as dear as she could be—and lonely, as though she were feeling her age. I really think we can do something now."

"All right, let's do something," Roger growled.

And Edith began to do something. Her hostility to her sister had completely disappeared. In its place was a friendly affection, an evident desire to please. She even drew Laura into the secret, and there was a gathering of the clan. There were consultations in Roger's den. "Deborah is to get married." The feeling of it crept through the house. Nothing was said to her, of course, but Deborah was made to feel that her two sisters had drawn close. And their influence upon her choice was more deep and subtle than she knew. For although Roger's family had split so wide apart, between his three daughters there were still mysterious bonds reaching far back into nursery days. And Deborah in deciding whether to marry Allan Baird was affected more than she was aware by the married lives of her sisters. All she had seen in Laura's ménage, all that she had ever observed in Edith's growing family, kept rising from time to time in her thoughts, as she vaguely tried to picture herself a wife and the mother of children.

So the family, with those subtle bonds from the past, began to press steadily closer and closer around this one unmarried daughter, and help her to make up her mind.

CHAPTER XVII

BUT she did not appear to care to be helped. Nor did Allan—he rarely came to the house, and he went to Edith's not at all. He was even absent from her Christmas tree for the children, a jolly little festivity which neither he nor Deborah had missed in years.

"What has got into him?" Roger asked. And shortly after Christmas he called the fellow up on the 'phone. "Drop in for dinner to-night," he urged. And he added distinctly, "I'm alone."

"Are you? I'll be glad to."

"Thank you, Baird, I want your advice." And as he hung up the receiver he said, "Now then!" to himself, in a tone of firm decision. But later, as the day wore on, he cursed himself for what he had done. "Don't it beat the devil," he thought, "how I'm always putting my foot in it?" And when Baird came into the room that night he loomed, to Roger's anxious eye, if anything taller than before. But his manner was so easy, his gruff voice so natural, and he seemed to take this little party of two so quietly as a matter of course, that Roger was soon reassured, and at table he and Allan got on even better than before. Baird talked of his life as a student, in Vienna, Bonn and Edinburgh, and of his first struggles in New York. His talk was full of human bits, some tragic, more amusing. And Roger's liking for the man increased with every story told.

"I asked you here," he bluntly began, when they had gone to the study to smoke, "to talk to you about Deborah." Baird gave him a friendly look.

138

"All right. Let's talk about her."

"It strikes me you were right last year," said Roger, speaking slowly. "She's already showing the strain of her work. She don't look to me as strong as she was."

"She looks to me stronger," Allan replied. "You know, people fool doctors now and then—and she seems to have taken a fresh start. I feel she may go on for years." Roger was silent a moment, chagrined and disappointed.

"Have you had a good chance to watch her?" he asked.

"Yes, and I'm watching her still," said Baird. "I see her down there at the school. She tells me you've been there yourself."

"Yes," said Roger, determinedly, "and I mean to keep on going. I'm trying not to lose hold of her," he added with harsh emphasis. Baird turned and frankly smiled at him.

"Then you have probably seen," he replied, "that to keep any hold at all on her, you must make up your mind as I have done that, strength or no strength, this job of hers is going to be a life career. When a woman who has held a job without a break for eleven years can feel such a flame of enthusiasm, you can be pretty sure, I think, it is the deepest part of her. At least I feel that way," he said. "And I believe the only way to keep near her—for the present, anyhow—is to help her in her work."

When Baird had gone, Roger found himself angry.

"I'm not in the habit, young man," he thought, "of throwing my daughter at gentlemen's heads. If you feel as calm and contented as that you can go to the devil! Far be it from me to lift a hand! In fact, as I come to think of it, you would probably make her a mighty poor husband!" He worked himself into quite a rage. But an hour later, when he had subsided, "Hold on," he thought. "Am I right about this? Is the man as contented as he talks? No, sir, not for a minute he isn't! But what can he do? If he tried making love to Deborah he'd simply be killing his chances. Not the slightest doubt in the world. She can't think of anything but her career. Yes, sir, when all's said and done, to marry a modern woman is no child's play, it means thought and care. And A. Baird has made up his mind to it. He has made up his mind to marry her by playing a long waiting game. He's just slowly and quietly nosing his way into her school, because it's her life. And a mighty shrewd way of going about it. You don't need any help from me, my friend; all you need is to be let alone."

In talks at home with Deborah, and in what he himself observed at school, Roger began to get inklings of "A. Baird's long waiting game." He found that several months before Allan had offered to start a free clinic for mothers and children in connection with the school, and that he alone had put it through, with only the most reluctant aid and gratitude from Deborah—as though she dreaded something. Baird took countless hours from his busy uptown practice; he hurt himself more than once, in fact, by neglecting rich patients to do this work. Where a sick or pregnant mother was too poor to carry out his advice, he followed her into her tenement home, sent one of his nurses to visit her, and even gave money when it was needed to ease the strain of her poverty until she should be well and strong. Soon scores of the mothers of Deborah's children were singing the praises of Doctor Baird.

Then he began coming to the house.

"I was right," thought Roger complacently.

He laid in a stock of fine cigars and some good port and claret, too; and on evenings when Baird came to dine, Roger by a genial glow and occasional jocular ironies would endeavor to drag the talk away from clinics, adenoids, children's teeth, epidemics and the new education. But no joke was so good that Deborah could not promptly match it with some amusing little thing which one of her children had said or done. For she had a mother's instinct for bragging fondly of her brood. It was deep, it was uncanny, this queer community motherhood.

"This poor devil," Roger thought, with a pitying glance at Baird, "might just as well be marrying a widow with three thousand brats."

But Baird did not seem in the least dismayed. On the contrary, his assurance appeared to be deepening every week, and with it Deborah's air of alarm. For his clinic, as it swiftly grew, he secured financial backing from his rich women patients uptown, many of them childless and only too ready to respond to the appeals he made to them. And one Saturday evening at the house, while dining with Roger and Deborah, he told of an offer he had had from a wealthy banker's widow to build a maternity hospital. He talked hungrily of all it could do in co-operation with the school. He said nothing of the obvious fact that it would require his whole time, but Roger thought of that at once, and by the expression on Deborah's face he saw she was thinking, too.

He felt they wanted to be alone, so presently he left them. From his study he could hear their voices growing steadily more intense. Was it all about work? He could not tell. "They've got working and living so mixed up, a man can't possibly tell 'em apart."

Then his daughter was called to the telephone, and Allan came in to bid Roger good-night. And his eyes showed an impatience he did not seem to care to hide.

"Well?" inquired Roger. "Did you get Deborah's consent?"

"To what?" asked Allan sharply.

"To your acceptance," Roger answered, "of the widow's mite." Baird grinned.

"She couldn't help herself," he said.

"But she didn't seem to like it, eh—"

"No," said Baird, "she didn't." Roger had a dark suspicion.

" By the way," he asked in a casual tone, "what's this philanthropic widow like?"

"She's sixty-nine," Baird answered.

"Oh," said Roger. He smoked for a time, and sagely added, "My daughter's a queer woman, Baird—she's modern, very modern. But she's still a woman, you understand—and so she's jealous—of her job." But A. Baird was in no joking mood.

"She's narrow," he said sternly. "That's what's the matter with Deborah. She's so centered on her job she can't see anyone else's. She thinks I'm doing all this work solely in order to help her school—when if she'd use some imagination and try to put herself in my shoes, she'd see the chance it's giving *me!*"

"How do you mean?" asked Roger, looking a bit bewildered.

"Why," said Baird with an impatient fling of his hand, "there are men in my line all over the country who'd leave home, wives and children for the chance I've blundered onto here! A hospital fully equipped for research, a free hand, an opportunity which comes to one man in a million! But can she see it? Not at all! It's only an annex to her school!"

"Yes," said Roger gravely, "she's in a pretty unnatural state. I think she ought to get married, Baird—" To his friendly and disarming twinkle Baird replied with a rueful smile.

"You do, eh," he growled. "Then tell her to plan her wedding to come before her funeral." As he rose to go, Roger took his hand.

"I'll tell her," he said. "It's sound advice. Good-night, my boy, I wish you luck."

A few moments later he heard in the hall their brief

good-nights to each other, and presently Deborah came in. She was not looking quite herself.

"Why are you eyeing me like that?" his daughter asked abruptly.

"Aren't you letting him do a good deal for you?"

Deborah flushed a little:

"Yes, I am. I can't make him stop."

Her father hesitated.

"You could," he said, "if you wanted to. If you were sure," he added slowly, "that you didn't love him—and told him so." He felt a little panic, for he thought he had gone too far. But his daughter only turned away and restlessly moved about the room. At last she came to her father's chair:

"Hadn't you better leave this to me?"

"I had, my dear, I most certainly had. I was all wrong to mention it," he answered very humbly.

From this night on, Baird changed his tack. Although soon busy with the plans for the hospital, to be built at once, he said little about it to Deborah. Instead, he insisted on taking her off on little evening sprees uptown.

"Do you know what's the matter with both of us?" he said to her one evening. "We've been getting too durned devoted to our jobs and our ideals. You're becoming a regular school marm and I'm getting to be a regular slave to every wretched little babe who takes it into his head to be born. We haven't one redeeming vice."

And again he took up dancing. The first effort which he made, down at Deborah's school one evening, was a failure quite as dismal as his attempts of the previous year. But he did not appear in the least discouraged. He came to the house one Friday night.

"I knew I could learn to dance," he said, "in spite of all your taunts and jibes. That little fiasco last Saturday night—"

"Was perfectly awful," Deborah said.

"Did not discourage me in the least," he continued severely. "I decided the only trouble with me was that I'm tall and I've got to bend—to learn to bend."

"Tremendously!"

"So I went to a lady professor, and she saw the point at once. Since then I've had five lessons, and I can fox-trot in my sleep. To-morrow is Saturday. Where shall we go?"

"To the theater."

"Good. We'll start with that. But the minute the play is over we'll gallop off to the Plaza Grill—just as the music is in full swing—"

"And we'll dance," she groaned, "for hours. And when I get home, I'll creep into bed so tired and sore in every limb—"

"That you'll sleep late Sunday morning. And a mighty good thing for you, too—if you ask my advice—"

"I don't ask your advice!"

"You're getting it, though," he said doggedly. "If you're still to be a friend of mine we'll dance at the Plaza to-morrow night—and well into the Sabbath."

"The principal of a public school—dancing on the Sabbath. Suppose one of my friends should see us there."

"Your friends," he replied with a fine contempt, "do not dance in the Plaza Grill. I'm the only roisterer you know."

"All right," she conceded grudgingly, "I'll roister. Come and get me. But I'd much prefer when the play is done to come home and have milk and crackers here."

"Deborah," he said cheerfully, "for a radical school reformer you're the most conservative woman I know."

CHAPTER XVIII

In Deborah's school, in the meantime, affairs had drawn to a climax. The moment had come for the city to say whether her new experiment should be dropped the following year or allowed to go on and develop. There came a day of sharp suspense when Deborah's friends and enemies on the Board of Education sat down to discuss and settle her fate. They were at it for several hours, but late in the afternoon they decided not only to let her go on the next year but to try her idea in four other schools and place her in charge with ample funds. The long strain came to an end at last in a triumph beyond her wildest hopes; when the news arrived she relaxed, grew limp, and laughed and cried a little. And her father felt her tremble as he held her a moment in his arms.

"Now, Baird," he thought, "your chance has come. For God's sake, take it while it's here!"

But in place of Baird that afternoon came men and women from the press, and friends and fellow workers. The door-bell and the telephone kept ringing almost incessantly. Why couldn't they leave her a moment's peace? Roger buried himself in his study. Later, when he was called to dinner, he found that Allan was there, too, but at first the conversation was all upon Deborah's victory. Flushed with success, for the moment engrossed in the wider field she saw ahead, she had not a thought for anything else. But after dinner the atmosphere changed.

"To hear me talk," she told them, "you'd think the whole world depended on me, and on my school and my

145

ideas. Me, me, me! And it has been me all winter long! What a time I've given both of you!"

She grew repentant and grateful, first to her father and then to Allan, and then more and more to Allan, with her happy eyes on his. And with a keen worried look at them both, Roger rose and left the room.

Baird was leaning forward. He had both her hands in his own.

"Well?" he asked. "Will you marry me now?"

Her eyes were looking straight into his. They kept moving slightly, searching his. Her wide, sensitive lips were tightly compressed, but did not quite hide their quivering. When she spoke her voice was low and a little queer and breathless:

"Do you want any children, Allan?"

"Yes."

"So do I. And with children, what of my work?"

"I don't want to stop your work. If you marry me we'll go right on. You see I know you, Deborah, I know you've always grown like that—by risking what you've got to-day for something more to-morrow."

"I've never taken a risk like this!"

"I tell you this time it's no risk! Because you're a grown woman—formed! I'm not making a saint of you. You're no angel down among the poor because you feel it's your duty in life—it's your happiness, your passion! You couldn't neglect them if you tried!"

"But the time," she asked him quickly. "Where shall I find the time for it all?"

"A man finds time enough," he answered, "even when he's married."

"But I'm not a man, I'm a woman," she said. And in a low voice which thrilled him, "A woman who wants a child of her own!" His lean muscular right hand contracted sharply upon hers. She winced, drew back a little.

"Oh—I'm sorry!" he whispered. Then he asked her again,

"Will you marry me now?" She looked suddenly up:

"Let's wait awhile, please! It won't be long—I'm in love with you, Allan, I'm sure of that now! And I'm not drawing back, I'm not afraid! Oh, I want you to feel I'm not running away! What I want to do is to face this square! It may be silly and foolish but—you see, I'm made like that. I want a little longer—I want to think it out by myself."

When Allan had gone she came in to her father. And her radiant expression made him bounce up from his chair.

"By George," he cried, "he asked you!"

"Yes!"

"And you've taken him!"

"No!"

Roger gasped.

"Look here!" he demanded, angrily. "What's the matter? Are you mad?" She threw back her head and laughed at him.

"No, I'm not—I'm happy!"

"What the devil about?" he snapped.

"We're going to wait a bit, that's all, till we're sure of everything!" she cried.

"Then," said Roger disgustedly, "you're smarter than your father is. I'm sure of nothing—nothing! I have never been sure in all my days! If I'd waited, you'd never have been born!"

"Oh, dearie," she begged him smilingly. "Please don't be so unhappy just now—"

"I've a right to be!" said Roger. "I see my house agog with this—in a turmoil—in a turmoil!"

But again he was mistaken. It was in fact astonishing how the old house quieted down. There came again one of those peaceful times, when his home to Roger's senses seemed to settle deep, grow still, and gather itself together. Day by day he felt more sure that Deborah was succeeding in making her work fit into her swiftly deepening passion for a full happy woman's life. And why shouldn't they live here, Allan and she? The thought of this dispelled the cloud which hung over the years he saw ahead. How smoothly things were working out. The monstrous new buildings around his house seemed to him to draw back as though balked of their prey.

On the mantle in Roger's study, for many years a bronze figure there, "The Thinker," huge and naked, forbidding in its crouching pose, the heavy chin on one clenched fist, had brooded down upon him. And in the years that had been so dark, it had been a figure of despair. Often he had looked up from his chair and grimly met its frowning gaze. But Roger seldom looked at it now, and even when it caught his eye it had little effect upon him. It appeared to brood less darkly. For though he did not think it out, there was this feeling in his mind:

"There is to be nothing startling in this quiet home of mine, no crashing deep calamity here."

Only the steadily deepening love between a grown man and a woman mature, both sensible, strong people with a firm control of their destinies. He felt so sure of this affair. For now, her tension once relaxed with the success which had come to her after so many long hard years, a new Deborah was revealed, more human in her yieldings. She let Allan take her off on the wildest little sprees uptown and out into the country. To Roger she seemed younger, more warm and joyous and more free. He loved to hear her laugh these nights, to catch the glad new tones in her voice.

"There is to be no tragedy here."

So, certain of this union and wistful for all he felt it would bring, Roger watched its swift approach. And when the news came, he was sure he'd been right. Because it came so quietly.

"It's settled, dear, at last it's sure. Allan and I are to be married." She was standing by his chair. Roger reached up and took her hand:

"I'm glad. You'll be very happy, my child."

She bent over and kissed him, and putting his arm around her he drew her down on the side of his chair.

"Now tell me all your plans," he said. And her answer brought him a deep peace.

"We're going abroad for the summer—and then if you'll have us we want to come here." Roger abruptly shut his eyes.

"By George, Deborah," he said, "you do have a way of getting right into the heart of things!" His arm closed about her with new strength and he felt all his troubles flying away.

"What a time we'll have, what a rich new life." Her deep sweet voice was a little unsteady. "Listen, dearie, how quiet it is." And for some moments nothing was heard but the sober tick-tick of the clock on the mantle. "I wonder what we're going to hear."

And they thought of new voices in the house.

CHAPTER XIX

Edith was radiant at the news.

"I do hope they're not going to grudge themselves a good long wedding trip!" she exclaimed.

"They're going abroad," said Roger.

"Oh, splendid! And the wedding! Church or home?"

"Home," said Roger blissfully, "and short and simple, not a frill. Just the family."

"Oh, that's so nice," sighed Edith. "I was afraid she'd want to drag in her school."

"School will be out by then," he said.

"Well, I hope it stays out—for the remainder of her days. She can't do both, and she'll soon see. Wait till she has a child of her own."

"Well, she wants one bad enough."

"Yes, but can she?" Edith asked, with the engrossed expression which came on her pretty florid face whenever she neared such a topic. She spoke with evident awkwardness. "That's the trouble. Is it too late? Deborah's thirty-one, you know, and she has lived her life so hard. The sooner she gives up her school the better for her chances."

The face of her father clouded.

"Look here," he said uneasily, "I wouldn't go talking to her—quite along those lines, my dear."

"I'm not such an idiot," she replied. "She thinks me homely enough as it is. And she's not altogether wrong. Bruce and I were talking it over last night. We want to be closer, after this, to Deborah and Allan. Bruce says it will do us *all* good, and for once I think he's right. I *have* given too much time to my children, and Bruce to his

150

office—I see it now. Not that I regret it, but—well, we're
going to blossom out."

She struck the same note with Deborah. And so did
Bruce.

"Oh, Deborah dear," he said smiling, when he found
a chance to see her alone, "if you knew how long I've
waited for this big fine thing to happen. A. Baird is my
best chum in the world. Don't yank him gently away
from us now. We'll keep close—eh?—all four of us."

"Very," said Deborah softly.

"And you mustn't get too solemn, you know. You
won't pull too much of the highbrow stuff."

"Heaven forbid!"

"That's the right idea. We'll have some fine little parties together. You and A. Baird will give us a hand and
get us out in the evenings. We need it, God knows, we've
been getting old." Deborah threw him a glance of affection.

"Why, Brucie," she said, in admiring tones, "I knew
you had it in you."

"So has Edith," he sturdily declared. "She only needs
a little shove. We'll show you two that we're regular
fellows. Don't you be all school and we won't be all home.
We'll jump out of our skins and be young again."

In pursuance of this gay resolve, Bruce planned frequent parties to theaters and musical shows, and to
Edith's consternation he even began to look about for a
teacher from whom he could learn to dance. "A. Baird,"
he told her firmly, "isn't going to be the only soubrette
in this family."

One of the most hilarious of these small celebrations
came early in June, when they dined all four together and
went to the summer's opening of "The Follies of 1914."
The show rather dragged a bit at first, but when Bert

Williams took the stage Bruce's laugh became so contagious that people in seats on every hand turned to look at him and join in his glee. Only one thing happened to mar the evening's pleasure. When they came outside the theater Bruce found in his car something wrong with the engine. He tinkered but it would not go. Allan hailed a taxi.

"Why not come with us?" asked Deborah.

"No, thanks," said Bruce. "I've got this car to look after."

"Oh, let it wait," urged Allan.

"It does look a little like rain," put in Edith. Bruce glanced up at the cloudy sky and hesitated a moment.

"Rain, piffle," he said good-humoredly. "Come on, wifey, stick by me. I won't be long." And he and Edith went back to his car.

"What a dear he is," said Deborah. Allan put his arm around her, and they looked at each other and smiled. It was only nine days to the wedding.

Out of the street's commotion came a sharp cry of warning. It was followed by a shriek and a crash. Allan looked out of the window, and then with a low exclamation he jumped from the taxi and slammed the door.

CHAPTER XX

Roger had been spending a long quiet evening at home. He had asked John to dine with him and they had chatted for a time. Then John had started up to his room. And listening to the slow shuffling step of the cripple going upstairs, Roger had thought of the quick eager feet and the sudden scampers that would be heard as the silent old house renewed its life. Later he had gone to bed.

He awakened with a start. The telephone bell was ringing.

"Nice time to be calling folks out of bed," he grumbled, as he went into the hall. The next moment he heard Deborah's voice. It was clear and sharp with a note of alarm.

"Father—it's I! You must come to Edith's apartment at once! Bruce is hurt badly! Come at once!"

When Roger reached the apartment, it was Deborah who opened the door. Her face had changed, it was drawn and gray. She took him into the living room.

"Tell me," he said harshly.

"It was just outside the theater. Bruce and Edith were out in the street and got caught by some idiot of a chauffeur. Bruce threw Edith out of the way, but just as he did it he himself got struck in the back and went under a wheel. Allan brought him here at once, while I telephoned for a friend of his—a surgeon. They're with Bruce now."

"Where's Edith?"

"She's trying to quiet the children. They all woke up—" Deborah frowned—"when he was brought in," she added.

"Well!" breathed Roger. "I declare!" Dazed and
stunned, he sank into a chair. Soon the door opened and
Allan came in.

"He's gone," he said. And Deborah jumped. "No,
no, I meant the doctor."

"What does he say?"

"Bruce can't live," said Allan gently. In the tense
silence there came a chill. "And he knows it," Allan
added. "He made me tell him—he said he must know—
for business reasons. He wants to see you both at once,
before Edith gets that child asleep."

As they entered the room they saw Bruce on his bed.
He was breathing quickly through his narrow tight-set
jaws and staring up at the ceiling with a straining fixed
intensity. As they entered he turned his head. His
eyes met theirs and lighted up in a hard and terrible
manner.

"I'm not leaving them a dollar!" he cried.

"We'll see to them, boy," said Roger, hoarsely, but
Bruce had already turned to Baird.

"I make you my executor, Allan—don't need it in writing—there isn't time." He drew a sudden quivering
breath. "I have no will," he muttered on. "Never made
one—never thought of this. Business life just starting—
booming!—and I put in every cent!" There broke from
him a low, bitter groan. "Made my money settling other
men's muddles! Never thought of making this mess of
my own! But even in mine—I could save something
still—if I could be there—if I could be there—"

The sweat broke out on his temples, and Deborah laid
her hand on his head. "Sh-h-h," she breathed. He shut
his eyes.

"Hard to think of anything any more. I can't keep
clear." He shuddered with pain. "Fix me for *them*," he
muttered to Baird. "George and his mother. Fix me
up—give me a couple of minutes clear. And Deborah—

when you bring 'em in—don't let 'em know. You understand? No infernal last good-byes!" Deborah sharply set her teeth.

"No, dear, no," she whispered. She followed her father out of the room, leaving Allan bending over the bed with a hypodermic in his hand. And when, a few moments later, George came in with his mother, they found Bruce soothed and quieted. He even smiled as he reached up his hand.

"They say I've got to sleep, old girl—just sleep and sleep—it'll do me good. So you mustn't stay in the room to-night. Stay with the kiddies and get 'em to sleep." He was still smiling up at her. "They say it'll be a long time, little wife—and I'm so sorry—I was to blame. If I'd done as you wanted and gone in their taxi. Remember? You said it might rain." He turned to George: "Look here, my boy, I'm counting on you. I'll be sick, you know—no good at all. You must stand by your mother."

George gulped awkwardly:

"Sure I will, dad." His father sharply pressed his hand:

"That's right, old fellow, I know what you are. Now good-night, son. Good-night, Edith dear." He looked at her steadily just for a moment, then closed his eyes. "Oh, but I'm sleepy," he murmured. "Good-night."

And they left him. Alone with Allan, Bruce looked up with a savage glare.

"Look here!" he snarled, between his teeth. "If you think I'm going to lie here and die you're mistaken! I won't! I won't let go! I'll show you chaps you can be wrong! Been wrong before, haven't you, thousands of times! Why be so damnably sure about *me?*" He fell back suddenly, limp and weak. "So damnably sure," he panted.

"We're never sure, my dear old boy," said Allan very

tenderly. Again he was bending close over the bed. "We're not sure yet—by any means. You're so strong, old chap, so amazingly strong. You've given me hope—"

"What are you sticking into my arm?" But Allan kept talking steadily on:

"You've given me hope you'll pull through still. But not like this. You've got to rest. Let go, and try to go to sleep."

"I'm afraid to," came the whisper. But soon, as again the drug took hold, he mumbled in a drowsy tone, "Afraid to go to sleep in the dark. . . . Say, Allan—get Deborah in here, will you—just for a minute. One thing more."

When she came, he did not open his eyes.

"That you, Deborah? Where's your hand? . . . Oh— there it is. Just one more point. You—you—" Again his mind wandered, but with an effort he brought it back. "You and Edith," he said in a whisper. "So—so—so different. Not—not like each other at all. But you'll stick together—eh? Always—always. Don't let go—I mean of my hand."

"No, dear, no."

And with her hand holding his, she sat for a long time perfectly still. Then the baby was heard crying, and Deborah went to the nursery.

"Now, Edith, I'll see to the children," she said. "Allan says you can go to Bruce if you like."

Edith looked up at Deborah quickly, and as quickly turned away. She went in to her husband. And there, hour by hour through the night, while he lay inert with his hand in hers, little by little she understood. But she asked no question of anyone.

At last Bruce stirred a little and began breathing deep and fast.

And so death came into the family.

CHAPTER XXI

Roger went through the next two days in a kind of a stupor. He remembered holding Edith and feeling her shudder as though from a chill. He remembered being stopped in the hall by George who had dressed himself with care in his first suit with long trousers. "I just wanted you to remember," the boy whispered solemnly, "that I'm nearly sixteen and I'll be here. He said to stand by her and I will." The rest of that ghastly time was a blank, punctuated by small quiet orders which Roger obeyed. Thank God, Deborah was there, and she was attending to everything.

But when at last it was over, and Roger had spent the next day in his office, had found it impossible to work and so had gone home early, Deborah came to him in his room.

"Now we must have a talk," she said. "Allan has gone through Bruce's affairs, and there are still debts to be settled, it seems."

"How much do they come to, Deborah?"

"About five thousand dollars," she said. And for a moment neither spoke. "I wish I could help you out," she went on, "but I have nothing saved and neither has Allan. We've both kept using our money downtown—except just enough for the trip abroad—and we'll need almost all of that to settle for the funeral."

"I can manage," Roger said, and again there was a silence.

"Edith will have to come here to live," Deborah said presently. Her father's heavy face grew stern.

"I'd thought of that," he answered. "But it will be hard on her, Deborah—"

"I know it will—but I don't see anything else to be done." The deep quiet voice of his daughter grew sweet with pity as she spoke. "At least we can try to make it a little easier for her. You can take her up to the mountains and I can close her apartment. But of course she won't agree to it unless she knows how matters stand." Deborah waited a little. "Don't you think you're the best one to tell her?"

"Yes," said Roger, after a pause.

"Then suppose we go to her. I'm sleeping up there for the next few nights."

They found Edith in her living room. She had sent the nurse out, put the children to bed, and left alone with nothing to do she had sat facing her first night. Her light soft hair was disheveled, her pretty features pale and set. But the moment Roger entered he saw that she had herself in hand.

"Well, father," she said steadily. "You'd better tell me about our affairs. *My* affairs," she corrected herself. When he had explained, she was silent a moment, and then in a voice harsh, bitter, abrupt, "That will be hard on the children," she said. On an impulse he started to take her hand, but she drew a little away from him.

"The children, my dear," he said huskily, "will be taken care of always."

"Yes." And again she was silent. "I've been thinking I'd like to go up to the mountains—right away," she continued.

"Just our idea," he told her. "Deborah will arrange it at once."

"That's good of Deborah," she replied. And after another pause: "But take her home with you—will you? I'd rather not have her here to-night."

"I think she'd better stay, my dear."

"All right." In a tone of weariness. "Madge Deering called me up to-night. She's coming in town to-morrow, and she means to stay till I go."

"I'm glad," he said approvingly. Madge had been a widow for years. Living out in Morristown with four daughters to bring up, she had determinedly fought her way and had not only regained her hold but had even grown in strength and breadth since the death of her husband long ago. "I'm glad," he said. "You and Madge —" he paused.

"Yes, we'll have a good deal in common," Edith finished out his thought. "You look tired, dad. Hadn't you better go home now?" she suggested after a moment.

"Yes," said Roger, rising. "Good-night, my child. Remember."

In the outer hallway he found Deborah with Laura. Laura had been here several times. She was getting Edith's mourning.

"There's a love of a hat at Thurn's," she was saying softly, "if only we can get her to wear it. It's just her type." And Laura drew an anxious breath. "Anything," she added, "to escape that hideous heavy crepe."

Roger slightly raised his brows. He noticed a faint delicious perfume that irritated him suddenly. But glancing again at his daughter, trim, fresh and so immaculate, the joy of life barely concealed in her eyes, he stopped and talked and smiled at her, as Deborah was doing, enjoying her beauty and her youth, her love and all her happiness. And though they spoke of her sister, she knew they were thinking of herself, and that it was quite right they should, for it gave them a little relief from their gloom. She was honestly sorry for Edith, but she was sorrier still for Bruce, who she knew had always liked her more than he would have cared to say. She was sorrier for Bruce because, while Edith had lost only her husband, Bruce had lost his very life. And life meant so much to Laura, these days, the glowing, coursing, vibrant life of her warm beautiful body. She was thinking of that as she stood in the hall.

In the evening, at home in his study, Roger heard a slight knock at the door. He looked up and saw John.

"May I come in, Mr. Gale, for a minute?"

"Yes, my boy." John hobbled in.

"Only a minute." His voice was embarrassed. "Just two or three things I thought of," he said. "The first was about your son-in-law. You see, I was his stenographer—and while I was in his office—this morning helping Doctor Baird—I found a good deal I can do there still—about things no one remembers but me. So I'll stay there awhile, if it's all right. Only—" he paused—"without any pay. See what I mean?"

"Yes, I see," said Roger. "And you'd better stay—in that way if you like."

"Thanks," said John. "Then about his wife and family. You're to take them up to the mountains, I hear —and—well, before this happened you asked *me* up this summer. But I guess I'd better not."

"I don't think you'd be in the way, my boy."

"I'd rather stay here, if you don't mind. When I'm through in your son-in-law's office I thought I might go back to yours. I could send you your mail every two or three days."

"I'd like that, John—it will be a great help."

"All right, Mr. Gale." John stopped at the door. "And Miss Deborah," he ventured. "Is she to get married just the same?"

"Oh, yes, I think so—later on."

"Good-night, sir."

And John went out of the room.

When *would* Deborah be married? It came over Roger, when he was alone, how his family had shifted its center.

Deborah would have come here to live, to love and be happy, a mother perhaps, but now she must find a home of her own. In her place would come Edith with her children. All would center on her in her grief.

And for no cause! Just a trick of chance, a street accident! And Roger grew bitter and rebelled. Bruce was not the one of the family to die. Bruce, so shrewd and vigorous, so vital, the practical man of affairs. Bruce had been going the pace that kills—yes, Roger had often thought of it. But that had nothing to do with this! If Bruce had died at fifty, say, as a result of the life he had chosen, the fierce exhausting city which he had loved as a man will love drink, then at least there would have been some sense of fairness in it all! If the town had let him alone till his time! But to be knocked down by an automobile! The devilish irony of it! No reason—nothing! Just hideous luck!

Well, life was like that. As for Edith and her children, he would be glad to have them here. Only, it would be different, the house would have to change again. He was sorry, too, for Deborah. No wedding trip as she had planned, no home awaiting her return.

So his mind went over his family.

But suddenly such thoughts fell away as trivial and of small account. For these people would still be alive. And Bruce was dead, and Roger was old. So he thought about Bruce and about himself, and all his children grew remote. "You will live on in our children's lives." Was there no other immortality? The clock ticked on the mantle and beside it "The Thinker" brooded down. And Roger looked up unafraid, but grim and gravely wondering.

CHAPTER XXII

BUT there was a rugged practical side to the character of Roger Gale, and the next morning he was ashamed of the brooding thoughts which had come in the night. He shook them off as morbid, and resolutely set himself to what lay close before him. There was work to be done on Bruce's affairs, and the work was a decided relief. Madge Deering, in the meantime, had offered to go with Edith and the children to the mountains and see them all well settled there. And a little talk he had with Madge relieved his mind still further. What a recovery *she* had made from the tragedy of years ago. How alert and wide-awake she seemed. If Edith could only grow like that.

Soon after their departure, one night when he was dining alone, he had a curious consciousness of the mingled presence of Edith and of Judith his wife. And this feeling grew so strong that several times he looked about in a startled, questioning manner. All at once his eye was caught by an old mahogany sideboard. It was Edith's. It had been her mother's. Edith, when she married, had wanted something from her old home. Well, now it was back in the family.

The rest of Edith's furniture, he learned from Deborah that night, had been stored in the top of the house.

"Most of it," she told him, "Edith will probably want to use in fitting up the children's rooms." With a twinge of foreboding, Roger felt the approaching change in his home.

"When do you plan to be married?" he asked.

"About the end of August. We couldn't very well

162

till then, without hurting poor Edith a little, you see. You know how she feels about such things—"

"Yes, I guess you're right," he agreed.

How everything centered 'round Edith, he thought. To pay the debts which Bruce had left would take all Roger had on hand; and from this time on his expenses, with five growing children here, would be a fast increasing drain. He would have to be careful and husband his strength, a thing he had always hated to do.

In the next few weeks, he worked hard in his office. He cut down his smoking, stayed home every evening and went to bed at ten o'clock. He tried to shut Deborah out of his mind. As for Laura, he barely gave her a thought. She dropped in one evening to bid him good-bye, for this summer again she was going abroad. She and her husband, she told him, were to motor through the Balkans and down into Italy. Her father gruffly answered that he hoped she would enjoy herself. It seemed infernally unfair that it should not be Deborah who was sailing the next morning. But when he felt himself growing annoyed, abruptly he put a check on himself. It was Edith he must think of now.

But curiously it happened, in this narrowing of his attention, that while he shut out two of his daughters, a mere outsider edged closer in.

Johnny Geer was a great help. He was back in Roger's office, and with the sharp wits he had gained in his eighteen years of fighting for a chance to stay alive, now at Roger's elbow John was watching like a hawk for all the little ways and means of pushing up the business. What a will the lad had to down bodily ills, what vim in the way he tackled each job. His shrewd and cheery companionship was a distraction and relief. John was so funny sometimes.

"Good-morning, Mr. Gale," he said, as Roger came into the office one day.

"Hello, Johnny. How are you?" Roger replied.

"Fine, thank you." And John went on with his work of opening the morning's mail. But a few minutes later he gave a cackling little laugh.

"What's so funny?" Roger asked.

"Fellers," was the answer. "Fellers. Human nature. Here's a letter from Shifty Sam."

"Who the devil is he? A friend of yours?"

"No," said John, "he's a 'con man.' He works about as mean a graft as any you ever heard of. He reads the 'ads' in the papers—see?—of servant girls who're looking for work. He makes a specialty of cooks. Then he goes to where they live and talks of some nice family that wants a servant right away. He claims to be the butler, and he's dressed to look the part. 'There ain't a minute to lose,' he says. 'If you want a chawnce, my girl, come quick.' He says 'chawnce' like a butler—see? 'Pack your things,' he tells her, 'and come right along with me.' So she packs and hustles off with him—Sam carrying her suit case. He puts her on a trolley and says, 'I guess I'll stay on the platform. I've got a bit of a headache and the air will do me good.' So he stays out there with her suit case—and as soon as the car gets into a crowd, Sam jumps and beats it with her clothes."

"I see," said Roger dryly. "But what's he writing *you* about?"

"Oh, it ain't me he's writing to—it's you," was John's serene reply. Roger started.

"What?" he asked.

"Well," said the boy in a cautious tone, vigilantly eyeing his chief, "you see, a lot of these fellers like Sam have been in the papers lately. They're being called a crime wave."

"Well?"

"Sam is up for trial this week—and half the Irish cooks in town are waiting 'round to testify. And Shifty seems to enjoy himself. His picture's in the papers—see? And he wants all the clippings. So he encloses a five dollar bill."

"He does, eh—well, you write to Sam and send his money back to him!" There was a little silence.

"But look here," said John with keen regret. "We've had quite a lot of these letters this week."

Roger wheeled and looked at him.

"John," he demanded severely, "what game have you been up to here?"

"No game at all," was the prompt retort. "Just getting a little business."

"How?"

"Well, there's a club downtown," said John, "where a lot of these petty crooks hang out. I used to deliver papers there. And I went around one night this month—"

"*To drum up business?*"

"Yes, sir." Roger looked at him aghast.

"John," he asked, in deep reproach, "do you expect this office to feed the vanity of thieves?"

"Where's the vanity," John rejoined, "in being called a crime wave?" And seeing the sudden tremor of mirth which had appeared on Roger's face, "Look here, Mr. Gale," he went eagerly on. "When every paper in the town is telling these fellers where they belong—calling 'em crooks, degenerates, and preaching regular sermons right into their faces—why shouldn't we help 'em to read the stuff? How do we know it won't do 'em good? It's church to 'em, that's what it is—and business for this office. Nine of these guys have sent in their money just in the last week or so—"

"Look out, my boy," said Roger, with slow and solemn emphasis. "If you aren't extremely careful you'll find yourself a millionaire."

"But wait a minute, Mr. Gale—"

"Not in this office," Roger said. "Send 'em back, every one of 'em! Understand?"

"Yes, sir," was the meek reply. And with a little sigh of regret John turned his wits to other kinds and conditions of New Yorkers who might care to see themselves in print.

As they worked together day by day, Roger had occasional qualms over leaving John here in the hot town while he himself went up to the mountains. He even thought of writing to Edith that he was planning to bring John, too. But no, she wouldn't like it. So he did something else instead.

"John," he said, one morning, "I'm going to raise your salary to a hundred dollars a month." Instantly from the lad's bright eyes there shot a look of triumph.

"Thanks, Mr. Gale," was his hearty response.

"And in the meantime, Johnny, I want you to take a good solid month off."

"All right, sir, thank you," John replied. "But I guess it won't be quite a month. I don't feel as if I needed it."

The next day at the office he appeared resplendent in a brand-new suit of clothes, a summer homespun of light gray set off by a tie of flaming red. There was nothing soft about that boy. No, Johnny knew how to look out for himself.

And Roger went up to the farm.

CHAPTER XXIII

GEORGE met him at the station, as he had done a year before. But at once Roger noticed a difference. In the short time since his father's death certain lines had come in the boy's freckled face, and they gave him a thoughtful, resolute look. George's voice was changing. One moment it was high and boyish, again a deep and manly bass. As he kept his eyes on the horses and talked about his mother, his grandfather from time to time threw curious side glances.

"Oh, yes," George was saying, "mother's all right, she's doing fine. It was pretty bad at first, though. She wouldn't let me sit up with her any—she treated me like a regular kid. But any fellow with any sense could see how she was feeling. She'd get thinking of the accident." George stopped short and clamped his jaws. "You know, my dad did a wonderful thing," he continued presently. "Even when he was dying, and mother and I were there by his bed, he remembered how she'd get thinking alone —all about the accident. You see he knew mother pretty darned well. So he told her to remember that he was the one to blame for it. If it hadn't been for him, he said, they would have gone home in the taxi. That's a pretty good point to keep in her mind. Don't you think so?" he inquired. And Roger glanced affectionately into the anxious face by his side.

"Yes," he said, "it's a mighty good point. Did you think of it?"

"Yes, sir," George replied. "I've told it to her a good many times—that and two other points I thought of."

"What are they, son?" asked Roger.

"First," the boy said awkwardly, "about how good she was to him. And second, that she let him buy the new car before he died. He had such a lot of fun out of that car—"

On the last words the lad's changing voice went from an impressive bass to a most undignified treble. He savagely scowled.

"Those three points," he continued, in more careful measured tones, "were about all I could think of. I had to use 'em over and over—on mother when things got bad, I mean." A flush of embarrassment came on his face. "And hold her and kiss her," he muttered. Then he whipped his horses. "We've had some pretty bad times this month," he continued, loud and manfully. "You see, mother isn't so young as she was. She's well on in her thirties." A glimmer of amusement appeared in Roger's heavy eyes. "But she don't cry often any more, and with you here we'll pull her through." He shot a quick look at his grandfather. "Gee, but I'm glad you're here!" he said.

"So am I," said Roger. And with a little pressure of his hand on George's shoulder, "I guess you've had about your share. Now tell me the news. How are things on the farm?"

With a breath of evident relief, the lad launched into the animal world. And soon he was talking eagerly.

In the next few days with his daughter Roger found that George was right. She had been through the worst of it. But she still had her reactions, her spells of emptiness, bleak despair, her moods of fierce rebellion or of sudden self-reproach for not having given Bruce more while he lived. And in such hours her father tried to comfort her with poor success.

"Remember, child, I'm with you, and I know how it

feels," he said. "I went through it all myself. When your mother died—"

"But mother was so much older!" He looked at his daughter compassionately.

"How old are you?" he inquired.

"Thirty-six."

"Your mother was thirty-nine," he replied. And at that Edith turned and stared at him, bewildered, shocked, brought face to face with a new and momentous fact in her life.

"Mother only my age when she died?"

"Yes," said Roger gently, "only three years older." With a twinge of pain he noticed two quite visible streaks of gray in his daughter's soft blonde hair. "And she felt as you do now—as though she were just starting out. And I felt the same way, my dear. If I'm not mistaken, everyone does. You still feel young—but the new generation is already growing up—and you can feel yourself being pushed on. And it is hard—it is very hard." Clumsily he took her hand. "Don't let yourself drop out," he said. "Be as your mother would have been if she had been left instead of me. Go straight on with your children."

To this note he could feel her respond. And at first, as he felt what a fight she was making, Roger glorified her pluck. As he watched her with her children at table, smiling at their talk with an evident effort to enter in, and again with her baby snug in her lap while she read bedtime stories to Bob and little Tad at her side, he kept noticing the resemblance between his daughter and his wife. How close were these two members of his family drawing together now, one of them living, the other dead.

But later, as the weeks wore on, she began to plan for her children. She planned precisely how to fit them all into the house in town, she planned the hours for their meals, for their going alone or with the nurse or a maid

to their different private schools, to music lessons, to
dancing school and uptown to the park to play. She
planned their fall clothes and she planned their friends.
And there came to her father occasional moods of anxiety.
He remembered Bruce's grim remarks about those "simple" schools and clothes, the kind that always cost the
most. And he began to realize what Bruce's existence
must have been. For scarcely ever in their talks did
Edith speak of anything outside of her family. Night
after night, with a tensity born of her struggle with her
grief, she talked about her children. And Roger was in
Bruce's place, he was the one she planned with. At moments with a vague dismay he glimpsed the life ahead in
his home.

George was hard at work each day down by the broken
dam at the mill. He had an idea he could patch it up, put
the old water-wheel back into place and make it run a
dynamo, by which he could light the house and barn and
run the machines in the dairy. In his new rôle as the man
of his family, George was planning out his career. He was
wrestling with a book entitled "Our New Mother Earth"
and a journal called "The Modern Farm." And to Roger
he confided that he meant to be a farmer. He wanted to
go in the autumn to the State Agricultural College. But
when one day, very cautiously, Roger spoke to Edith of
this, with a hard and jealous smile which quite transformed
her features, she said,

"Oh, I know all about that, father dear. It's just a
stage he's going through. And it's the same way
with Elizabeth, too, and her crazy idea of becoming
a doctor. She took that from Allan Baird, and George
took his from Deborah! They'll get over it soon
enough—"

"They won't get over it!" Roger cried. "Their
dreams are parts of something new! Something I'm quite
vague about—but some of it has come to stay! You're

losing all your chances—just as I did years ago! You'll
never know your children!"

But he uttered this cry to himself alone. Outwardly
he only frowned. And Edith had gone on to say,

"I do hope that Deborah won't come up this summer.
She's been very good and kind, of course, and if she comes
she'll be doing it entirely on my account. But I don't
want her here—I want her to marry, the sooner the better,
and come to her senses—be happy, I mean. And I wish
you would tell her so."

Within a few days after this Deborah wrote to her
father that she was coming the next week. He said nothing to Edith about it at first, he had William saddled and
went for a ride to try to determine what he should do.
But it was a ticklish business. For women were queer
and touchy, and once more he felt the working of those
uncanny family ties.

"Deborah," he reflected, "is coming up here because
she feels it's selfish of her to stay away. If she marries
at once, as she told me herself, she thinks Edith will
be hurt. Edith won't be hurt—and if Deborah comes,
there'll be trouble every minute she stays. But can I
tell her so? Not at all. I can't say, 'You're not
wanted here.' If I do, *she'll* be hurt. Oh Lord, these
girls! And Deborah knows very well that if she does
get married this month, with Laura abroad and Edith
up here and only me at the wedding, Edith will smile to
herself and say, 'Now isn't that just like Deborah?'"

As Roger slowly rode along a steep and winding mountain road, gloomily he reflected to what petty little troubles
a family of women could descend, so soon after death itself. And he lifted his eyes up to the hills and decided to
leave this matter alone. If women would be women, let
them settle their own affairs. Deborah was due to arrive
on the following Friday evening. All right, let her come,
he thought. She would soon see she was in the way, and

then in a little affectionate talk he would suggest that she marry right off and have a decent honeymoon before the school year opened.

So he dismissed it from his mind. And as he listened in the dusk to the numberless murmuring voices of living creatures large and small which rose out of the valley, and as from high above him the serenity of the mountains there towering over thousands of years stole into his spirit, Roger had a large quieting sense of something high and powerful looking down upon the earth, a sense of all humanity honeycombed with millions upon millions of small sorrows, absorbing joys and hopes and fears, and in spite of them all the Great Life sweeping on, with no Great Death to check its course, no immense catastrophe, all these little troubles like mere tiny specks of foam upon the surface of the tide.

Deborah's visit, the following week, was as he had expected. Within an hour after her coming he could feel the tension grow. Deborah herself was tense, both from the work she had left in New York where she was soon to have five schools, and from the thought of her marriage, only a few weeks ahead. She said nothing about it, however, until as a sisterly duty Edith tried to draw her out by showing an interest in her plans. But the cloud of Bruce's death was there, and Deborah shunned the topic. She tried to talk of the children instead. But Edith at once was on the defensive, vigilant for trouble, and as she unfolded her winter plans she grew distinctly brief and curt.

"If Deborah doesn't see it now, she's a fool," her father told himself. "I'll just wait a few days more, and then we'll have that little talk."

CHAPTER XXIV

I⊤ had rained so hard for the past two days that no one had gone to the village, which was nearly three miles from the farm. But when the storm was over at last, George and Elizabeth tramped down and came back at dusk with a bag full of mail. Their clothes were mud-bespattered and they hurried upstairs to change before supper, while Roger settled back in his chair and spread open his New York paper. It was July 30, 1914.

From a habit grown out of thirty odd years of business life, Roger read his paper in a fashion of his own. By instinct his eye swept the page for news dealing with individual men, for it was upon people's names in print that he had made his living. And so when he looked at this strange front page it gave him a swift twinge of alarm. For the news was not of men but of nations. Austria was massing her troops along the Serbian frontier, and Germany, Italy, Russia, France and even England, all were in a turmoil, with panics in their capitals, money markets going wild.

Edith came down, in her neat black dress with its narrow white collar, ready for supper. She glanced at her father.

"Why, what's the matter?"

"Look at this." And he tossed her a paper.

"Oh-h-h," she murmured softly. "Oh, how frightful that would be." And she read on with lips compressed. But soon there came from a room upstairs the sudden cry of one of her children, followed by a shrill wail of distress. And dropping the paper, she hurried away.

Roger continued his reading.

173

Deborah came. She saw the paper Edith had dropped, picked it up and sat down to read, and there were a few moments of absolute silence. Then Roger heard a quivering breath, and glancing up he saw Deborah's eyes, intent and startled, moving down the columns of print in a swift, uncomprehending way.

"Pretty serious business," he growled.

"It can't happen!" she exclaimed.

And they resumed their reading.

In the next three days, as they read the news, they felt war like a whirlpool sucking in all their powers to think or feel, felt their own small personal plans whirled about like leaves in a storm. And while their minds—at first dazed and stunned by the thought of such appalling armies, battles, death and desolation—slowly cleared and they strove to think, and Roger thought of business shivered to atoms in every land, and Deborah thought of schools by thousands all over Europe closing down, in cities and in villages, in valleys and on mountain sides, of homes in panic everywhere, of all ideals of brotherhood shaken, bending, tottering—war broke out in Europe.

"What is this going to mean to me?"

Millions of people were asking that. And so did Roger and Deborah. The same night they left for New York, while Edith with a sigh of relief settled back into her family.

The next morning at his office Roger found John waiting with misery stamped on his face. John had paid small heed to war. Barely stopping for sleep in the last two days he had gone through scores and hundreds of papers, angrily skipping all those names of kings and emperors and czars, and searching instead for American names, names of patrons—business! Gone! Each hour he had been opening mail and piling up letters cancelling contracts, ordering service discontinued.

Roger sat down at his desk. As he worked and figured and dictated letters, glancing into the outer rooms he saw the long rows of girls at tables obviously trying to pretend that there was work for them to do. He felt them anxiously watching him—as in other offices everywhere millions of other employees kept furtively glancing at their chiefs.

"War," he thought. "Shall I close down?" He shrank from what it would mean to those girls. "Business will pick up again soon. A few days—weeks—that's all I need."

And he went to his bank. No credit there. He tried other sources, all he could think of, racking his brains as he went about town, but still he could not raise a loan. Finally he went to the firm which had once held a mortgage on his house. The chief partner had been close to Bruce, an old college friend. And when even this friend refused him aid, "It's a question of Bruce's children," Roger muttered, reddening. He felt like a beggar, but he was getting desperate. The younger man had looked away and was nervously tapping his desk with his pen.

"Bad as that, eh," he answered. "Then I guess it's got to be done." He looked anxiously up at Roger, who just at that moment appeared very old. "Don't worry, Mr. Gale," he said. "Somehow or other we'll carry you through."

"Thank you, sir." Roger rose heavily, feeling weak, and took his departure. "This is war," he told himself, "and I've got to look after my own."

But he had a sensation almost of guilt, as upon his return to his office he saw those suddenly watchful faces. He walked past them and went into his room, and again he searched for ways and means. He tried to see his business as it would be that autumn, to see the city, the nation, the world as it would be in the months ahead.

Repeatedly he fought off his fears. But slowly and inexorably the sense of his helplessness grew clear.

"No, I must shut down," he thought.

On his way home that evening, in a crush at a turbulent corner he saw a big truck jam into a taxi, and with a throb of rebellion he thought of his son-in-law who was dead. Just the turn of a hair and Bruce might have lived and been here to look after the children! At the prospect of the crisis, the strain he saw before him, Roger again felt weak and old. He shook off his dread and strode angrily on.

In his house, the rooms downstairs were still dismantled for the summer. There was emptiness and silence but no serenity in them now, only the quiet before the storm which he could feel from far and near was gathering about his home. He heard Deborah on the floor above, and went up and found her making his bed, for the chambermaid had not yet come. Her voice was a little unnatural.

"It has been a hard day, hasn't it. I've got your bathroom ready," she said. "Don't you want a nice cool bath? Supper will be ready soon."

When, a half hour later, somewhat refreshed, Roger came down to the table, he noticed it was set for two.

"Isn't Allan coming?" he asked. Her mobile features tightened.

"Not till later," she replied.

They talked little and the meal was short. But afterwards, on the wooden porch, Deborah turned to her father,

"Now tell me about your office," she said.

"There's not enough business to pay the rent."

"That won't last—"

"I'm not so sure."

"I am," she said determinedly. Her father slowly turned his head.

"Are you, with this war?" he asked. Her eyes met his

and moved away in a baffled, searching manner. "She has troubles of her own," he thought.

"How much can we run the house on, Deborah?" he asked her. At first she did not answer. "What was it—about six thousand last year?"

"I think so," she said restlessly. "We can cut down on that, of course—"

"With Edith and the children here?"

"Edith will have to manage it! There are others to be thought of!"

"The children in your schools, you mean."

"Yes," she answered with a frown. "It will be a bad year for the tenements. But please go on and tell me. What have you thought of doing?"

"Mortgage the house again," he replied. "It hasn't been easy, for money is tight, but I think I'll be able to get enough to just about carry us through the year. At home, I mean," he added.

"And the office?"

"Shut down," he said. She turned on him fiercely.

"You won't do that!"

"What else can I do?"

"Turn all those girls away?" she cried. At her tone his look grew troubled.

"How can I help myself, Deborah? If I kept open it would cost me over five hundred a week to run. Have I five hundred dollars a week to lose?"

"But I tell you it won't last!" she cried, and again the baffled, driven expression swept over her expressive face. "Can't you see this is only a panic—and keep going somehow? Can't you see what it means to the tenements? Hundreds of thousands are out of work! They're being turned off every day, every hour—employers all over are losing their heads! And City Hall is as mad as the rest! They've decided already down there to retrench!"

He turned with a quick jerk of his head:

"Are they cutting you down?" She set her teeth:

"Yes, they are. But the work in my schools is going on—every bit of it is—for every child! I'm going to find a way," she said. And he felt a thrill of compassion.

"I'm sorry to hear it," he muttered.

"You needn't be." She paused a moment, smiled and went on in a quieter voice: "Don't think I'm blind— I'm sensible—I see you can't lose five hundred a week. But why not try what other employers, quite a few, have decided to do? Call your people together, explain how it is, and ask them to choose a committee to help you find which ones need jobs the most. Keep all you can—on part time, of course—but at least pay them something, carry them through. You'll lose money by it, I haven't a doubt. But you've already found you can mortgage the house, and remember besides that I shall be here. I'm not going to marry now"—her father looked at her quickly —"and of course I'll expect to do my share toward meeting the expenses. Moreover, I know we can cut down."

"Retrench," said Roger grimly. "Turn off the servants instead of the clerks."

"No, only one of them, Martha upstairs—and she is to be married. We'll keep the cook and the waitress. Edith will have to give up her nurse—and it will be hard on her, of course—but she'll have to realize this is war," Deborah said sharply. "Besides," she urged, "it's not going to last. Business everywhere will pick up—in a few weeks or months at most. The war *can't* go on—it's too horribly big!" She broke off and anxiously looked at him. Her father was still frowning.

"I'm asking you to risk a good deal," she continued, her voice intense and low. "But somehow, dearie, I always feel that this old house of ours is strong. It can *stand* a good deal. We can all of us stand so much, as soon as we know we have to." The lines of her wide sensitive mouth tightened firmly once again. "It's all so vague and uncertain, I know. But one thing at least is sure. This is no time for people with money—no matter how little—to shut themselves up in their own little houses and let the rest starve or beg or steal. This is the time to do our share."

And she waited. But he made no reply.

"Every nation at war is doing it, dad—become like one big family—with everyone helping, doing his share. Must a nation be at war to do that? Can't we be brothers without the guns? Can't you see that we're all of us stunned, and trying to see what war will mean to all the children in the world? And while we're groping, groping, can't we give each other a hand?"

Still he sat motionless there in the dark. At last he stirred heavily in his chair.

"I guess you're right," he told her. "At least I'll think it over—and try to work out something along the lines you spoke of."

Again there was a silence. Then his daughter turned to him with a little deprecating smile.

"You'll forgive my—preaching to you, dad?"

"No preaching," he said gruffly. "Just ordinary common sense."

A little later Allan came in, and Roger soon left them and went to bed. Alone with Baird she was silent a moment.

"Well? Have you thought it over?" she asked. "Wasn't I right in what I said?" At the anxious ring in her low clear voice, leaning over he took her hand; and he felt it hot and trembling as it quickly closed on his. He stroked it slowly, soothingly. In the semi-darkness he seemed doubly tall and powerful.

"Yes, I'm sure you were right," he said.

"Spring at the latest—I'll marry you then—"

Her eyes were intently fixed on his.

"Come here!" she whispered sharply, and Baird bent

over and held her tight. "Tighter!" she whispered. "Tighter! . . . There! . . . I said, spring at the latest! I can't lose you, Allan—now—"

She suddenly quivered as though from fatigue.

"I'm going to watch you close down there," he said in a moment, huskily.

CHAPTER XXV

Roger saw little of Deborah in the weeks that followed. She was gathering her forces for the long struggle she saw ahead. And his own worries filled his mind. On his house he succeeded in borrowing five thousand dollars at ten per cent, and in his office he worked out a scheme along the lines of Deborah's plan. At first it was only a struggle to save the remnants of what was left. Later the tide began to turn, new business came into the office again. But only a little, and then it stopped. Hard times were here for the winter.

Soon Edith would come with the children. He wondered how sensible she would be. It was going to mean a daily fight to make ends meet, he told himself, and guiltily he decided not to let his daughter know how matters stood in his office. Take care of your own flesh and blood, and then be generous as you please—that had always been his way. And now Deborah had upset it by her emotional appeal. "How dramatic she is at times!" he reflected in annoyance. "Just lets herself out and enjoys herself!" He grew angry at her interference, and more than once he resolved to shut down. But back in the office, before those watchful faces, still again he would put it off.

"Wait a little. We'll see," he thought.

In the meantime, in this interplay, these shifting lights and shadows which played upon the history of the life of Roger's home, there came to him a diversion from an unexpected source. Laura and Harold returned from abroad. Soon after landing they came to the house, and talking fast and eagerly they told how they had eluded the war.

For them it had been a glorious game. In Venice in early August, Harold had seen a chance for a big stroke of business. He had a friend who lived in Rome, an Italian close to his government. At once they had joined forces, worked day and night, pulled wires, used money judiciously here and there, and so had secured large orders for munitions from the U. S. A. Then to get back to God's country! There came the hitch, they were too late. Naples, Genoa, and Milan, all were filled with tourist mobs. They took a train for Paris, and reaching the city just a week before the end of the German drive they found it worse than Italy. But there Hal had a special pull—and by the use of those wits of his, not to be downed by refusals, he got passage at last for Laura, himself and his new Italian partner. At midnight, making their way across the panic-stricken city, and at the station struggling through a wild and half crazed multitude of men and women and children, they boarded a train and went rushing westward right along the edge of the storm. To the north the Germans were so close that Laura was sure she could hear the big guns. The train kept stopping to take on troops. At dawn some twenty wounded men came crowding into their very car, bloody and dirty, pale and worn, but gaily smiling at the pain, and saying, "Ça n'fait rien, madame." Later Harold opened his flask for some splendid Breton soldier boys just going into action. And they stood up with flashing eyes and shouted out the Marseillaise, while Laura shivered and thrilled with delight.

"I nearly kissed them all!" she cried.

Roger greatly enjoyed the evening. He had heard so much of the horrors of war. Here was something different, something bright and vibrant with youth and adventure! Here at last was the thrill of war, the part he had always read about!

He glanced now and then at Deborah and was annoyed by what he saw. For although she said nothing and forced a smile, he could easily tell by the set of her lips that Deborah thoroughly disapproved. All right, that was her way, he thought. But this was Laura's way, shedding the gloom and the tragic side as a duck will shed water off its back, a duck with bright new plumage fresh from the shops of the Rue de la Paix and taking some pleasure out of life! What an ardent gleaming beauty she was, he thought as he watched this daughter of his. And underneath his enjoyment, too, though Roger would not have admitted it, was a sense of relief in the news that at least one man in the family was growing rich instead of poor. Already Hal and his partner—a fascinating creature according to Laura's description—were fast equipping shrapnel mills. Plainly they expected a tremendous rush of business. And no matter how you felt about war, the word "profits" at least had a pleasant sound.

"How has the war hit you, sir?" Harold asked his father-in-law.

"Oh, so-so, I'll get on, my boy," was Roger's quiet answer. For Harold was not quite the kind he would ever like to ask for aid. Still, if the worst came to the worst, he would have someone to turn to.

Long after they had left the house, he kept thinking over all they had said. What an amazing time they had had, the two young scalawags.

Deborah was still in the room. As she sat working at her desk, her back was turned and she did not speak. But little by little her father's mood changed. Of course she was right, he admitted. For now they were gone, the spell they had cast was losing a part of its glamor. Yes, their talk had been pretty raw. Sheer unthinking selfishness, a bold rush for plunder and a dash to get away, trampling over people half crazed, women and children in panicky crowds, and leaving behind them, so to speak, Laura's joyous rippling laugh over their own success

in the game. Yes, there was no denying the fact that
Hal was rushing headlong into a savage dangerous game,
a scramble and a gamble, with adventurers from all over
Europe gathering here and making a little world of their
own. He would work and live at a feverish pitch, and
Laura would go it as hard as he. Roger thought he could
see their winter ahead. How they would pile up money
and spend!

All at once, as though some figure silent and invisible
were standing close beside him, from far back in his childhood a memory flashed into his mind of a keen and clear
October night, when Roger, a little shaver of nine, had
stood with his mother in front of the farmhouse and listened to the faint sharp roll of a single drum far down in
the valley. And his mother's grip had hurt his hand, and
a lump had risen in his throat—as Dan, his oldest brother,
had marched away with his company of New Hampshire
mountain boys. "We are coming, Father Abraham, three
hundred thousand more." Dan had been killed at Shiloh.

And it must be like that now in France. No, he did not
like the look which he had seen on Laura's face as she
had talked about the war and the fat profits to be made.
Was this all we Yankees had to say to the people over in
Europe?

Frowning and glancing at Deborah's back, he saw that
she was tired. It was nearly midnight, but still she kept
working doggedly on, moving her shoulder muscles at
times as though to shake off aches and pains, then bending
again to her labor, her fight against such heavy odds in
the winter just beginning for those children in the tenements. He recalled a fragment of the appeal she had made
to him only the month before:

"Can't you see that we're all of us stunned, and trying
to see what war will mean to all the children in the world?
And while we're groping, groping, can't we give each other
a hand?"

And as he looked at his daughter, she made him think
of her grandmother, as she had so often done before. For
Deborah, too, was a pioneer. She, too, had lived in the
wilderness. Clearing roads through jungles? Yes. And
freeing slaves of ignorance and building a nation of new
men. And now she was doggedly fighting to save what she
had builded—not from the raids of the Indians but from
the ravages of this war which was sweeping civilization
aside. With her school behind her, so to speak, she stood
facing this great enemy with stern and angry, steady eyes.
Her pioneer grandmother come to life.

So, with the deep craving which was a part of his inmost
self, Roger tried to bind together what was old and what
was new. But his thoughts grew vague and drifting. He
realized how weary he was, and said good-night and went
to bed. There, just before he fell asleep, again he had a
feeling of relief at the knowledge that one at least in the
family was to be rich this year. With a guilty sensation
he shook off the thought, and within a few moments after
that his harsh regular breathing was heard in the room.

CHAPTER XXVI

IT was only a few days later that Edith arrived with her children.

Roger met her at the train at eight o'clock in the evening. The fast mountain express of the summer had been taken off some time before, so Edith had had to be up at dawn and to change cars several times on the trip. "She'll be worn out," he thought as he waited. The train was late. As he walked about the new station, that monstrous sparkling hive of travel with its huge halls and passageways, its little village of shops underground and its bewildering levels for trains, he remembered the interest Bruce had shown in watching this immense puzzle worked out, the day and night labor year after year without the stopping of a train, this mighty symbol of the times, of all the glorious power and speed in an age that had been as the breath to his nostrils. How Bruce had loved the city! As Roger paced slowly back and forth with his hands clasped behind his back, there came over his heavy visage a look of affection and regret which made even New Yorkers glance at him as they went nervously bustling by. From time to time he smiled to himself. "The Catskills will be Central Park! All this city needs is speed!"

But suddenly he remembered that Bruce had always been here before to meet his wife and children, and that Edith on her approaching train must be dreading her arrival. And when at last the train rolled in, and he spied her shapely little head in the on-coming throng of travellers, Roger saw by her set steady smile and the strained expression on her face that he had guessed right. With a

186

quick surge of compassion he pressed forward, kissed her awkwardly, squeezed her arm, then hastily greeted the children and hurried away to see to the trunks. That much of it was over. And to his relief, when they reached the house, Edith busied herself at once in helping the nurse put the children to bed. Later he came up and told her that he had had a light supper prepared.

"Thank you, dear," she answered, "it was so thoughtful in you. But I'm too tired to eat anything." And then with a little assuring smile, "I'll be all right—I'm going to bed."

"Good-night, child, get a fine long sleep."

And Roger went down to his study, feeling they had made a good start.

"What has become of Martha?" Edith asked her father at breakfast the next morning.

"She left last month to be married," he said.

"And Deborah hasn't replaced her yet?" In her voice was such a readiness for hostility toward her sister, that Roger shot an uneasy glance from under his thick grayish brows.

"Has Deborah left the house?" he asked, to gain time for his answer. Edith's small lip slightly curled.

"Oh, yes, long ago," she replied. "She had just a moment to see the children and then she had to be off to school—to her office, I mean. With so many schools on her hands these days, I don't wonder she hasn't had time for the servants."

"No, no, you're mistaken," he said. "That isn't the trouble, it's not her fault. In fact it was all my idea."

"*Your* idea," she retorted, in an amused affectionate tone. And Roger grimly gathered himself. It would be extremely difficult breaking his unpleasant news.

"Yes," he answered. "You see this damnable war. abroad has hit me in my business."

"Oh, father! How?" she asked him. In an instant she was all alert. "You don't mean seriously?" she said.

"Yes, I do," he answered, and he began to tell her why. But she soon grew impatient. Business details meant nothing to Edith. "I see," she kept saying, "yes, yes, I see." She wanted him to come to the point.

"So I've had to mortgage the house," he concluded. "And for very little money, my dear. And a good deal of that—" he cleared his throat—"had to go back into the business."

"I see," said Edith mechanically. Her mind was already far away, roving over her plans for the children. For in Roger's look of suspense she plainly read that other plans had been made for them in her absence. "Deborah's in this!" flashed through her mind. "Tell me what it will mean," she said.

"I'm afraid you'll have to try to do without your nurse for a while."

"Let Hannah go? Oh, father!" And Edith flushed with quick dismay. "How can I, dad? Five children— five! And two of them so little they can't even dress themselves alone! And there are all their meals—their baths—and the older ones going uptown to school! I can't let them go way uptown on the 'bus or the trolley without a maid—"

"But, Edith!" he interrupted, his face contracting with distress. "Don't you see that they can't go to school?" She turned on him. "Uptown, I mean, to those expensive private schools."

"Father!" she demanded. "Do you mean you want my children to go to common public schools?" There was rage and amazement upon her pretty countenance, and with it an instant certainty too. Yes, this was Deborah's planning! But Roger thought that Edith's look was all directed at himself. And for the first time in his life he felt the shame and humility of the male provider no longer able to provide. He reddened and looked down at his plate.

"You don't understand," he said. "I'm strapped, my child—I can't help it—I'm poor."

"Oh. Oh, dad. I'm sorry." He glanced up at his daughter and saw tears welling in her eyes. How utterly miserable both of them were.

"It's the war," he said harshly and proudly. This made a difference to his pride, but not to his daughter's anxiety. She was not interested in the war, or in any other cause of the abyss she was facing. She strove to think clearly what to do. But no, she must do her thinking alone. With a sudden quiet she rose from the table, went around to her father's chair and kissed him very gently.

"All right, dear—I see it all now—and I promise I'll try my best," she said.

"You're a brave little woman," he replied.

But after she had gone, he reflected. Why had he called her a brave little woman? Why had it all been so intense, the talk upon so heroic a plane? It would be hard on Edith, of course; but others were doing it, weren't they? Think of the women in Europe these days! After all, she'd be very comfortable here, and perhaps by Christmas times would change.

He shook off these petty troubles and went to his office for the day.

As she busied herself unpacking the trunks, Edith strove to readjust her plans. By noon her head was throbbing, but she took little notice of that. She had a talk with Hannah, the devoted Irish girl who had been with her ever since George was born. It was difficult, it was brutal. It was almost as though in Edith's family there had been two mothers, and one was sending the other away.

"There, there, poor child," Edith comforted her, "I'll find you another nice family soon where you can stay till

I take you back. Don't you see it will not be for long?"
And Hannah brightened a little.

"But how in the wide wurrld," she asked, "will you
ever do for the children, me gone?"

"Oh, I'll manage," said Edith cheerfully. And that
afternoon she began at once to rearrange her whole intricate schedule, with Hannah and school both omitted, to
fit her children into the house. But instead of this, as
the days wore on, nerve-racking days of worry and toil,
sternly and quite unconsciously she fitted the house to her
children. And nobody made her aware of the fact. All
summer long in the mountains, everyone by tacit consent
had made way for her, had deferred to her grief in the
little things that make up the everyday life in a home.
And to this precedent once established Edith now clung
unawares.

Her new day gave her small time to think. It began at
five in the morning, when Roger was awakened by the
gleeful cries of the two wee boys who slept with their
mother in the next room, the room which had been Deborah's. And Edith was busy from that time on. First
came the washing and dressing and breakfast, which was
a merry, boisterous meal. Then the baby was taken out
to his carriage on the porch at the back of the house.
And after that, in her father's study from which he had
fled with his morning cigar, for two hours Edith held school
for her children, trying her best to be patient and clear,
with text-books she had purchased from their former
schools uptown. For two severe hours, shutting the
world all out of her head, she tried to teach them about it.
At eleven, their nerves on edge like her own, she sent
them outdoors "to play," intrusting the small ones to
Betsy and George, who took them to Washington Square
nearby with strict injunctions to keep them away from
all other children. No doubt there were "nice" children
there, but she herself could not be along to distinguish

the "nice" from the "common"—for until one o'clock she was busy at home, bathing the baby and making the beds, and then hurrying to the kitchen to pasteurize the baby's milk and keep a vigilant oversight on the cooking of the midday meal. And the old cook's growing resentment made it far from easy.

After luncheon, thank heaven, came their naps. And all afternoon, while again they went out, Edith would look over their wardrobes, mend and alter and patch and contrive how to make last winter's clothes look new. At times she would drop her work in her lap and stare wretchedly before her. This was what she had never known; this was what made life around her grim and hard, relentless, frightening; this was what it was to be poor. How it changed the whole city of New York. Behind it, the sinister cause of it all, she thought confusedly now and then of the Great Death across the sea, of the armies, smoking battle-fields, the shrieks of the dying, the villages blazing, the women and children flying away. But never for more than a moment. The war was so remote and dim. And soon she would turn back again to her own beloved children, whose lives, so full of happiness, so rich in promise hitherto, were now so cramped and thwarted. Each day was harder than the last. It was becoming unbearable!

No, they must go back to school. But how to manage it? How? How? It would cost eight hundred dollars, and this would take nearly all the money she would be able to secure by the sale of her few possessions. And then what? What of sickness, and the other contingencies which still lay ahead of her? How old her father seemed, these days! In his heavy shock of hair the flecks of white had doubled in size, were merging one into the other, and his tall, stooping, massive frame had lost its look of ruggedness. Suppose, suppose. . . . Her breath came fast. Was his life insured, she wondered.

On such afternoons, in the upstairs room as the dusk crept in and deepened, she would bend close to her sewing —planning, planning, planning. At last she would hear the children trooping merrily into the house. And making a very real effort, which at times was in truth heroic, to smile, she would rise and light the gas, would welcome them gaily and join in their chatter and bustle about on the countless tasks of washing them, getting their suppers, undressing the small ones and hearing their prayers. With smiling good-night kisses she would tuck her two babies into their cribs. Afterward, just for a moment or two, she would linger under the gas jet, her face still smiling, for a last look. A last good-night. Then darkness.

Darkness settling over her spirit, together with loneliless and fatigue. She would go into Betsy's room and throw herself dressed on her daughter's bed, and a dull complete indifference to everything under the moon and the stars would creep from her body up into her mind. At times she would try to fight it off. To-night at dinner she must not be what she knew she had been the night before, a wet blanket upon all the talk. But if they only knew how hard it was—what a perfect—hell it was! Her breath coming faster, she would dig her nails into the palms of her hands. One night she noticed and looked at her hand, and saw the skin was actually cut and a little blood was appearing. She had read of women doing this, but she had never done it before—not even when her babies were born. She had gripped Bruce's hand instead.

CHAPTER XXVII

ROGER found her like that one evening. He heard what he thought was a sob from the room, for she had forgotten to close the door. He came into the doorway but drew back, and closed the door with barely a sound. Frowning and irresolute, he stood for a moment in the hall, then turned and went into his room. Soon he heard Deborah enter the house and come slowly up the stairs. She too had had a hard day, he recalled, a day all filled with turbulence, with problems and with vexing toil, in her enormous family. And he felt he could not blame her for not being of more help at home. Still, he had been disappointed of late in her manner toward her sister. He had hoped she would draw closer to Edith, now that again they were living together in their old home where they had been born. But no, it had worked just the opposite way. They were getting upon each other's nerves. Why couldn't she make overtures, small kindly proffers of help and advice and sympathy, the womanly things?

From his room he heard her knock softly at the same door he had closed. And he heard her low clear voice:

"Are you there, Edith dear?" He listened a moment intently, but he could not hear the reply. Then Deborah said, "Oh, you poor thing. I'm awfully sorry. Edith— don't bother to come downstairs—let me bring you up your supper." A pause. "I wish you would. I'd love to."

He heard Deborah come by his door and go up the second flight of stairs to the room she had taken on the third floor.

"I was wrong," he reflected, "she has been trying—but it doesn't do any good. Women simply haven't it in 'em to see each other's point of view. Deborah doesn't admire Edith—she can't, she only pities her and puts her down as out of date. And Edith feels that, and it gets her riled, and she sets herself like an angry old hen against all Deborah's new ideas. Why the devil can't they live and let live?"

And he hesitated savagely between a pearl gray and a black cravat. Then he heard another step on the stairs. It was much slower than Deborah's, and cautious and dogged, one foot lifted carefully after the other. It was John, who had finished his kitchen supper and was silently making his way up through the house to his room at the top, there to keep out of sight for the evening. And it came into Roger's mind that John had been acting in just this fashion ever since Edith had been in the house.

"We'll have trouble there, too!" he told himself, as he jerked the black satin cravat into place, a tie he thoroughly disliked. Yes, black, by George, he felt like it to-night! These women! These evenings! This worry! This war! This world gone raving, driveling mad!

And frowning with annoyance, Roger went down to his dinner.

As he waited he grew impatient. He had eaten no lunch, he was hungry; and he was very tired, too, for he had had his own hard day. Pshaw! He got up angrily. *Somebody* must be genial here. He went into the dining room and poured himself a good stiff drink. Roger had never been much of a drinker. Ever since his marriage, cigars had been his only vice. But of late he had been having curious little sinking spells. They worried him, and he told himself he could not afford to get either too tired or too faint.

Nevertheless, he reflected, it was setting a bad example for George. But glancing into his study he saw that the lad was completely absorbed. With knees drawn up, his long lank form all hunched and huddled on the lounge, hair rumpled, George was reading a book which had a cover of tough gray cloth. At the sight of it his grandfather smiled, for he had seen it once before. Where George had obtained it, the Lord only knew. Its title was "Bulls and Breeding." A thoroughly practical little book, but nothing for George's mother to see. As his grandfather entered behind him, the boy looked up with a guilty start, and resumed with a short breath of relief.

Young Elizabeth, too, had a furtive air, for instead of preparing her history lesson she was deep in the evening paper reading about the war abroad. Stout and florid, rather plain, but with a frank, attractive face and honest, clear, appealing eyes, this curious creature of thirteen was sitting firmly in her chair with her feet planted wide apart, eagerly scanning an account of the work of American surgeons in France. And again Roger smiled to himself. (He was feeling so much better now.) So Betsy was still thinking of becoming a surgeon. He wondered what she would take up next. In the past two years in swift succession she had made up her mind to be a novelist, an actress and a women's college president. And Roger liked this tremendously.

He loved to watch these two in the house. Here again his family was widening out before him, with new figures arising to draw his attention this way and that. But these were bright distractions. He took a deep, amused delight in watching these two youngsters caught between two fires, on the one side their mother and upon the other their aunt; both obviously drawn toward Deborah, a figure who stood in their regard for all that thrilling outside world, that heaving sparkling ocean on which they too would soon embark; both sternly repressing their eagerness as an insult to their mother, whom they loved and pitied so, regarding her as a brave and dear but rapidly ageing creature "well on in her thirties," whom they must

cherish and preserve. They both had such solemn thoughts
as they looked at Edith in her chair. But as Roger watched
them, with their love and their solemnity, their guilt and
their perplexity, with quiet enjoyment he would wait to
see the change he knew would come. And it always
did. The sudden picking up of a book, the vanishing of
an anxious frown, and in an instant their young minds had
turned happily back into themselves, into their own
engrossing lives, their plans, their intimate dreams and
ambitions, all so curiously bound up with memories of
small happenings which had struck them as funny that
day and at which they would suddenly chuckle aloud.

And this was only one stage in their growth. What
would be the next, he asked, and all the others after that?
What kind of world would they live in? Please heaven,
there would be no wars. Many old things, no doubt,
would be changed, by the work of Deborah and her kind—
but not too many, Roger hoped. And these young people,
meanwhile, would be bringing up children in their turn.
So the family would go on, and multiply and scatter wide,
never to unite again. And he thought he could catch
glimpses, very small and far away but bright as patches
of sunlight upon distant mountain tops, into the widening
vista of those many lives ahead. A wistful look crept
over his face.

"In their lives too we shall be there, the dim strong
figures of the past."

Deborah came into the room, and at once the whole
atmosphere changed. Her niece sprang up delightedly.

"Why, Auntie, how lovely you look!" she exclaimed.
And Roger eyed Deborah in surprise. Though she did
not believe in mourning, she had been wearing dark
gowns of late to avoid hurting Edith's feelings. But
to-night she had donned bright colors instead; her dress
was as near décolleté as anything that Deborah wore,

and there was a band of dull blue velvet bound about her hair.

"Thanks, dearie," she said, smiling. "Shall we go in to dinner now?" she added to her father. "Edith said not to wait for her—and I'll have to be off rather early this evening."

"What is it to-night?" he inquired.

"A big meeting at Cooper Union."

And at dinner she went on to say that in her five schools the neighborhood clubs had combined to hold this meeting, and she herself was to preside. At once her young niece was all animation.

"Oh, I wish I could go and hear you!" she sighed.

"Afraid you can't, Betsy," her aunt replied. And at this, with an instinctive glance toward the door where her mother would soon come in to stop by her mere presence all such conversation, Elizabeth eagerly threw out one inquiry after the other, pell mell.

"How on earth do you do it?" she wanted to know. "How do you get a speech ready, Aunt Deborah—how much of it do you write out ahead? Aren't you just the least bit nervous—now, I mean—this minute? And how will you feel on the platform? *What on earth do you do with your feet?*"

As the girl bent forward there with her gaze fixed ardently on her aunt, her grandfather thought in half comic dismay, "Lord, now she'll want to be a great speaker—like her aunt. And she will tell her mother so!"

"What's the meeting all about?" he inquired. And Deborah began to explain.

In her five schools the poverty was rapidly becoming worse. Each week more children stayed away or came to school ragged and unkempt, some without any overcoats, small pitiful mites wearing shoes so old as barely to stick on their feet. And when the teachers and visitors followed these children into their homes they found bare, dirty, chilly rooms where the little folk shivered and wailed for food and the mothers looked distracted, gaunt and sullen and half crazed. Over three hundred thousand workers were idle in the city. Meanwhile, to make matters worse, half the money from uptown which had gone in former years into work for the tenements was going over to Belgium instead. And the same relentless drain of war was felt by the tenement people themselves; for all of them were foreigners, and from their relatives abroad, in those wide zones of Europe already blackened and laid waste, in endless torrents through the mails came wild appeals for money.

In such homes her children lived. And Deborah had set her mind on vigorous measures of relief. Landlords must be made to wait and the city be persuaded to give work to the most needy, food and fuel must be secured. As she spoke of the task before her, with a flush of animation upon her bright expressive face at the thought that in less than an hour she would be facing thousands of people, the gloom of the picture she painted was dispelled in the spirit she showed.

"These things always work out," she declared, with an impatient shrug of her shoulders. And watching her admiringly, young Betsy thought, "How strong she is! What a wonderful grown-up woman!" And Roger watching thought, "How young."

"What things?" It was Edith's voice at the door, and among those at the table there was a little stir of alarm. She had entered unnoticed and now took her seat. She was looking pale and tired. "What things work out so finely?" she asked, and with a glance at Deborah's gown, "Where are you going?" she added.

"To a meeting," Deborah answered.

"Oh." And Edith began her soup. In the awkward pause that followed, twice Deborah started to speak to her sister, but checked herself, for at other dinners just like this she had made such dismal failures.

"By the way, Edith," she said, at last, "I've been thinking of all that furniture of yours which is lying in storage." Her sister looked up at her, startled.

"What about it?" she asked.

"There's so much of it you don't care for," Deborah answered quietly. "Why don't you let a part of it go? I mean the few pieces you've always disliked."

"For what purpose?"

"Why, it seems such a pity not to have Hannah back in the house. She would make things so much easier." Roger felt a glow of relief.

"A capital plan!" he declared at once.

"It would be," Edith corrected him, "if I hadn't already made *other* plans." And then in a brisk, breathless tone, "You see I've made up my mind," she said, "to sell not only part but *all* my furniture—very soon—and a few other belongings as well—and use the money to put George and Elizabeth and little Bob back in the schools where they belong."

"Mother!" gasped Elizabeth, and with a prolonged "Oh-h" of delight she ran around to her mother's chair.

"But look here," George blurted worriedly, "I don't like it, mother, darned if I do! You're selling everything —just for school!"

"School is rather important, George," was Edith's tart rejoinder. "If you don't think so, ask your aunt."

"What do you think of it, Auntie?" he asked. The cloud which had come on Deborah's face was lifted in an instant.

"I think, George," she answered gently, "that you'd better let your mother do what she thinks best for you. It *will* make things easier here in the house," she added, to her sister, "but I wish you could have Hannah, too."

"Oh, I'll manage nicely now," said Edith. And with a slight smile of triumph she resumed her dinner.

"The war won't last forever," muttered Roger uneasily. And to himself: "But suppose it *should* last—a year or more." He did not approve of Edith's scheme. "It's burning her bridges all at once, for something that isn't essential," he thought. But he would not tell her so.

Meanwhile Deborah glanced at the clock.

"Oh! It's nearly eight o'clock! I must hurry or I'll be late," she said. "Good-night, all—."

And she left them.

Roger followed her into the hall.

"What do you think of this?" he demanded. Her reply was a tolerant shrug.

"It's her own money, father—"

"All her money!" he rejoined. "Every dollar she has in the world!"

"But I don't just see how it can be helped."

"Can't you talk to her, show her what folly it is?"

"Hardly," said Deborah, smiling. Already she had on her coat and hat and was turning to go. And her father scowled with annoyance. She was always going, he told himself, leaving him to handle her sister alone. He would like to go out himself in the evenings—yes, by George, this very night—it would act like a tonic on his mind. Just for a moment, standing there, he saw Cooper Union packed to the doors, he heard the ringing speeches, the cheers. But no, it was not to be thought of. With this silent war going on in his house he knew he must stay neutral. Watchful waiting was his course. If he went out with Deborah, Edith would be distinctly hurt, and sitting all evening here alone she would draw still deeper into herself. And so it would be night after night, as it had been for many weeks. He would be cooped up at home while Deborah did the running about. . . . In half the time it takes to tell it, Roger had worked himself into a state where he felt like a mighty badly used man.

"I wish you *would* speak to her," he said. "I wish you could manage to find time to be here more in the evenings. Edith worries so much and she's trying so hard. A little sympathy now and then—"

"But she doesn't seem to want any from me," said his daughter, a bit impatiently. "I know it's hard—of course it is. But what can I do? She won't let me help. And besides—there are other families, you know—thousands— really suffering—for the lack of all that we have here." She smiled and kissed him quickly. "Good-night, dad dear, I've got to run."

And the door closed behind her.

CHAPTER XXVIII

AFTER dinner that night, in the living room the two older children studied their lessons and Edith sat mending a pair of rompers for little Tad. Presently Roger came out from his den with the evening paper in his hand and sat down close beside her. He did this conscientiously almost every evening. With a sigh he opened his paper to read, again there was silence in the room, and in this silence Roger's mind roamed far away across the sea.

For the front page of his paper was filled with the usual headlines, tidings which a year before would have made a man's heart jump into his throat, but which were getting commonplace now. Dead and wounded by the thousands, famine, bombs and shrapnel, hideous atrocities, submarines and floating mines, words once remote but now familiar, always there on the front page and penetrating into his soul, becoming a part of Roger Gale, so that never again when the war was done would he be the same man he was before. For he had forever lost his faith in the sanity and steadiness of the great mind of humanity. Roger had thought of mankind as mature, but there had come to him of late the same feeling he had had before in the bosom of his family. Mankind had suddenly unmasked and shown itself for what it was—still only a precocious child, with a terrible precocity. For its growth had been one sided. Its strength was growing at a speed breathless and astounding. But its vision and its poise, its sense of human justice, of kindliness and tolerance and of generous brotherly love, these had been neglected and were being left behind. Vaguely he thought of its ships of steel, its railroads and its flaming mills, its miracles, its prodigies. And the picture rose in his mind of a child, standing there of giant's size with dangerous playthings in its hands, and boastfully declaring,

"I can thunder over the earth, dive in the ocean, soar on the clouds! I can shiver to atoms a mountain, I can drench whole lands with blood! I can look up and laugh at God!"

And Roger frowned as he read the news. What strange new century lay ahead? What convulsing throes of change? What was in store for his children? Tighter set his heavy jaw.

"It shall be good," he told himself with a grim determination. "For them there shall be better things. Something great and splendid shall come out of it at last. They will look back upon this time as I look on the French Revolution."

He tried to peer into that world ahead, dazzling, distant as the sun. But then with a sigh he returned to the news, and little by little his mind again was gripped and held by the most compelling of all appeals so far revealed in humanity's growth, the appeal of war to the mind of a man. He frowned as he read, but he read on. Why didn't England send over more men?

The clock struck nine.

"Now, George. Now, Elizabeth," Edith said. With the usual delay and reluctance the children brought their work to an end, kissed their mother and went up to bed. And Edith continued sewing. Presently she smiled to herself. Little Tad had been so droll that day.

On the third page of his paper, Roger's glance was arrested by a full column story concerning Deborah's meeting that night. And as in a long interview he read here in the public print the same things she had told him at supper, he felt a little glow of pride. Yes, this daughter of his was a wonderful woman, living a big useful life, taking a leading part in work which would certainly brighten the lives of millions of children still unborn. Again he felt the tonic of it. Here was a glimmer of hope in the world, here was an antidote to war. He finished the column and glanced up.

Edith was still sewing. He thought of her plan to sell all she possessed in order to put her children back in their expensive schools uptown.

"Why can't she save her money?" he thought. "God knows there's little enough of it left. But I can't tell her that. If I do she'll sell everything, hand me the cash and tell me she's sorry to be such a burden. She'll sit like a thundercloud in my house."

No, he could say nothing to stop her. And over the top of his paper her father shot a look at her of keen exasperation. Why risk everything she had to get these needless frills and fads? Why must she cram her life so full of petty plans and worries and titty-tatty little jobs? For the Lord's sake, leave their clothes alone! And why these careful little rules for every minute of their day, for their washing, their dressing, their eating, their napping, their play and the very air they breathed! He crumpled his paper impatiently. She was always talking of being old-fashioned. Well then, why not be that way? Let her live as her grandmother had, up there in the mountain farmhouse. *She* had not been so particular. With one hired girl she had thought herself lucky. And not only had she cooked and sewed, but she had spun and woven too, had churned and made cheese and pickles and jam and quilts and even mattresses. Once in two months she had cut Roger's hair, and the rest of the time she had let him alone, except for something really worth while— a broken arm, for example, or church. She had stuck to the essentials! . . . But Edith was not old-fashioned, nor was she alive to this modern age. In short, she was neither here nor there!

Then from the nursery above, her smallest boy was

heard to cry. With a little sigh of weariness, quickly she
rose and went upstairs, and a few moments later to Roger's
ears came a low, sweet, soothing lullaby. Years ago Edith
had asked him to teach her some of his mother's cradle
songs. And the one which she was singing to-night was
a song he had heard when he was small, when the mountain storms had shrieked and beat upon the rattling old
house and he had been frightened and had cried out and
his mother had come to his bed in the dark. He felt as
though she were near him now. And as he listened to the
song, from the deep well of sentiment which was a part
of Roger Gale rose memories that changed his mood, and
with it his sense of proportions.

Here was motherhood of the genuine kind, not orating
in Cooper Union in the name of every child in New York,
but crooning low and tenderly, soothing one little child to
sleep, one of the five she herself had borne, in agony, without complaint. How Edith had slaved and sacrificed, how
bravely she had rallied after the death of her husband.
He remembered her a few hours ago on the bed upstairs,
spent and in anguish, sobbing, alone. And remorse came
over him. Deborah's talk at dinner had twisted his thinking, he told himself. Well, that was Deborah's way of
life. She had her enormous family and Edith had her
small one, and in this hell of misery which war was spreading over the earth each mother was up in arms for her
brood. And, by George, of the two he didn't know but
that he preferred his own flesh and blood. All very noble,
Miss Deborah, and very dramatic, to open your arms to
all the children under the moon and get your name in the
papers. But there was something pretty fine in just sitting
at home and singing to one.

"All right, little mother, you go straight ahead.
This is war and panic and hard times. You're perfectly
right to look after your own."

He would show Edith he did not begrudge her this

use of her small property. And more than that, he would
do what he could to take her out of her loneliness. How
about reading aloud to her? He had been a capital reader,
during Judith's lifetime, for he had always enjoyed it
so. Roger rose and went to his shelves and began to look
over the volumes there. Perhaps a book of travel. . . .
Stoddard's "Lectures on Japan."

Meanwhile Edith came into the room, sat down and
took up her sewing. As she did so he turned and glanced
at her, and she smiled brightly back at him. Yes, he
thought with a genial glow, from this night on he would
do his part. He came back to his chair with a book in
his hand, prepared to start on his new course.

"Father," she said quietly. Her eyes were on the work
in her lap.

"Yes, my child, what is it?"

"It's about John," she answered. And with a movement of alarm he looked at his daughter intently.

"What's the matter with John?" he inquired.

"He has tuberculosis," she said.

"He has no such thing!" her father retorted. "John has
Pott's Disease of the spine!"

"Yes, I know he has," she replied. "And I'm sorry for
him, poor lad. But in the last year," she added, "certain
complications have come. And now he's tubercular as
well."

"How do you know? He doesn't cough—his lungs are
sound as yours or mine!"

"No, it's—" Edith pursed her lips. "It's different,"
she said softly.

"Who told you?" he demanded.

"Not Deborah," was the quick response. "She knew
it, I'm certain, for I find that she's been having Mrs.
Neale, the woman who comes in to wash, do John's things
in a separate tub. I found her doing it yesterday, and she
told me what Deborah had said."

"It's the first I'd heard of it," Roger put in.

"I know it is," she answered. "For if you'd heard of it before, I don't believe you'd have been as ready as Deborah was, apparently, to risk infecting the children here." Edith's voice was gentle, slow and relentless. There was still a reflection in her eyes of the tenderness which had been there as she had soothed her child to sleep. "As time goes on, John is bound to get worse. The risk will be greater every week."

"Oh, pshaw!" cried her father. "No such thing! You're just scaring yourself over nothing at all!"

"Doctor Lake didn't think I was." Lake was the big child specialist in whose care Edith's children had been for years. "I talked to him to-day on the telephone, and he said we should get John out of the house."

Roger heartily damned Doctor Lake!

"It's easy to find a good home for the boy," Edith went on quietly, "close by, if you like—in some respectable family that will be only too thankful to take in a boarder."

"How about the danger to that family's children?" Roger asked malignantly.

"Very well, father, do as you please. Take any risk you want to."

"I'm taking no risk," he retorted. "If there were any risk they would have told me—Allan and Deborah would, I mean."

"They wouldn't!" burst from Edith with a vehemence which startled him. "They'd take the same risk for my children they would for any street urchin in town! All children are the same in their eyes—and if you feel as they do—"

"I don't feel as they do!"

"Don't you? Then I'm telling you that Doctor Lake said there was very serious risk—every day this boy remains in the house!" Roger rose angrily from his chair:

"So you want me to turn him out! To-night!"

"No, I want you to wait a few days—until we can find him a decent home."

"All right, I won't do it!"

"Very well, father—it's your house, not mine."

For a few moments longer she sat at her sewing, while her father walked the floor. Then abruptly she rose, her eyes brimming with tears, and left the room. And he heard a sob as she went upstairs.

"Now she'll shut herself up with her children," he reflected savagely, "and hold the fort till I come to terms!" Rather than risk a hair on their heads, Edith would turn the whole world out of doors! He thought of Deborah and he groaned. She would have to be told of this; and when she was, what a row there would be! For Johnny was one of *her* family. He glanced at the clock. She'd be coming home soon. Should he tell her? Not to-night! Just for one evening he'd had enough!

He picked up the book he had meant to read—Stoddard's "Lectures on Japan." And Roger snorted wrathfully. By George, how *he'd* like to go to Japan—or to darkest Africa! Anywhere!

CHAPTER XXIX

But later in the evening, when Allan and Deborah came in, Roger, who in the meantime had had a good hour in Japan and was somewhat relaxed and soothed, decided at once this was the time to tell her and have done with it. For Deborah was flushed with triumph, the meeting had been a huge success. Cooper Union had been packed to the walls, with an overflow meeting out on the street; thousands of dollars had been pledged and some big politicians had promised support; and men and women, rich and poor, had volunteered their services. She started to tell him about it, but noticed his troubled expression and asked him what was on his mind.

"Oh, nothing tremendous," Roger said. "I hate to be any damper to-night. I hadn't meant to tell you to-night—but I think I will now, for you look as though you could find a solution for anything."

"Then I must look like an idiot," his daughter said good-humoredly. "What is it?" she demanded.

"It's about John." Her countenance changed.

"Oh. Is he worse?"

"Edith thinks he is—and she says it's not safe."

"I see—she wants him out of the house. Tell me what she said to you." As he did so she listened intently, and turning to Allan at the end, "What do you say to this, Allan?" she asked. "Is there any real risk to the children?"

"A little," he responded. "As much as they take every day in the trolley going to school."

"They never go in the trolley," Deborah answered dryly. "They always go on the top of the 'bus." She was

209

silent for a moment. "Well, there's no use discussing it. If Edith feels that way, John must go. The house won't be livable till he does."

Roger looked at her in surprise. He felt both relieved and disappointed. "John's only one of thousands to her," he told himself aggrievedly. "He isn't close to her, she hasn't room, she has a whole mass meeting in her head. But I haven't, by George, I like the boy—and I'm the one who will have to tell him to pack up and leave the house! Isn't it the very devil, how things all come back on me?"

"Look here, father," Deborah said, "suppose you let me manage this." And Roger's heavy visage cleared.

"You mean you'll tell him?"

"Yes," she replied, "and he'll understand it perfectly. I think he has been expecting it. I have, for a good many weeks," she added, with some bitterness. "And I know some people who will be glad enough to take him in. I'll see that he's made comfortable. Only—" her face clouded.

"It has meant a lot to him, being here," her father put in gruffly.

"Oh, John's used to getting knocks in this world." Her quiet voice grew hard and stern. "I wasn't thinking of John just now. What frightens me at times like this is Edith," she said slowly. "No, not just Edith—mother-hood. I see it in so many mothers these days—in the women downtown, in their fight for their children against all other children on earth. It's the hardest thing we have to do—to try to make them see and feel outside of their own small tenement homes—and help each other—pull together. They can't see it's their only chance! And all because of this mother love! It's so blind sometimes, like an animal!" She broke off, and for a moment she seemed to be looking deep into herself. "And I suppose we're all like that, we women are," she muttered, "when we marry and have children. If the pinch is ever hard enough—"

"*You* wouldn't be," said Allan. And a sudden sharp uneasiness came into Roger's mind.

"When are you two to be married?" he asked, without stopping to think. And at once he regretted his question. With a quick impatient look at him, Allan bent over a book on the table.

"I don't know," Deborah answered. "Next spring, I hope." The frown was still on her face.

"Don't make it too long," said her father brusquely. He left them and went up to bed.

Deborah sat motionless. She wished Allan would go, for she guessed what was coming and did not feel equal to it to-night. All at once she felt tired and unnerved from her long exciting evening. If only she could let go of herself and have a good cry. She locked her hands together and looked up at him with impatience. He was still at the table, his back was turned.

"Don't you *know* I love you?" she was thinking fiercely. "Can't you see it—haven't you seen it—growing, growing —day after day? But I don't want you here to-night! Why can't you see you must leave me alone? Now! This minute!"

He turned and came over in front of her, and stood looking steadily down.

"I wonder," he said slowly, "how well you understand yourself."

"I think I do," she muttered. With a sudden twitching of her lip she looked quickly up at him. "Go on, Allan—let's talk it all over now if you must!"

"Not if you feel like that," he said. At his tone of displeasure she caught his hand.

"Yes, yes, I want to! Please!" she cried. "It's better —really! Believe me, it is—"

He hesitated a moment, his wide generous mouth set hard, and then in a tone as sharp as hers he demanded,

"Are you sure you'll marry me next spring? Are you sure you *hope* you will next spring? Are you sure this sister of yours in the house, on your nerves day and night, with this blind narrow motherhood, this motherhood which frightens you—isn't frightening you too much?"

"No—a little—but not too much." Her deep sweet voice was trembling. "You're the one who frightens me. If you only knew! When you come like this—with all you've done for me back of you—"

"Deborah! Don't be a fool!"

"Oh, I know you say you've done nothing, except what you've been glad to do! You love me like that! But it's just that love! Giving up all your practice little by little, and your reputation uptown—all for the sake of me, Allan, me!"

"You're wrong," he replied. "Compared to what I'm getting, I've given up nothing! Can't you see? You're just as narrow in your school as Edith is right here in her home! You look upon my hospital as a mere annex to your schools, when the truth of it is that the work down there is a chance I've wanted all my life! Can't you understand," he cried, "that instead of your being in debt to me it's I who am in debt to you? You're a suffragist, eh, a feminist—whatever you want to call it! All right! So you want to be equal with man! Then, for God's sake, why not begin? *Feel* equal! I'm no annex to you, nor you to me! It has happened, thank God, that our work fits in—each with the other!"

He stopped and stared, seemed to shake himself; he walked the floor. And when he turned back his expression had changed.

"Look here, Deborah," he asked, with an appealing humorous smile, "will you tell me what I'm driving at?"

Deborah threw back her head and laughed, and her laughter thrilled with relief. "How sure I feel now that I love him," she thought.

"You've proved I owe you nothing!" she cried. "And that men and women of our kind can work on splendidly side by side, and never bother our poor little heads about anything else—even marriage!"

"We will, though!" he retorted. The next moment she was in his arms. "Now, Deborah, listen to reason, child. Why can't you marry me right away?"

"Because," she said, "when I marry you I'm going to have you all to myself—for weeks and weeks as we planned before! And afterwards, with a wonderful start—and with the war over, work less hard and the world less dark and gloomy—we're going to find that at last we can live! But this winter it couldn't be like that. This winter we've got to go on with our work—and without any more silly worries or talk about whether or not we're in love. *For we are!*" Her upturned face was close to his, and for some moments nothing was said, "Well?" she asked. "Are you satisfied?"

"No—I want to get married. But it is now a quarter past one. And I'm your physician. Go straight to bed."

She stopped him a minute at the front door:

"Are you sure, absolutely, you understand?"

He told her he did. But as he walked home he reflected. How tense she had been in the way she had talked. Yes, the long strain was telling. "Why was she so anxious to get me out of the house," he asked, "when we were alone for the first time in days? And why, if she's really sure of her love, does she hate the idea that she's in my debt?"

He walked faster, for the night was cold. And there was a chill, too, in this long waiting game.

Roger heard Deborah come up to bed, and he wondered what they had been talking about. Of the topic he himself had broached—each other, love and marriage?

"Possibly—for a minute or two—but no more," he grumbled. "For don't forget there's work to discuss, there's that mass meeting still on her mind. And God knows a woman's mind is never any child's play. But when you load a mass meeting on top—"

Here he yawned long and noisily. His head ached, he felt sore and weak—"from the evening's entertainment my other daughter gave me." No, he was through, he had had enough. They could settle things to suit themselves. Let Edith squander her money on frills, the more expensive the better. Let her turn poor Johnny out of the house, let her give full play to her motherhood. And if that scared Deborah out of marrying, let her stay single and die an old maid. He had worried enough for his family. He wanted a little peace in his house.

Drowsily he closed his eyes, and a picture came into his mind of the city as he had seen it only a few nights before. It had been so cool, so calm and still. At dusk he had been in the building of the great tower on Madison Square; and when he had finished his business there, on an impulse he had gone up to the top, and through a wide low window had stood a few moments looking down. A soft light snow was falling; and from high up in the storm, through the silent whirling flakes, he had looked far down upon lights below, in groups and clusters, dancing lines, between tall phantom buildings, blurred and ghostly, faint, unreal. From all that bustle and fever of life there had risen to him barely a sound. And the town had seemed small and lonely, a little glow in the infinite dark, fulfilling its allotted place for its moment in eternity. Suddenly from close over his head like a brazen voice out of the sky, hard and deafening and clear, the great bell had boomed the hour. Then again had come the silence, and the cool, soft, whirling snow.

Like a dream it faded all away, and with a curious smile on his face presently Roger fell asleep.

CHAPTER XXX

AND now he felt the approach at last of another season of quiet, one of those uneventful times which come in family histories. As he washed and dressed for dinner, one night a little later, he thought with satisfaction, "How nicely things are smoothing out." His dressing for dinner, as a rule, consisted in changing his low wing collar and his large round detachable cuffs; but to-night he changed his cravat as well, from a black to a pearl gray one. He hoped the whole winter would be pearl gray.

The little storm which Edith had raised over John's presence in the house had been allayed. Deborah had talked to John, and had moved him with his belongings to a comfortable sunny room in the small but neat apartment of a Scotch family nearby. And John had been so sensible. "Oh, I'm fine, thank you," he had answered simply, when in the office Roger had asked him about his new home. So that incident was closed. Already Edith was disinfecting John's old room to her heart's content, for George was to occupy it now. She was having the woodwork repainted and a new paper put on the walls. She had already purchased a small new rug, and a bed and a bureau and one easy chair, and was making a pair of fresh pretty curtains. All right, let her do it—if only there could be peace in the house.

With his cravat adjusted and his thick-curling silver hair trim from having just been cut by "Louis" over at the Brevoort, Roger went comfortably down to his dinner. Edith greeted him with a smile.

"Deborah's dining out," she said.

"Very well," he replied, "so much the better. We'll

go right in—I'm hungry. And we'll have the evening to
ourselves. No big ideas nor problems. Eh, daughter?"
He slipped his hand in hers, and she gave it a little affectionate squeeze. With John safely out of the way, and not
only the health of her children but their proper schooling
assured, Edith was herself again, placid, sweet and kindly.
And dinner that night was a cheerful meal. Later, in the
living room, as Roger contentedly lit his cigar, Edith gave
an appreciative sniff.

"You do smoke such good cigars, father," she said,
smiling over her needle. And glancing up at her daughter,
"Betsy, dear," she added, "go and get your grandfather's
evening paper."

In quiet perusal of the news he spent the first part of
his evening. The war did not bother him to-night, for
there had come a lull in the fighting, as though even war
could know its place. And times were better over here.
As, skipping all news from abroad his eye roved over the
pages for what his business depended upon, Roger began
to find it now. The old familiar headliness were reappear-
ing side by side—high finance exposures, graft, the antics
and didos cut up by the sons and daughters of big mil-
lionaires; and after them in cheery succession the Yale-
Harvard game, a new man for the Giants, a new college
building for Cornell, a new city plan for Seattle, a woman
senator in Arizona and in Chicago a "sporting mayor."
In brief, all over the U. S. A., men and women old and
new had risen up, to power, fame, notoriety, whatever you
chose to call it. Men and women? Hardly. "Children"
was the better word. But the thought did not trouble
Roger to-night. He had instead a heartening sense of
the youth, the wild exuberance, the boundless vigor in his
native land. He could feel it rising once again. Life was
soon to go on as before; people were growing hungry
to see the names of their countrymen back in the headlines
where they belonged. And Roger's business was picking

up. He was not sure of the figure of his deficit last week—
he had always been vague on the book-keeping side—but
he knew it was down considerably.

When Betsy and George had gone to bed, Roger put
down his paper.

"Look here, Edith," he proposed, "how'd you like me
to read aloud while you sew?" She looked up with a
smile of pleased surprise.

"Why, father dear, I'd love it." At once, she bent over
her needle again, so that if there were any awkwardness
attending this small change in their lives it did not reveal
itself in her pretty countenance. "What shall we read?"
she affably asked.

"I've got a capital book," he replied. "It's about travel
in Japan."

"I'd like nothing better," Edith replied. And with a
slight glow of pride in himself Roger took his book in hand.
The experiment was a decided success. He read again the
next night and the next, while Edith sat at her sewing.
And so this hour's companionship, from nine to ten in the
evening, became a regular custom—just one hour and no
more, which Roger spent with his daughter, intimately
and pleasantly. Yes, life was certainly smoothing out.

Edith's three older children had been reinstated in
school. And although at first, when deprived of their aid,
she had found it nearly impossible to keep her two small
boys amused and give them besides the four hours a day of
fresh air they required, she had soon met this trouble by
the same simple process as before. Of her few possessions
still unsold, she had disposed of nearly all, and with a small
fund thus secured she had sent for Hannah to return. The
house was running beautifully.

Christmas, too, was drawing near. And though Roger
knew that in Edith's heart was a cold dread of this season,
she bravely kept it to herself; and she set about so determinedly to make a merry holiday, that her father ad-

miring her pluck drew closer still to his daughter. He
entered into her Christmas plans and into all the conspiracies which were whispered about the house. Great se-
crets, anxious consultations, found in him a ready listener.

So passed three blessed quiet weeks, and he had high
hopes for the winter.

CHAPTER XXXI

IF there wére any cloud upon his horizon, it was the
thought of Laura. She had barely been to the house
since Edith had come back to town; and at times, especially in the days when things had looked dark for Roger,
he had caught himself reproaching this giddy-gaddy
youngest child, so engrossed in her small "ménage" that
apparently she could not spare a thought for her widowed
sister. Laura on her return from abroad had brought as
a gift for Edith a mourning gown from Paris, a most
alluring creation—so much so, in fact, that Edith had
felt it simply indecent, insulting, and had returned it to
her sister with a stilted note of thanks. But Roger did
not know of this. There were so many ways, he thought,
in which Laura might have been nice to Edith. She had a
gorgeous limousine in which she might so easily have come
and taken her sister off on little trips uptown. But no,
she kept her car to herself. And from her small apartment,
where a maid whom she had brought from Rome dressed
her several times each day, that limousine rushed her
noiselessly forth, gay and wild as ever, immaculate and
elegant, radiant and very rich. To what places did she
go? What new friends was she making? What was Laura
up to?

He did not like her manner, one evening when she came
to the house. As he helped her off with her cloak, a sleek
supple leopard skin which fitted her figure like a glove, he
asked,

"Where's Hal this evening?" And she answered lightly,
"Oh, don't ask *me* what he does with himself."

"You mean, I suppose," said Edith, with quiet dis-

approval, "that he is rushed to death this year with all
this business from the war."

"Yes, it's business," Laura replied, as she deftly
smoothed and patted her soft, abundant, reddish hair.
"And it's war, too," she added.

"What do you mean?" her father asked. He knew what
she meant, war with her husband. But before Laura
could answer him, Edith cut in hastily, for two of her
children were present. At dinner she turned the talk to
the war. But even on this topic, Laura's remarks were
disturbing. She did not consider the war wholly bad—
by no means, it had many good points. It was clearing
away a lot of old rubbish, customs, superstitions and
institutions out of date. "Musty old relics," she called
them. She spoke as though repeating what someone else
had told her. Laura with her chicken's mind could never
have thought it all out by herself. When asked what
she meant, she was smilingly vague, with a glance at
Edith's youngsters. But she threw out hints about the
church and even Christianity, as though it were falling
to pieces. She spoke of a second Renaissance, "a glorious
pagan era" coming. And then she exploded a little bomb
by inquiring of Edith,

"What do you think the girls over there are going to do
for husbands, with half the marriageable men either killed
or hopelessly damaged? They're not going to be nuns
all their lives!"

Again her sister cut her off, and the rest of the brief
evening was decidedly awkward. Yes, she was changing,
growing fast. And Roger did not like it. Here she was
spending money like water, absorbed in her pleasures,
having no baby, apparently at loose ends with her husband,
and through it all so cocksure of herself and her out-
rageous views about war, and smiling about them with
such an air, and in her whole manner such a tone of amused
superiority. She talked about a world for the strong,

bits of gabble from Nietzsche and that sort of rot; she spoke blithely of a Rome reborn, the "Wings of the Eagles" heard again. This part of it she had taken, no doubt, from her new Italian friend, her husband's shrapnel partner.

Pshaw! What was Laura up to?

But that was only one evening. It was not repeated, another month went quickly by, and Roger had soon shaken it from him, for he had troubles enough at home. One daughter at a time, he had thought. And as the dark clouds close above him had cleared, the other cloud too had drifted away, until it was small, just on the horizon, far away from Roger's house. What was Laura up to? He barely ever thought of that now.

But one night when he came home, Edith, who sat in the living room reading aloud to her smaller boys, gave him a significant look which warned him something had happened. And turning to take off his overcoat, in the hall he almost stumbled upon a pile of hand luggage, two smart patent leather bags, a hat trunk and a sable cloak.

"Hello," he exclaimed. "What's this? Who's here?"

"Laura," Edith answered. "She's up in Deborah's room, I think—they've been up there for over an hour." Roger looked indignantly in at his daughter.

"What has happened?" he asked.

"I'm afraid I can't tell you," Edith replied. "They didn't seem to need me. They made it rather plain, in fact. Another quarrel, I presume. She came into the house like a whirlwind, asked at once for Deborah and flew up to Deborah's room."

"Pshaw!" Roger heavily mounted the stairs. He at least did not feel like flying. A whirlwind, eh—a nice evening ahead!

Meanwhile, in her room upstairs Deborah sat motionless, sternly holding her feelings down, while in a tone now kindly but more often full of a sharp dismay, she threw out question after question to Laura who was walking the floor in a quick, feverish sort of way, with gestures half hysterical, her voice bursting with emotions of mingled fright and rage.

"No, this time it's divorce!" she declared, at the end of her first outburst, in which she had told in fragments of her husband's double life. "I've stood it long enough! I'm through!"

"You mean you don't care for him," Deborah said. She was fighting for time to think it out. "You want a divorce. Very well, Laura dear—but how do you think you are going to get it? The laws are rather strict in this state. They allow but one cause. Have you any proofs?"

"No, I haven't—but I don't need any proofs! He wants it as badly as I do! Wait—I'll give you his very words!" Laura's face grew white with fury. "'It's entirely up to you, Sweetie'—the beast!—'You can have any kind of divorce you like. You can let me bring suit on the quiet or you can try to fight me in court, climb up into the witness chair in front of the reporters and tell them all about yourself!'"

"*Your husband is to bring suit against you?*" Deborah's voice was loud and harsh. "For God's sake, Laura, what do you mean?"

"Mean? I mean that *he has proofs!* He has used a detective, the mean little cur, and he's treating me like the dirt under his feet! Just as though it were one thing for a man, and another—quite—for a woman! He even had the nerve to be mad, to get on a high horse, call me names! Turn me!—turn me out on the street!" Deborah winced as though from a blow. "Oh, it was funny, funny!" Laura was almost sobbing now.

"Stop, this minute!" Deborah said. "You say that you've been doing—what he has?" she demanded.

"Why shouldn't I? What do you know about it? Are you going to turn against me, too?"

"I am—pretty nearly—"

"Oh, good God!" Laura tossed up her hands and went on with her walking.

"Quiet! Please try to be clear and explain."

"Explain—to you? How can I? *You* don't understand—you know nothing about it—all you know about is schools! You're simply a nun when it comes to this. I see it now—I didn't before—I thought you a modern woman—with your mind open to new ideas. But it isn't, it seems, when it comes to a pinch—it's shut as tight as Edith's is—"

"Yes, tight!"

"Thank you very much! Then for the love of Heaven will you kindly leave me alone! I'll have a talk with father!"

"You will *not* have a talk with father— "

"I most certainly will—and he'll understand! He's a man, at least—and he led a man's life before he was married!"

"Laura!"

"*You* can't see it in him—*but I can!*"

"You'll say not a word to him, not one word! He has had enough this year as it is!"

"Has he? Then I'm sorry! If *you* were any help to me—instead of acting like a nun—"

"Will you please stop talking like a fool?"

"I'm not! I'm speaking the truth and you know it! You know no more about love like mine than a nun of the middle ages! You needn't tell me about Allan Baird. You think you're in love with him, don't you? Well then, I'll tell you that you're not—your love is the kind that can wait for years—because it's cold, it's cold, it's cold—it's all in your mind and your reason! And so I say you're no help to me now! Here—look at yourself in the glass over there! You're just plain angry—frightened!"

"Yes—I am—I'm frightened." While she strove to
think clearly, to form some plan, she let her young sister
talk rapidly on:

"I know you are! And you can't be fair! You're like
nearly all American women—married or single, young or
old—you're all of you scared to death about sex—just as
your Puritan mothers were! And you leave it alone—you
keep it down—you never give it a chance—you're afraid!
But I'm not afraid—and I'm living my life! And let me
tell you I'm not alone! There are hundreds and thousands
doing the same—right here in New York City to-night!
It's been so abroad for years and years—in Rome and
Berlin, in Paris and London—and now, thank God, it
has come over here! If our husbands can do it, why can't
we? And we are—we're starting—it's come with the war!
You think war is hell and nothing else, don't you—but
you're wrong! It's not only killing men—it's killing a lot
of hypocrisies too—it's giving a jolt to marriage! You'll
see what the women will do soon enough—when there
aren't enough men any longer—"

"Suppose you stop this tirade and tell me exactly what
you've done," Deborah interrupted. A simple course of
action had just flashed into her mind.

"All right, I will. I'm not ashamed. I've given you
this 'tirade' to show you exactly how I feel—that it's not
any question of sin or guilt or any musty old rubbish
like that! I know I'm right! I know just what I'm
doing!"

"Who's the man? That Italian?"

"Yes."

"Where is he?"

"Right here in New York."

"Does he mean to stand by you?"

"Of course he does."

"Will he marry you, Laura?"

"Yes, he will—the minute I'm free from my beast of a husband!"

"And your husband will keep his suit quiet, you said, if you agree not to fight him."

"Yes."

Deborah rose abruptly.

"Then will you stay right here to-night, and leave this matter to me?" she asked.

"What do *you* mean to do?"

"See your husband."

"What for? When?"

"To-night, if I can. I want to be sure."

Laura looked for the moment nonplussed.

"And what of my wishes?" she inquired.

"*Your* wishes," said Deborah steadily. "You want a divorce, don't you—so do I. And you want it quiet—and so do I. I want it so hard that I want to make sure." Deborah's tone was kinder now, and she came over close to her sister. "Look here, Laura, if I've been hard, forgive me—please—and let me help. I'm not so narrow as you think. I've been through a good deal of this before—downtown, I mean, with girls in my school. They come to me, we have long talks. Maybe I *am* a nun—as you say—but I'm one with a confessional. Not for sins," she added, as Laura looked up angrily. "Sins don't interest me very much. But troubles do. And heaven knows that marriage is one," she said with a curious bitterness. "And when it has failed and there's no love left—as in your case—I'm for divorce. Only—" her wide sensitive lips quivered just a little, "I'm sorry it had to come like this. But I love you, dear, and I want to help, I want to see you safely through. And while I'm doing it, if we can, I want to keep dad out of it—at least until it's settled." She paused a moment. "So if you agree, I'll go to your husband. I want to be sure, absolutely, just what we can count on. And until I come back, stay here in my room. You don't want to talk to father and Edith—"

"Most certainly not!" Laura muttered.

"Good. Then stay here until I return. I'll send you up some supper."

"I don't want any, thank you."

Laura went and threw herself on the bed, while her sister finished dressing.

"It's decent of you, Deborah." Her voice was muffled and relaxed. "I wasn't fair," she added. "I'm sorry for some of the things I said."

"About me and marriage?" Deborah looked at herself in the glass in a peculiar searching way. A slight spasm crossed her features. "I'm not sure but that you were right. At times I feel far from certain," she said. Laura lifted her head from the pillow, watched her sister a moment, dropped back.

"Don't let this affect *you*, Deborah."

"Oh, don't worry, dearie." And Deborah moved toward the door. "My affair is just mine, you see, and this won't make any difference."

But in her heart she knew it would. What an utter loathing she had to-night for all that people meant by sex! Suddenly she was quivering, her limbs and her whole body hot.

"You say I'm cold," she was thinking. "Cold toward Allan, calm and cool, nothing but mind and reason! You say it means little to me, all that! But if I had had trouble with Allan, would I have come running home to talk? Wouldn't I have hugged it tight? And isn't that love? What do *you* know of me and the life I've led? Do you know how it feels to want to work, to be something yourself, without any man? And can't *that* be a passion? Have you had to live with Edith here and see what motherhood can be, what it can do to a woman? And now you come with *another* side, just as narrow as hers, devouring

everything else in sight! And because I'm a little afraid
of that, for myself and all I want to do, you say I don't
know what love is! But I do! And my love's worth more
than yours! It's deeper, richer, it will last! . . . Then
why do I loathe it *all* to-night? . . . But I don't, I only
loathe *your* side! . . . But yours is the very heart of it!
. . . All right, then what am I going to do?"

She was going slowly down the stairs. She stopped for
a moment, frowning.

CHAPTER XXXII

On the floor below she met her father, who was coming out of his room. He looked at her keenly:

"What's the trouble?"

"Laura's here," she answered. "Trouble again with her husband. Better leave her alone for the present—she's going to stay in my room for a while."

"Very well," her father grunted, and they went down to dinner. There Deborah was silent, and Edith did most of the talking. Edith, quite aware of the fact that Laura and all Laura's ways were in disgrace for the moment, and that she and her ways with her children shone by the comparison, was bright and sweet and tactful. Roger glanced at her more than once, with approval and with gratitude for the effort she was making to smooth over the situation. Deborah rose before they had finished.

"Where are you off to?" Roger asked.

"Oh, there's something I have to attend to—"

"School again this evening, dear?" inquired Edith cheerfully, but her sister was already out of the room. She looked at her father with quiet concern. "I'm sorry she has to be out to-night—to-night of all nights," she murmured.

"Humph!" ejaculated her father. This *eternal* school business of Deborah's was beginning to get on his nerves. Yes, just a little on his nerves! Why couldn't she give up one evening, just one, and get Laura out of this snarl she was in? He heard her at the telephone, and presently she came back to them.

"Oh, Edith," she said casually, "don't send any supper

228

up to Laura. She says she doesn't want any to-night. And ask Hannah to put a cot in my room. Will you?"

"Yes, dear, I'll attend to it."

"Thanks." And again she left them. In silence, when the front door closed, Edith looked at her father. This must be rather serious, Roger thought excitedly. So Laura was to stay all night, while Deborah gallivanted off to those infernal schools of hers! He had little joy in his paper that night. The news of the world had such a trick of suddenly receding a million miles away from a man the minute he was in trouble. And Roger was in trouble. With each slow tick of the clock in the hall he grew more certain and more disturbed. An hour passed. The clock struck nine. With a snort he tossed his paper aside.

"Well, Edith," he said glumly, "how about some chess this evening?" In answer she gave him a quick smile of understanding and sympathy.

"All right, father dear." And she fetched the board.

But they had played only a short time when Deborah's latchkey was heard in the door. Roger gave an angry hitch to his chair. Soon she appeared in the doorway.

"May I talk to you, father?" she asked.

"I suppose so." Roger scowled.

"You'll excuse us, Edith?" she added.

"Oh, assuredly, dear." And Edith rose, looking very much hurt. "Of course, if I'm not needed—"

At this her father scowled again. Why couldn't Deborah show her sister a little consideration?

"What is it?" he demanded.

"Suppose we go into the study," she said.

He followed her there and shut the door.

"Well?" he asked, from his big leather chair. Deborah had remained standing.

"I've got some bad news," she began.

"What is it?" he snapped. "School burnt down?"
Savagely he bit off a cigar.

"I've just had a talk with Harold," she told him. He
shot a glance of surprise and dismay.

"Have, eh—what's it all about?"

"It's about a divorce," she answered.

The lighted match dropped from Roger's hand. He
snatched it up before it was out and lit his cigar, and
puffing smoke in a vigilant way again he eyed his
daughter.

"I've done what I could," she said painfully, "but they
seem to have made up their minds."

"Then they'll unmake 'em," he replied, and he leaned
forward heavily. "They'll unmake 'em," he repeated,
in a thick unnatural tone. "I'm not a'goin' to hear to
it!" In a curious manner his voice had changed. It
sounded like that of a man in the mountains, where he had
been born and raised. This thought flashed into Deborah's
mind and her wide resolute mouth set hard. It would be
very difficult.

"I'm afraid this won't do, father dear. Whether you
give your consent or not—"

"Wun't, wun't it! You wait and see if it wun't!"
Deborah came close to him.

"Suppose you wait till you understand," she admonished sternly.

"All right, I'm waiting," he replied. She felt herself
trembling deep inside. She did not want him to understand, any more than she must to induce him to keep out
of this affair.

"To begin with," she said steadily, "you will soon see
yourself, I think, that they fairly loathe the sight of each
other—that there is no real marriage left."

"That's fiddlesticks!" snapped Roger. "Just modern
talk and new ideas—ideas you're to blame for! Yes, you
are—you put 'em in her head—you and your gabble about

woman's rights!" He was angry now. He was glad he
was angry. He'd just begun!

"If you want me to leave her alone," his daughter cut
in sharply, "just say so! I'll leave it all to you!" And
she saw him flinch a little. "What would be *your* idea?"
she asked.

"My idea? She's to go straight home and make up
with him!"

She hesitated. Then she said:

"Suppose there's another woman."

"Then he's a beast," growled Roger.

"And yet you want her to live with him?"

He scowled, he felt baffled, his mind in a whirl. And a
wave of exasperation suddenly swept over him.

"Well, why shouldn't she?" he cried. "Other wives
have done it—millions! Made a devilish good success of
it, too—made new men of their husbands! Let her show
him she's ready to forgive! That's only Christian, ain't it?
Hard? Of course it's hard on her! But can you tell me
one hard thing she has ever had to do in her life? Hasn't
it been pleasure, pleasure from the word go? Can't
she stand something hard? Don't we all of us have to?
I do—God knows—with all of you!" And he puffed his
cigar in a fury. His daughter smiled. She saw her chance.

"Father," she said, in a low clear voice, "You've had so
many troubles. Why not leave this one to me? You
can't help—no matter how hard you try—you'll only
make it worse and worse. And you've been through so
much this year—you've earned the right to be quiet. And
that's what *they* want, both of them—they both want it
quiet, without any scandal." Her father glared, for he
knew about scandal, he handled it in his office each day.
"Let me manage this—please," she said. And her offer
tempted him. He struggled for a moment.

"No, I wun't!" he burst out in reply. "I want quiet
right enough, but not at the price of her peace with her

God!" This sounded foolish, he felt that it did, and he
flushed and grew the angrier. "No, I wun't," he said
stubbornly. "She'll go back to him if I take her myself.
And what's more," he added, rising, "she's to go straight
back to-night!"

"She is not going back to-night, my dear." And Deborah caught her father's arm. "Sit down, please—"

"I've heard enough!"

"I'm afraid you haven't," she replied.

"Very well." His smile was caustic. "Give me some
more of it," he said.

"Her husband won't have her," said Deborah bluntly.
"He told me so himself—to-night."

"Did, eh—then *I'll* talk to him!"

"He thinks," she went on in a desperate tone, "that
Laura has been leading—'her own little life'—as he put
it to me."

"*Eh?*"

"He is bringing suit himself."

"*Oh! He is!*" cried Roger hoarsely. "Then I *will*
talk to this young man!" But she put out a restraining
hand:

"Father! Don't try to fight this suit!"

"You watch me!" he snarled. Tears showed in her
eyes:

"Think! Oh, please! Think what you're doing! Have
you ever seen a divorce-court—here, in New York? Do
you know what it's like? What it *can* be like?"

"Yes," Roger panted. He did know, and the picture
came vividly into his mind—a mass of eager devouring
eyes fixed on a girl in a witness chair. "To-morrow I see a
lawyer!" he said.

"No—you won't do that, my dear," Deborah told
him sadly. "Laura's husband has got proofs."

Her father looked up slowly and glared into his
daughter's face.

"I've seen them myself," she added. "And Laura has admitted it, too."

Still for a moment he stared at her. Then slowly he settled back in his chair, his eyes dropped in their sockets, and very carefully, with a hand which was trembling visibly, he lifted his cigar to his lips. It had gone nearly out, but he drew on it hard until it began to glow again.

"Well," he asked simply, "what shall we do?"

Sharply Deborah turned away. To be quiet, to be matter of fact, to act as though nothing had happened at all—she knew this was what he wanted now, what he was silently begging her to be for his sake, for the family's sake. For he had been raised in New England. And so, when she turned back to him, her voice was flat and commonplace.

"Keep her here," she said. "Let him do what he likes. There'll be nothing noisy, he promised me that. But keep her here till it's over."

Roger smoked for a moment, and said,

"There's Edith and her children."

"The children needn't know anything—and Edith only part of it."

"The less, the better," he grunted.

"Of course." She looked at him anxiously. This tractable mood of his might not last. "Why not go up and see her now—and get it all over—so you can sleep."

Over Roger's set heavy visage flitted a smile of grim relish at that. Sleep! Deborah was funny. Resolutely he rose from his chair.

"You'll be careful, of course," she admonished him, and he nodded in reply. At the door he turned back:

"Where's the other chap?"

"I don't know," she answered. "Surely you don't want to see *him*—" Her father snorted his contempt:

"See him? No. Nor she neither. *She's* not to see him. Understand?"

"I wouldn't tell her that to-night."

"Look here." Roger eyed his daughter a moment.
"You've done well. I've no complaint. But don't try to
manage everything."

He went out and slowly climbed the stairs. Outside
the bedroom door he paused. When had he stood like
this before? In a moment he remembered. One evening
some two years ago, the night before Laura's wedding,
when they had had that other talk. And so it had come to
this, had it. Well, there was no use making a scene.
Again, with a sigh of weariness, Laura's father knocked
at her door.

"Come in, Deborah," she said.

"It isn't Deborah, it's I." There was a little silence.

"Very well, father, come in, please." Her voice
sounded tired and lifeless. He opened the door and
found the room dark. "I'm over on the bed," she said.
"I've had a headache this evening."

He came over to the bedside and he could just see
her there, a long shadow upon the white. She had
not taken off her clothes. He stood a moment help-
lessly.

"Please don't *you* talk to me!" His daughter fiercely
whispered. "I can't stand any more to-night!"

"I won't," he answered. "It's too late." Again there
was a pause.

"What time is it?" she asked him. But he did not
answer.

"Well, Laura," he said presently, "your sister has told
me everything. She has seen your husband—it's all
arranged—and you're to stay here till it's over. . . .
You want to stay here, don't you?"

"Yes."

"Then it's settled," he went on. "There's only one
thing—the other man. I don't know who he is and I
don't want to know. And I don't want you to know him

again. You're not to see him. Understand?" For a moment Laura was silent.

"I'm going to marry him, father," she said. And standing in the darkened room Roger stiffened sharply.

"Well," he answered, after a pause, "that's your affair. You're no longer a child. I wish you were," he added.

Suddenly in the darkness Laura's hand came out clutching for his. But he had already turned to the door.

"Good-night," he said, and left her.

In the hallway below he met Deborah, and to her questioning look he replied, "All right, I guess. Now I'm going to bed." He went into his room and closed the door.

As soon as Roger was alone, he knew this was the hardest part—to be here by himself in this intimate room, with this worn blue rug, these pictures and this old mahogany bed. For he had promised Judith his wife to keep close to the children. What would she think of him if she knew?

Judith had been a broad-minded woman, sensible, bighearted. But she never would have stood for this. Once, he recollected, she had helped a girl friend to divorce her husband, a drunkard who ran after chorus girls. But that had been quite different. There the wife had been innocent and had done it for her children. Laura was guilty, she hadn't a child, she was already planning to marry again. And then what, he asked himself. "From bad to worse, very likely. A woman can't stop when she's started downhill." His eye was caught by the picture directly before him on the wall—the one his wife had given him—two herdsmen with their cattle high up on a shoulder of a sweeping mountain side, tiny blue figures against the dawn. It had been like a symbol of their lives, always beginning clean glorious days. What was Laura beginning?

"Well," he demanded angrily, as he began to jerk off his clothes, "what can I do about it? Try to keep her from re-marrying, eh? And suppose I succeeded, how long would it last? She wouldn't stay here and I couldn't keep her. She'll be independent now—her looks will be her bank account. There'd be some other chap in no time, and he might not even marry her!" He tugged ferociously at his boots. "No, let well enough alone!"

He finished undressing, opened the window, turned out the gas and got into bed. Wearily he closed his eyes. But after a time he opened them and stared long through the window up at the beetling cliff of a building close by, with its tier upon tier of lighted apartments, a huge garish hive of homes. Yes, the town was crowding down on him to-night, on his house and on his family. He realized it had never stopped, and that his three grown children, each one of them a part of himself, had been struggling with it all the time. Laura—wasn't she part of himself? Hadn't he, too, had his little fling, back in his early twenties? "You will live on in our children's lives." She was a part of him gone wild. She gave it free rein, took chances. God, what a chance she had taken this time! The picture of that court he had seen, with the girl in the witness chair and those many rows of eyes avidly fixed upon her, came back to his mind so vividly they seemed for a moment right here in the room, these eyes of the town boring into his house. Angrily he shut out the scene. And alone in the darkness, Roger said to his daughter all the ugly furious things he had not said to her upstairs —until at last he was weary of it.

"Why am I working myself all up? I've got to take this. It's my medicine."

CHAPTER XXXIII

But as he watched Laura in the house, Roger's first emotions were complicated more and more by a feeling of bewilderment. At dinner the next evening he noticed with astonishment that she appeared like her natural self. "She's acting," he decided. But this explanation he soon dismissed. No, it was something deeper. She was actually unashamed, unafraid. That first display of feelings, the night of her arrival, had been only the scare of an hour. Within a few days she was back on her feet; and her cure for her trouble, if trouble she felt, was not less but more pleasure, as always. She went out nearly every evening now; and when she had spent what money she had, she sold a part of her jewelry to the little old Galician Jew in the shop around the corner. Yes, she was her natural self. And she was as before to her father. Her attitude said plainly,

"It isn't fair to you, poor dear, to expect you to fully understand how right I am in this affair. And considering your point of view, you're acting very nicely."

Often as she talked to him a note of good-humored forgiveness crept into his daughter's voice. And looking at her grimly out of the corner of his eye, he saw that she looked down on him, far, far down from heights above.

"Yes," he thought, "this is modern." Then he grew angry all at once. "No," he added, "this is wrong! You can't fool me, young woman, you know it as well as I do myself! You're not going to carry this off with an air— not with your father! No, by George!"

And he would grow abrupt and stern. But days would

237

pass and in spite of himself into their talks would creep
a natural friendly tone.   Again he found himself friends
with her—friends as though nothing whatever had happened!   Could it be that a woman who had so sinned could
go right on?   Here was Laura, serenely unconscious of
guilt, and smiling into her future, dreaming still of happiness, quite plainly sure of it, in fact!   With a curious
dismayed relief Roger would scowl at this daughter of his
—a radiant enigma in his quiet sober house.

But Edith was not at all perplexed.   When she learned
from Deborah that there was soon to be a divorce, she
came at once to her father.   Her face was like a thundercloud.

"A nice example for my children!" she indignantly
exclaimed.

"I'm sorry, my dear.   But what can I do?"

"You can make her go back to her husband, can't
you?"

"No, I can't," he flatly replied.

"Then I'd better try it myself!"

"You'll do no such thing!" he retorted.   "I've gone
clear to the bottom of this—and I say you're to leave her
alone!"

"Very well," she answered.   And she did leave her sister
alone, so severely that Laura soon avoided being home for
lunch or dinner.   She had taken the room which George had
occupied ever since John had been turned out, and there
she breakfasted late in bed, until Edith put a stop to it.
They barely spoke to each other now.   Laura still smiled
defiance.

Days passed.   Christmas came at last, and despite
Edith's glum resolution to make it a happy time for the
children, the happiness soon petered out.   After the tree
in the morning, the day hung heavy on the house.   Roger
buried himself in his study.   Laura had motored off into
the country with a gay party of her friends.   Or was this

just a ruse, he wondered, and was she spending the day with her lover? Well, what if she was? Could he lock her in?

About twilight he thought he heard her return, and later from his bedroom he heard her voice and Edith's. Both voices sounded angry, but he would not interfere.

At the Christmas dinner that evening Laura did not put in an appearance, but Edith sat stiff and silent there; and despite the obvious efforts which Deborah and Allan made to be genial with the children, the very air in the room was charged with the feeling of trouble close ahead. Again Roger retreated into his den, and presently Laura came to him.

"Good-night—I'm going out," she said, and she pressed her cheek lightly to his own. "What a dear you've been to me, dad," she murmured. And then she was gone.

A few minutes later Edith came in. She held a small note in her hand, which Roger saw was addressed to himself.

"Well, father, I learned this afternoon what you've been keeping from me," she said. Roger gave her a steady look.

"You did, eh—Laura told you?"

"Yes, she did!" his daughter exclaimed. "And I can't help wondering, father—"

"Why did she tell you? Have you been at her again to-day?"

"Again? Not at all," she answered. "I've done as you asked me to, let her alone. But to-day—mother's day—I got thinking of _her_."

"Leave your mother out of it, please. What did you say to Laura?"

"I tried to make her go back, of course—"

"And she told you—"

"He wouldn't have her! And then in a perfect tantrum she went on to tell me why!" Edith's eyes were cold with disgust. "And I'm wondering why you let her stay here—in the same house with my children!"

Roger reached out his hand.

"Give me that note," he commanded. He read it quickly and handed it back. The note was from Laura, a hasty good-bye.

"Edith will explain," she wrote, "and you will see I cannot stay any longer. It is simply too impossible. I am going to the man I love—and in a few days we shall sail for Naples. I know you will not interfere. It will make the divorce even simpler and everything easier all round. Please don't worry about me. We shall soon be married over there. You have been so dear and sensible and I do so love you for it." Then came her name scrawled hastily. And at the bottom of the page: "I have paid every bill I can think of."

Edith read it in silence, her color slowly mounting.

"All right," said her father, "your children are safe."

She gave him a quick angry look, burst into tears and ran out of the room.

Roger sat without moving, his heavy face impassive. And so he remained for a long time. Well, *Laura* was gone—no mistake about that—and this time she was gone for good. She was going to live in Rome. Try to stop her? No. What good would it do? Wings of the Eagles, Rome reborn. That was it, she had hit it, struck the keynote of this new age. Rome reborn, all clean, old-fashioned Christian living swept away by millions of men at each others' throats like so many wolves. And at last quite openly to himself Roger admitted that he felt old. Old and beaten, out of date. Moments passed, and hours—he took little note of time. Nor did he see on the mantle the dark visage of "The Thinker" there, resting on the huge clinched fist and brooding down upon him. Lower, imperceptibly, he sank into his leather chair.

Quiet had returned to his house.

CHAPTER XXXIV

BUT the quiet was dark to Roger now. Each night he spent in his study alone, for instinctively he felt the need of being by himself for a while, of keeping away from his children—out of whose lives he divined that other events would soon come forth to use up the last of the strength that was in him.

And Roger grew angry with the world. Why couldn't it let a man alone, an old man in a silent house alive for him with memories? Repeatedly in such hours his mind would go groping backward into the years behind him. What a long and winding road, half buried in the jungle, dim, almost impenetrable, made up of millions of small events, small worries, plans and dazzling dreams, with which his days had all been filled. But the more he recalled the more certain he grew that he was right. Life had never been like this: the world had never come smashing into his house, his very family, with its dirty teeming tenements, its schools, its prisons, electric chairs, its feverish rush for money, its luxuries, its scandals. These things had existed in the world, but remote and never real, mere things which he had read about. War? Did he not remember wars that had come and gone in Europe? But they hadn't come into his home like this, first making him poor when he needed money for Edith and her children, then plunging Deborah into a struggle which might very probably ruin her life, and now taking Laura and filling her mind with thoughts of pagan living. Why was every man, woman and child, these days, bound up in the whole life of the world? What would come of it all? A

new day out of this deafening night? Maybe so. But
for him it would come too late.

"What have I left to live for?"

One night with a sigh he went to his desk, lit a cigar
and laid his hand upon a pile of letters which had been
mounting steadily. It was made up of Laura's bills, the
ones she had not remembered. Send them after her to
Rome for that Italian fellow to pay? No, it could not be
thought of. Roger turned to his dwindling bank account.
He was not yet making money, he was still losing a little
each week. But he would not cut expenses. To the few
who were left in his employ, to be turned away would
mean dire need. And angrily he determined that they
should not starve to pay Laura's bills. "The world for
the strong, eh? Not in my office!" In Rome or Berlin
or Vienna, all right! But not over here!

Grimly, when he had made out the checks, Roger eyed
his balance. By spring he would be penniless. And he
had no one to turn to now, no rich young son-in-law who
could aid.

He set himself doggedly to the task of forcing up his
business, and meanwhile in the evenings he tried with
Edith to get back upon their former footing. To do this
was not easy at first, for his bitterness still rankled deep:
"When you were in trouble I took you in, but when she
was in trouble you turned her out, as you turned out John
before her." In the room again vacated, young George
had been reinstalled. One night Edith found her father
there looking in through the open doorway, and the look on
his massive face was hard.

"Better have the room disinfected again," he muttered when he saw her. He turned and went slowly
down the stairs. And she was late for dinner that
night.

But Edith had her children. And as he watched her
night by night hearing their lessons patiently, reading them

fairy stories and holding them smilingly in her arms, the old appeal of her motherhood regained its hold upon him. One evening when the clock struck nine, putting down his paper he suggested gruffly,

"Well, daughter, how about some chess?"

Edith flushed a little:

"Why, yes, dear, I'd be glad to."

She rose and went to get the board. So the games were resumed, and part at least of their old affection came to life. But only a part. It could never be quite the same again.

And though he saw little of Deborah, slowly, almost unawares to them both, she assumed the old place she had had in his home—as the one who had been right here in the house through all the years since her mother had died, the one who had helped and never asked help, keeping her own troubles to herself. He fell back into his habit of going before dinner to his daughter's bedroom door to ask whether she would be home that night. At one such time, getting no response and thinking Deborah was not there, he opened the door part way to make sure. And he saw her at her dresser, staring at herself in the glass, rigid as though in a trance. Later in the dining room he heard her step upon the stairs. She came in quietly and sat down; and as soon as dinner was over, she said her good-nights and left the house. But when she came home at midnight, he was waiting up for her. He had foraged in the kitchen, and on his study table he had set out some supper. While she sat there eating, her father watched her from his chair.

"Things going badly in school?" he inquired.

"Yes," she replied. There was silence.

"What's wrong?"

"To-night we had a line of mothers reaching out into the street. They had come for food and coal—but we had to send most of them home empty-handed. Some of them cried—and one of them fainted. She's to have a baby soon."

"Can't you get any money uptown?" he asked.

"I have," she answered grimly. "I've been a beggar —heaven knows—on every friend I can think of. And I've kept a press agent hard at work trying to make the public see that Belgium is right here in New York." She stopped and went on with her supper. "But it's a bad time for work like mine," she continued presently. "If we're to keep it going we must above all keep it cheap. That's the keynote these days, keep everything cheap— at any cost—so that men can expensively kill one another." Her voice had a bitter ring to it. "You try to talk peace and they bowl you over, with facts on the need of pre- paredness—for the defence of your country. And that doesn't appeal to me very much. I want a bigger pre- paredness—for the defence of the whole world—for democ- racy, and human rights, no matter who the people are! I'd like to train every child to that!"

"What do you mean?" her father asked.

"To teach him what his life can be!" she replied in a hard quivering tone. "A fight? Oh yes! So long as he lives—and even with guns if it must be so! But a fight for all the people on earth!—and a world so full of happy lives that men will think hard—before ever again letting themselves be led by the nose—into war and death— for a place in the sun!" She rose from her chair, with a weary smile: "Here I am making a speech again. I've made so many lately it's become a habit. I'm tired out, dad, I'm going to bed." Her father looked at her anxiously.

"You're seeing things out of proportion," he said. "You've worked so hard you're getting stale. You ought to get out of it for a while."

"I can't!" she answered sharply. "You don't know— you don't even guess—how it takes every hour—all the demands!"

"Where's Allan these days?"

"Working," was her harsh reply. "Trying to keep his hospital going with half its staff. The woman who was backing him is giving her money to Belgium instead."

"Do you see much of him?"

"Every day. Let's drop it. Shall we?"

"All right, my dear—"

And they said good-night. . . .

In the meantime, in the house, Edith had tried to scrimp and save, but it was very difficult. Her children had so many needs, they were all growing up so fast. Each month brought fresh demands on her purse, and the fund from the sale of her belongings had been used up long ago. Her sole resource was the modest allowance her father gave her for running the house, and she had not asked him for more. She had put off trouble from month to month. But one evening early in March, when he gave her the regular monthly check, she said hesitatingly:

"I'm very sorry, father dear, but I'm afraid we'll need more money this month." He glanced up from his paper:

"What's the matter?" She gave him a forced little smile, and her father noticed the gray in her hair.

"Oh, nothing in particular. Goodness knows I've tried to keep down expenses, but—well, we're a pretty large household, you know—"

"Yes," said Roger kindly, "I know. Are the month's bills in?"

"Yes."

"Let me see them." She brought him the bills and he looked relieved. "Not so many," he ventured.

"No, but they're large."

"Why, look here, Edith," he said abruptly, "these are bills for two months—some for three, even four!"

"I know—that's just the trouble. I couldn't meet them at the time."

"Why didn't you tell me?"

"Laura was here—and I didn't want to bother you— you had enough on your mind as it was. I've done the best I could, father dear—I've sold everything, you know —but I've about come to the end of my rope." And her manner said clearly, "I've done my part. I'm only a woman. I'll have to leave the rest to you."

"I see—I see." And Roger knitted his heavy brows. "I presume I can get it somehow." This would play the very devil with things!

"Father." Edith's voice was low. "Why don't you let Deborah help you? She does very little, it seems to me—compared to the size of her salary."

"She can't do any more than she's doing now," was his decisive answer. Edith looked at him, her color high. She hesitated, then burst out:

"I saw her check book the other day, she had left it on the table! She's spending thousands—every month!"

"That's not her own money," Roger said.

"No—it's money she gets for her fads—her work for those tenement children! She can get money enough for *them!*" He flung out his hand:

"Leave her out of this, please!"

"Very well, father, just as you say." And she sat there hurt and silent while again he looked slowly through the bills. He jotted down figures and added them up. They came to a bit over nine hundred dollars. Soon Deborah's key was heard in the door, and Roger scowled the deeper. She came into the room, but he did not look up. He heard her voice:

"What's the matter, Edith?"

"Bills for the house."

"Oh." And Deborah came to her father. "May I see what's the trouble, dear?"

"I'd rather you wouldn't. It's nothing," he growled. He wanted her to keep out of this.

"Why shouldn't she see?" Edith tartly inquired. "Deborah is living here—and before I came she ran the house. In her place I should certainly want to know."

Deborah was already glancing rapidly over the bills.

"Why, Edith," she exclaimed, "most of these bills go back for months. Why didn't you pay them when they were due?"

"Simply because I hadn't the money!"

"You've had the regular monthly amount."

"That didn't last long—"

"Why didn't you tell us?"

"Laura was here."

Deborah gave a shrug of impatience, and Roger saw how tired she was, her nerves on edge from her long day.

"Never mind about it now," he put in.

"What a pity," Deborah muttered. "If we had been told, we could have cut down."

"I don't agree with you!" Edith rejoined. "I have already done that myself! I've done nothing else!"

"Have the servants been paid?" her sister asked.

"No, they haven't—"

"Since when?"

"Three months!"

Roger got up and walked the room. Deborah tried to speak quietly:

"I can't quite see where the money has gone."

"Can't you? Then look at my check book." And Edith produced it with a glare. Her sister turned over a few of the stubs.

"What's this item?"

"Where?"

"Here. A hundred and twenty-two dollars."

"The dentist," Edith answered. "Not extravagant, is it—for five children?"

"I see," said Deborah. "And this?"

"Bedding," was Edith's sharp response. "A mattress

and more blankets. I found there weren't half enough in the house."

"You burned John's, didn't you?"

"Naturally!"

All at once both grew ashamed.

"Let's be sensible," Deborah said. "We must do something, Edith—and we can't till we're certain where we stand."

"Very well—"

They went on more calmly and took up the items one by one. Deborah finished and was silent.

"Well, father, what's to be done?" she asked.

"I don't know," he answered shortly.

"Somehow or other," Deborah said, "we've got to cut our expenses down."

"I'm afraid that's impossible," Edith rejoined. "I've already cut as much as I can."

"So did I, in my school," said her sister. "And when I thought I had reached the end, I called in an expert. And he showed me ways of saving I had never dreamed of."

"What kind of expert would you advise here?" Edith's small lip curled in scorn.

"Domestic science, naturally—I have a woman who does nothing else. She shows women in their homes just how to make money count the most."

"What women? And what homes? Tenements?"

"Yes. She's one of my teachers."

"Thank you!" said Edith indignantly. "But I don't care to have my children brought down to tenement standards!"

"I didn't mean to *have* them! But I know she could show you a great many things you can buy for less!"

"I'm afraid I shouldn't agree with her!"

"Why not, Edith?"

"Because she knows only tenement children—nothing of children bred like mine!"

Deborah drew a quick short breath, her brows drew tight and she looked away. She bit her lip, controlled herself:

"Very well, I'll try again. This house is plenty large enough so that by a little crowding we could make room for somebody else. And I know a teacher in one of my schools who'd be only too glad—"

"Take a boarder, you mean?"

"Yes, I do! We've got to do something!"

"No!"

Deborah threw up her hands:

"All right, Edith, I'm through," she said. "Now what do *you* propose?"

"I can try to do without Hannah again—"

"That will be hard—on *all* of us. But I guess you'll have to."

"So it seems."

"But unfortunately that won't be enough."

Edith's face grew tenser:

"I'm afraid it will have to be—just now—I've had about all I can stand for one night!"

"I'm sorry," Deborah answered. For a moment they confronted each other. And Edith's look said to Deborah plainly, "You're spending thousands, thousands, on those tenement children! You can get money enough for them, but you won't raise a hand to help with mine!" And as plainly Deborah answered, "My children are starving, shivering, freezing! What do yours know about being poor?" Two mothers, each with a family, and each one baffled, brought to bay. There was something so insatiable in each angry mother's eyes.

"I think you'd better leave this to me," said Roger very huskily. And both his daughters turned with a start, as though in their bitter absorption they had forgotten his presence there. Both flushed, and now the glances of all three in that room avoided each other. For they felt how sordid it had been. Deborah turned to her sister.

"I'm sorry, Edith," she said again, and this time there were tears in her eyes.

"So am I," said Edith unsteadily, and in a moment she left the room. Deborah stood watching her father.

"I'm ashamed of myself," she said. "Well? Shall we talk it over?"

"No," he replied. "I can manage it somehow, Deborah, and I prefer that you leave it to me."

Roger went into his study and sank grimly into his chair. Yes, it had been pretty bad; it had been ugly, ominous. He took paper and pencil and set to work. How he had come to hate this job of wrestling with figures. Of the five thousand dollars borrowed in August he had barely a thousand left. The first semi-annual interest was due next week and must be paid. The balance would carry them through March and on well into April. By that time he hoped to be making money, for business was better every week. But what of this nine hundred dollars in debts? Half at least must be paid at once. Lower and lower he sank in his chair. But a few moments later, his blunt heavy visage cleared, and with a little sigh of relief he put away his papers, turned out the lights and went upstairs. The dark house felt friendly and comforting now.

In his room he opened the safe in the corner where his collection of curious rings had lain unnoticed for many months. He drew out a tray, sat down by the light and began to look them over. At first only small inanimate objects, gradually as from tray after tray they glittered duskily up at him, they began to yield their riches as they had so often done before. Spanish, French, Italian, Bohemian, Hungarian, Russian and Arabian, rings small and rings enormous, religious rings and magic rings, poison rings, some black with age for all his careful polishing

—again they stole deep into Roger's imagination with suggestions of the many hands that had worn them through the centuries, of women kneeling in old churches, couples in dark crooked streets, adventures, love, hate, jealousy. Youth and fire, dreams and passion. . . .

At last he remembered why he was here. He thought of possible purchasers. He knew so many dealers, but he knew, too, that the war had played the devil with them as with everyone else. Still, he thought of several who would find it hard to resist the temptation. He would see them to-morrow, one by one, and get them bidding, haggling. Roger frowned disgustedly.

No help for it, though, and it was a relief. It would bring a truce in his house for a time.

But the truce was brief.

On the afternoon when he sold his collection Roger came home all out of sorts. He had been forced to haggle long; it had been a mean inglorious day; one of the brightest paths in his life had ended in a pigstie. But at least he had bought some peace in his home! Women, women, women! He shut the front door with a slam and went up to his room for a little rest, a little of what he had paid for! On the stairs he passed young Betsy, and he startled the girl by the sudden glare of reproach he bestowed upon her. Savagely he told himself he was no "feminist" that night!

The brief talk he had with Edith was far from reassuring. With no Deborah there to wound her pride, Edith quickly showed herself friendly to her father; but when he advised her to keep her nurse, she at once refused to consider it.

"I want you to," he persisted, with an anxious note in his voice. He had tried life without Hannah here and he did not care to try it again.

"It is already settled, father, I sent her away this morning."

"Then you get her right back!" he exclaimed. But Edith's face grew obstinate.

"I don't care to give Deborah," she replied, "another chance to talk as she did."

Roger looked at her gloomily. "You will, though," he was thinking. "You two have only just begun. Let any little point arise, which a couple of men would settle offhand, and you two will get together and go it! There'll be no living in the house!"

With deepening displeasure he watched the struggle between them go on. Sometimes it seemed to Roger there was not a topic he could bring up which would not in some way bring on a clash. One night in desperation he proposed the theatre.

"I'm afraid we can't afford it," said Edith, glancing at Deborah. And she had the same answer, again and again, for the requests her children made, if they involved but the smallest expense. "No, dear, I'm afraid we can't afford that," she would say gently, with a sigh. And under this constant pressure, these nightly little thrusts and jabs, Deborah would grow rigid with annoyance and impatience.

"For Heaven's sake, Edith," she burst out, one night when the children had gone to their lessons, "can you think of nothing on earth, except your own little family?"

"Here it comes again," thought Roger, scowling into his paper. He heard Edith's curt reply:

"No, I can't, not nowadays. Nobody *else* seems to think of them."

"You mean that I don't!"

"Do you?"

"Yes! I'm thinking of George! Do you want him killed in the trenches—in a war with Germany or Japan?"

"Are you utterly mad?" demanded Edith.

"No, I'm awake—my eyes are open! But yours are shut so tight, my dear, you can't see what has happened!"

You know this war has made us poor and your own life harder, but that's all. The big thing it has done you know nothing about!"

"Suppose you teach me," Edith said, with a prim provoking little smile. Deborah turned on her angrily:

"It has shown that all such mothers as you are out of date and have got to change! That we're bound together —all over the world—whether we like it or whether we don't! And that if we want to keep out of war, we've got to do it by coming right out of our own little homes—*and thinking, Edith, thinking!*"

"Votes for women," Edith said. Deborah looked at her, rose with a shrug.

"All right, Edith, I give up."

"Thank you. I'm not worth it. You'd better go back to your office now and go on with your work of saving the world. And use every hour of your time and every dollar you possess. I'll stay here and look after my children."

Deborah had gone into the hall. Roger, buried deep in his paper, heard the heavy street door close. He looked up with a feverish sigh—and saw at the open door of his study George and Betsy standing, curious, solemn and wide eyed. How long had they been listening?

CHAPTER XXXV

THERE came a season of sleet and rain when the smaller children were shut indoors and it was hard to keep them amused. They did not look well, and Edith was worried. She had always dreaded the spring, and to carry her family safely through she had taken them, in former years, to Atlantic City for two weeks. That of course was impossible now. Trouble was bound to come, she thought. And it was not long in coming. Bobby, who was ten years old and went to school with his brother George, caught a wretched cold one day. Edith popped him into bed, but despite her many precautions he gave his cold to Bruce and Tad.

"Suppose I ask Allan Baird to come," Deborah suggested. "He's wonderful with children, you know."

Edith curtly accepted his services. She felt he had been sent for to prevent her getting Doctor Lake. But she said nothing. She would wait. Through long hard days and longer nights she slaved upstairs. All Deborah's proffers of aid she declined. She kept Elizabeth home from school to help her with the many meals, the medicines and the endless task of keeping her lively patients in bed. She herself played with them by the hour, while the ache in her head was a torment. At night she was up at the slightest sound. Heavy circles came under her eyes. Within a few days her baby, Bruce, had developed pneumonia.

That evening after dinner, while Deborah was sitting with Roger in the living room, she heard her sister coming downstairs. She listened acutely, and glancing around she saw that Roger was listening, too. Edith passed the doorway and went on down the hall, where they heard her voice at the telephone. She came back and looked in at the door.

"I've called Doctor Lake," she said. "I've just taken Bruce's temperature. It's a hundred and five and two fifths." Deborah glanced up with a start.

"Oh, Edith!" she said softly. Her sister turned and looked at her.

"I ought to have had him before," she said. "When he comes, please bring him right up to the room." And she hurried upstairs.

"Pshaw!" breathed Roger anxiously. He had seen Bruce an hour ago; and the sight of the tiny boy, so exhausted and so still, had given him a sudden scare. Could it be that *this* would happen? Roger rose and walked the floor. Edith was right, he told himself, they should have had Lake long before. And they would have, by George, if it had not been for Deborah's interference! He glanced at her indignantly. Bringing in Baird to save money, eh? Well, it was just about time they stopped saving money on their own flesh and blood! What had Bruce to do with tenement babies? But he had had tenement treatment, just that! Deborah had had her way at last with Edith's children, and one of them might have to pay with its life! Again Roger glared at his silent daughter. And now, even in his excited state, he noticed how still and rigid she was, how unnatural the look she bent on the book held tightly in her hands.

Still Deborah said nothing. She could feel her father's anger. Both he and Edith held her to blame. She felt herself in a position where she could not move a hand. She was stunned, and could not think clearly. A vivid picture was in her mind, vivid as a burning flame which left everything else in darkness. It was of Bruce, one adorable baby, fighting for breath. "What would I do if he were mine?"

When the doctor arrived she took him upstairs and then came down to her father.

"Well?" he demanded.

"I don't know. We'll have to wait." And they both sat silent. At last they heard a door open and close, and presently steps coming down the stairs. Roger went out into the hall:

"Come right in here, doctor, won't you? I want to hear about this myself."

"Very well, sir." And Lake entered the room, with Edith close behind him. He took no notice of anyone else. "Write this down," he said to her. "And give it to the nurse when she comes." A heavy man of middle age, with curious dark impassive eyes that at times showed an ironic light, Lake was a despot in a world of mothers to whom his word was law. He was busy to-night, with no time to waste, and his low harsh voice now rattled out orders which Edith wrote down in feverish haste—an hourly schedule, night and day. He named a long list of things needed at once. "Night nurse will be here in an hour," he ended. "Day nurse, to-morrow, eight a. m. Get sleep yourself and plenty of it. As it is you're not fit to take care of a cat." Abruptly he turned and left the room. Edith followed. The street door closed, and in a moment after that his motor was off with a muffled roar. Edith came back, picked up her directions and turned to her sister:

"Will you go up and sit with Bruce? I'll telephone the druggist," she said.

Deborah went to the sick room. Bruce's small face, peaked and gray in the soft dim light, turned as she entered and came to the bed.

"Well, dear?" she whispered. The small boy's eyes, large and heavy with fever, looked straight into hers.

"Sick," said the baby hoarsely. The next instant he tossed up his hands and went through a spasm, trying to breathe. It passed, he relaxed a little, and again stared solemnly at his aunt. "Sick," he repeated. "Wery sick."

Deborah sat silent. The child had another fight for his breath; and this time as he did so, Deborah's body contracted, too. A few moments later Edith came in. Deborah returned downstairs, and for over an hour she sat by herself. Roger was in his study, Betsy and George had gone to bed. The night nurse arrived and was taken upstairs. Still Deborah's mind felt numb and cold. Instinctively again and again it kept groping toward one point: "If I had a baby as sick as that, what would I do? What would I do?"

When the doorbell rang again, she frowned, rose quickly and went to the door. It was Allan.

"Allan—come in here, will you?" she said, and he followed her into the living room.

"What is it?" he inquired.

"Bruce is worse."

"Oh—I'm sorry. Why didn't Edith let me know?"

"She had Lake to-night," said Deborah. He knitted his brows in annoyance, then smiled.

"Well, I don't mind that," he replied. "I'm rather glad. She'll feel easier now. What did he tell her?"

"He seemed to consider it serious—by the number of things he ordered."

"Two nurses, of course—"

"Yes, day and night." Deborah was silent a moment. "I may be wrong," she continued, "but I still feel sure the child will live. But I know it means a long hard fight. The expense of it all will be heavy."

"Well?"

"Whatever it is, I'll meet it," she said. "Father can't, he has reached the end. But even if he could help still, it wouldn't make much difference in what I've been deciding. Because when I was with Bruce to-night,

I saw as clear as I see you now that if I had a child like that—as sick as that—I'd sacrifice anything—everything—schools, tenement children, thousands! I'd use the money which should have been theirs, and the time and the attention! I'd shut them all out, they could starve if they liked! I'd be like Edith—exactly! I'd center on this one child of mine!"

Deborah turned her eyes to his, stern and gleaming with her pain. And she continued sharply:

"But I don't mean to shut those children out! And so it's clear as day to me that I can't ever marry you! That baby to-night was the finishing stroke!"

She made a quick restless movement. Baird leaned slowly forward. Her hands in her lap were clenched together. He took them both and held them hard.

"No, this isn't clear," he said. "I can feel it in your hands. This is nerves. This is the child upstairs. This is Edith in the house. This is school, the end of the long winter's strain."

"No, it's what I've decided!"

"But this is the wrong decision," Allan answered steadily.

"It's made!"

"Not yet, it isn't, not to-night. We won't talk of it now, you're in no condition." Deborah's wide sensitive lips began to quiver suddenly:

"We *will* talk of it now, or never at all! I want it settled—done with! I've had enough—it's killing me!"

"No," was Allan's firm reply, "in a few days things will change. Edith's child will be out of danger, your other troubles will clear away!"

"But what of next winter, and the next? What of Edith's children? Can't you see what a load they are on my father? Can't you see he's ageing fast?"

"Suppose he dies," Baird answered. "It will leave them on your hands. You'll have *these* children, won't you, whether you marry or whether you don't! And so will I! I'm their guardian!"

"That won't be the same," she cried, "as having children of our own—"

"Look into my eyes."

"I'm looking—" Her own eyes were bright with tears.

"Why are you always so afraid of becoming a mother?" Allan asked. In his gruff low voice was a fierce appeal. "It's this obsession in your mind that you'll be a mother like Edith. And that's absurd! You never will! You say you're afraid of not keeping school the first thing in your life! But you always do and you always will! You're putting it ahead of me now!"

"Yes, I can put it ahead of *you!* But I couldn't put it ahead of *my child!*" He winced at this and she noticed it. "Because you are strong, and the child would be weak! The child would be like Bruce to-night!"

"Are you sure if you marry you must have a child?"

"Yes," she answered huskily, "if I married you I'd want a child. And that want in me would grow and grow until it made both of us wretched. I'm that kind of a woman. That's why my work has succeeded so far— because I've a passion for children! They're not my work, they're my very life!" She bowed her head, her mouth set hard. "But so are you," she whispered. "And since this is settled, Allan, what do you think? Shall we try to go on—working together side by side— seeing each other every day as we have been doing all these months? Rather hard on both of us, don't you think? I do, I feel that way," she said. Again her features quivered. "The kind of feeling I have—for you—would make that rather—difficult!"

His grip tightened on her hands.

"I won't give you up," he said. "Later you will change your mind."

He left the room and went out of the house. Deborah

sat rigid. She trembled and the tears came. She brushed them angrily away. Struggling to control herself, presently she grew quieter. Frowning, with her clear gray eyes intently staring before her, she did not see her father come into the doorway. He stopped with a jerk at sight of her face.

"What's the matter?" he asked. She started.

"Nothing's the matter! How is Bruce?"

"I don't know. Who went out a few minutes ago?"

"Allan Baird," she answered.

"Oh. You explained to him, of course, about Lake—"

"Yes, he understands," she said. "He won't come here after this—"

Roger looked at her sharply, wondering just what she meant. He hesitated. No, he would wait.

"Good-night," he said, and went upstairs.

CHAPTER XXXVI

On the morrow Bruce did not grow better. If anything, the child grew worse. But by the next morning the crisis had passed. In the house the tension relaxed, and Roger suddenly felt so weak that he went to see his own physician. They had a long and serious talk. Later he went to his office, but he gave little heed to his work. Sitting there at his desk, he stared through the window far out over the city. A plan was forming in his mind.

At home that night, at dinner, he kept watching Deborah, who looked tired and pale and rather relaxed. And as soon as she was out of the house he telephoned Allan to come at once.

"It's something which can't wait," he urged.

"Very well, I'll come right up."

When Baird arrived a little later, Roger opened the door himself, and they went back into his study.

"Sit down," he said. "Smoke, Allan?"

"No, thanks." Baird looked doubly tall and lean, his face had a gaunt appearance; and as he sat down, his lithe supple right hand slowly closed on the arm of his chair.

"Now then," began Roger, "there are two things we want to get clear on. The first is about yourself and Deborah. There has been trouble, hasn't there?"

"Yes."

"She has made up her mind not to marry you."

"Yes."

"I guessed as much." And Roger paused. "Do you mind my asking questions?"

"No—"

"Are you still in love with her, Allan?"

"I am."

"And she with you?"

"I think so."

"Then it's the same old trouble."

"Yes." And he told a part of what she had said. As he talked in clear, terse, even tones, Baird's steady eyes had a tortured light, the look of a man who has almost reached the end of his endurance. Roger smoked in silence.

"What do you propose to do?"

"Wait," said Allan, "a few days more. Then try again. If I fail I'm through." Roger shot a quick look at him.

"I don't think you'll fail, my boy—and what's more I think I can help you. This is a large house, Allan—there's more in it than you know. My second point concerns myself. I'm going to die within a year."

As Baird turned on him suddenly, Roger grimly smiled and said, "We won't go into the details, but I've been examined lately and I have quite positive knowledge of what I've suspected for some time. So far, I have told no one but you. And I'm telling you only because of the bearing it has on Deborah." Roger leaned forward heavily. "She's the one of my daughters who means the most, now that I'm so near the end. When I die next year that may be all—I may simply end—a blank, a grave—I am not sure. But I've made up my mind above everything else to see Deborah happy before I go. And I mean to do it by setting her free—so free I think it will frighten her."

Roger went on to explain his plan, and they talked together for some time.

Another week had soon gone by. Bruce still recovered rapidly, and the other sick children were up and about. Deborah, in the meantime, had barely been in the house at all. But late on Saturday evening Roger found her in her room. She was working. He came behind her.

"What is it, dad?"

"Busy, eh?" He hesitated, and laid his hand on her shoulder with a little affectionate pressure. "You've kept so busy lately," he said, "I haven't had time to see anything of you. How's your work going?"

"Much better, thanks—now that the winter is over."

He questioned her about her schools. And then after a brief pause,

"Well, daughter," he said, "it has been a great fight, and I'm proud of you for it. And if I've got anything to say—" his hand was still on her shoulder, and he felt her tighten suddenly—"it isn't by way of criticism—please be sure of that ahead. In this damnable war my faith in men has been badly shaken up. Humanity seems to me still a child—a child who needs to go to school. God knows we need men and women like you—and I'm proud of all you've accomplished, I'd be the last man to hold you back. I only want to help you go on—by seeing to it that you are free—from anything which can hinder you."

He stopped again for a moment.

"To begin with," he said, "I understand you're not going to marry Allan Baird." She stirred slightly:

"Did he tell you so?"

"Yes—I asked him," Roger replied. "I had Allan here a few nights ago, and he told me you had decided to give up your happiness for the sake of all those children in that big family of yours. You felt you must keep yourself free for them. Very well, if that is your decision I propose to clear the way." She looked intently up at his face. "You're not free now," he continued. "We have Edith and her children here. And I'm growing old—that has got to be thought of—I don't want to leave them on your hands. So as soon as the baby is well enough, I'm going to move them up to the mountains—not only for the summer—they are to stay the whole year 'round. From this time on they're to make it their home."

"Father! But they can't do that! Think of the winters!" Deborah cried.

"It's already settled," he answered. "I've talked to Edith and she has agreed. She has always loved the farm, and it will be good for her children. In the meantime I've been talking to George. 'George,' I told him, 'I'm going to talk to you, man to man, about a man's job I want you to tackle.'"

"The farm? But, dearie! He's only a boy!"

"He's nearly seventeen," said Roger, "and a young moose for his age. And old Dave Royce will still be there. It's the work George has been dreaming about ever since he was a child. You should have seen how he was thrilled by the scheme. I told him we'd spend the summer together up there laying all our plans, investing our money carefully to make every dollar count."

"What money?" Deborah sharply asked. But her father was talking steadily on:

"We already have a fine lot of cattle. We'll add to it and enlarge the barn and put in some new equipment. In short, we'll put it in fine shape, make it a first class dairy farm. 'And then, George,' I said to him, 'I'm going to turn it over to you. I shall give the farm to your mother, and the rest of the money I have I mean to invest in her name down here, so that she'll have a small income until you can make your dairy pay.'"

"What money are you speaking of?" Deborah's voice was thick and hard, her sensitive lips were parted and she was breathing quickly.

"I've sold the house," he told her. Convulsively she gripped his arms:

"Then tell me where *you* mean to live!"

"I'm not going to live—I'm going to die—very soon—I have definite knowledge."

Without speaking Deborah rose; her face went white. Her father kept tight hold of her hands, and he felt them trembling, growing cold.

"You're soon to be free of everyone," he continued painfully. "I know this is hurting you, but I see so plain, so plain, my child, just what it is I've got to do. I'm trying to clear the way for you to make a simple definite choice— a choice which is going to settle your life one way or the other. I want to make sure you see what you're doing. Because you mean so much to me. We're flesh and blood—eh, my daughter?—and in this family of ours we've been the closest ones of all!" She seemed to sway a little.

"*You're not going to die!*" she whispered.

"So it hurts you to lose me," he replied. "It will be hard to be so free. Would you rather not have had me at all? I've been quite a load on your back, you know. A fearful job you had of it, dragging me up when I was down. And since then Edith and Bruce and the rest, what burdens they have been at times. What sharp worries, heavy sorrows, days and nights you and I have gone through, when we should have been quietly resting—free—to keep up our strength for our next day's work. Suppose you had missed them, lived alone, would you have worked better? You don't know. But you will know soon, you're to give it a trial. For I've cleared the way—so that if you throw over Baird to be free you shall get the freedom you feel you need!"

"Father! Please! Is this fair? Is this kind?" She asked in a harsh frightened tone. Her eyes were wet with angry tears.

"This isn't a time to be kind, my dear." His voice was quivering like her own. "I'm bungling it—I'm bungling it—but you must let me stumble along and try to show you what I mean. You will have your work, your crowded schools, to which you'll be able to give your life. But I look ahead, I who know you—and I don't see you happy, I don't even see you whole. For you there will be no family. None of the intimate sorrows and joys that have been in this house will come to you. I look back and I see them all—for a man who has come so near the end gets a larger vision." He shut his eyes, his jaw set tight. "I look into my family back and back, and I see how it has been made of many generations. Certain figures stand out in my mind—they cover over a hundred years. And I see how much they've meant to me. I see that I've been one of them—a link in a long chain of lives—all inter-bound and reaching on. In my life they have all been here—as I shall be in lives to come.

"And this is what I want for you." He held her close a moment. The tears were rolling down her cheeks. "Until now you have been one of us, too. You have never once been free. You have been the one in this house to step in and take hold and try to decide what's best to be done. I'm not putting you up on a pedestal, I don't say you've made no mistakes—but I say you're the kind of a woman who craves what's in a family. You're the one of my daughters who has loved this house the most!"

"Yes," she said, "I've loved this house—"

"But now for you all this will stop—quite suddenly," he told her. "This house of ours will soon be sold. And within a few months I shall be dead, and your family will have dropped out of your life."

"Stop! Can't you? Stop! It's brutal! It isn't true about you!" she cried. "I won't believe it!" Her voice broke.

"Go and see my physician," he said.

"How long have you known it? Why didn't you tell me?"

"Because we had troubles enough as it was, other things to think of. But there's only one thing now, this freedom you are facing."

"Please! Please!" she cried imploringly. "I don't want to talk of myself but of you! This physician—"

"No," he answered with stern pain, "you'll have to hear me out, my child. We're talking of you—of you alone when I am gone. How will it be? Are you quite sure? You will have your work, that vision of yours, and I know how close it has been to you, vivid and warm, almost like a friend. But so was my business once like that, when I was as young as you. And the business grew and it got cold—impersonal, a mere machine. Thank God I had a family. Isn't your work growing too? Are you sure it won't become a machine? And won't you lose touch with the children then, unless you have a child of your own? Friends won't be enough, you'll find, they're not bound up into yourself. The world may reach a stage at last where we shall live on in the lives of all—we may all be one big family. But that time is still far off—we hold to our own flesh and blood. And so I'm sure it will be with you. You see you have been young, my dear, and your spirit has been fresh and new. But how are you going to keep it so, without the ties you've always had?" He felt the violent clutch of her hand.

"*You won't die!*" she whispered. But he went on relentlessly:

"And what will you do without Allan Baird? For you see you have not even worked alone. You have had this man who has loved you there. I've seen how much he has helped you—how you have grown and he has grown since you two got together. And if you throw him over now, it seems to me you are not only losing what has done the most for your work, but you're running away from life as well. You've never won by doing that, you've always won by meeting life, never evading it, taking it all, living it full, taking chances! If you marry Baird, I see you both go on together in your work, while in your home you struggle through the troubles, tangles, joys and griefs which most of us mortals know so well! I see you in a world of children, but with children, too, of your own—to keep your spirit always young! Living on in your children's lives!"

Roger stopped abruptly. He groped for something more to say.

"On the one side, all that," he muttered, "and on the other, a lonely life which will soon grow old."

There fell a dangerous silence. And sharply without warning, the influence, deep and invisible, of many generations of stolid folk in New England made itself felt in each of them. Father and daughter grew awkward, both. The talk had been too emotional. Each made, as by an instinct, a quick strong effort at self-control, and felt about for some way to get back upon their old easy footing. Roger turned to his daughter. Her head was still bent, her hands clasped tight, but she was frowning down at them now, although her face was still wet with tears. She drew a deep unsteady breath.

"Well, Deborah," he said simply, "here I've gone stumbling on like a fool. I don't know what I've said or how you have listened."

"I've listened," she said thickly.

"I have tried," he went on in a steadier tone, "to give you some feeling of what is ahead—and to speak for your mother as well as myself. And more than that—much more than that—for the world has changed since she was here. God knows I've tried to be modern." A humorous glint came into his eyes, "Downright modern," he declared. "Have I asked you to give up your career? Not at all, I've asked you to marry Baird, and go right on with him in your work. And if you can't marry Allan Baird, after what he has done for you, how in God's name can you modern women ever marry anyone? Now what do you say? Will you marry him? Don't laugh at me! I'm serious! Talk!"

But Deborah was laughing—although her father felt her hands still cold and trembling in his. Her gray eyes, bright and luminous, were shining up into his own.

"What a time you've been having, haven't you, dear!" his daughter cried unsteadily. "Fairly lying awake at night and racking your brains for everything modern I've ever said—to turn it and twist it and use it against me!"

"Well?" he demanded. "How does it twist?"

"It twists hard, thank you," she declared. "You've turned and twisted me about till I barely see how I can live at all!"

"You can, though! Marry Allan Baird!"

"I'll think it over—later on."

"What is there left to think about? Can you point to one hole in all I've said?"

"Yes, a good many—and one right off."

"Out with it!"

"You're not dying," Deborah told him calmly, "I feel quite certain you'll live for years."

"Oh, you do, eh—then see my physician!"

"I will, I'll see him to-morrow. How long did you give yourself? Just a few months?"

"No, he said it might be more," admitted Roger grudgingly. "If I had no worries to wear me out—"

"Me, you mean."

"Exactly."

"Well, you've worried quite enough. You're going to leave it to me to decide."

"Very well," he agreed. He looked at her. "You have listened—hard?" he gruffly asked.

"Yes, dear." Her hands slowly tightened on his. "But don't speak of this again. You're to leave it to me. You promise?"

"Yes."

And Roger left her.

He went to bed but he could not sleep. With a sudden sag in his spirits he felt what a bungler he had been. He was not used to these solemn talks, he told himself irately. What a fool to try it! And how had Deborah taken it all? He did not mind her laughter, nor that lighter tone of hers. It was only her way of ending the talk, an easy way out for both of them. But what had she thought underneath? Had his points gone home? He tried to remember them. Pshaw! He had been too excited, and he could recall scarcely anything. He had not meant to speak of Baird—he had meant to leave him out! Yes, how he must have bungled it! Doubtless she was smiling still. Even the news about himself she had not taken seriously.

But as he thought about that news, Roger's mood completely changed. The talk of the evening grew remote, his family no longer real, mere little figures, shadowy, receding swiftly far away. . . Much quieter now, he lay a long time listening to the life of the house, the occasional sounds from the various rooms. From the nursery adjoining came little Bruce's piping laugh, and Roger could hear the nurse moving about. Afterwards for a long time he could hear only creaks and breathings. Never had the old house seemed so like a living creature. For nearly forty years it had held all that he had loved and known, all he had been sure of. Outside of it was the strange, the new, the uncertain, the vast unknown, stretching away to infinity. . . .

Again he heard Bruce's gay little laugh. What did it remind him of? He puzzled. Then he had it. Edith had been a baby here. Her cradle had been in this very room, close by the bed. And how she had laughed! What gurgles and ripples of bursting glee! The first child in his family. . . .

CHAPTER XXXVII

On the next day, which was Sunday, Deborah made an appointment with her father's physician, and had a long talk with him at his house. Upon her return she went to her room and stayed there until evening, but when she came down to supper her manner was as usual. At the table she joined in the talk of Edith and the children, already deep in their preparations for the move up to the farm. George could hardly wait to start. That life would be a change indeed in Edith's plans for her family, and as they talked about it now the tension of hostility which had so long existed between the two sisters passed away. Each knew the clash had come to an end, that they would live together no more; and as though in remorse they drew close, Deborah with her suggestions, Edith in her friendly way of taking and discussing each one. Then Deborah went again to her room. Her room was just over Roger's, and waking several times in the night he heard his daughter walking the floor.

The next day she was up early and off to her school before he came down. It was a fine spring morning, Roger had had a good night's sleep, and as he walked to his office he was buoyed up by a feeling both of hope for his daughter and of solid satisfaction in himself as he remembered all that he had said to her. Curiously enough he could recall every word of it now. Every point which he had made rose up before him vividly. How clear he had been, how simple and true, and yet with what a tremendous effect he had piled the points one on the other. "By George," he thought with a little glow, "for a fellow who's never been in a pulpit I put up a devilish strong appeal." And he added sagely, "Let it work on the girl, give it a chance. She'll come out of this all right. This idea some fellows have, that every woman is born a fool, isn't fair, it isn't true. Just let a line of argument be presented to her strong and clear—straight from the shoulder—by some man—"

And again with a tingle of pleasure his mind recurred to his sermon. His pleasures had been few of late, so he dwelt on this little glow of pride and made the most of it while it was here.

At the office, as he entered his room, he stopped with a slight shock of surprise. John, standing on his crutches in front of a large table, had been going through the morning's mail, sorting out the routine letters Roger did not need to see. To-day he had just finished and was staring at the window. The light fell full on his sallow face and showed an amazing happiness. At Roger's step he started.

"Well, Johnny, how goes it this morning?"

"Fine, thank you," was the prompt reply. And John hobbled briskly over to his typewriter in the corner. Roger sat down at his desk. As he did so he glanced again at the cripple and felt a little pang of regret. "What will become of him," he asked, "when I close out my business?" He still thought of him as a mere boy, for looking at the small crooked form it was difficult to remember that John was twenty years of age. The lad had worked like a Trojan of late. Even Roger, engrossed as he had been in family anxieties, had noticed it in the last few weeks. He would have to make some provision for John. Deborah would see to it. . . . Roger went slowly through his mail. One letter was from the real estate firm through whom he was to sell the house. The deal had not been closed as yet, there were certain points still to be settled. So Roger called John to his desk and dictated a reply. When he finished there was a brief pause.

"That's all," said Roger gruffly.

"So you're sellin' the house," John ventured.

"Yes."

The lad limped back to his corner and went to work at his machine. But presently he came over again and stood waiting awkwardly.

"What is it, Johnny?" Roger inquired, without looking up.

"Say, Mr. Gale," the boy began, in a carefully casual tone, "would you mind talking business a minute or two?"

"No. Fire ahead."

"Well, sir, you've had your own troubles lately, you haven't had much time for things here. The last time you went over the books was nearly a couple of weeks ago." John paused and his look was portentous.

"Well," asked Roger, "what about it? Business been picking up any since then?"

"Yes, sir!" was the answer. "We didn't lose a cent last week! We made money! Fifteen dollars!"

"Good Lord, Johnny, we're getting rich."

"But that's nothing," John continued. "The fact of the matter is, Mr. Gale, I have been working lately on a new line I thought of. And now it's got agoing so fast it's getting clean away from me!" Again he stopped, and swallowed hard.

"Out with it, then," said Roger.

"I got it from the war," said John. "The papers are still half full of war news, and that's what's keeping our business down—because we ain't adopting ourselves to the new war conditions. So I figured it like this. Say there are a million people over here in America who've got either friends or relations in the armies over there. Say that all of 'em want to get news—not just this stuff about battles, but real live news of what's happened to Bill. Has Bill still got his legs and arms? Can he hold down a job when he gets home? News which counts for something! See? A big new market! Business for us! So I tried to see what I could do!" John excitedly shifted his crutches. Roger was watching intently.

"Go on, Johnny."

"Sure, I'll go on! One night I went to a library where they have English papers. I went over their files for about a month. I took one Canadian regiment—see?—and traced it through, and I got quite a story. Then I used some of the money I've saved and bought a whole bunch of papers. I piled 'em up in the room where I sleep and went through 'em nights. I hired two kids to help me. Well, Mr. Gale, the thing worked fine! In less than a week I had any amount of little bunches of clippings. See how I mean? Each bunch was the story of one regiment for a month. So I knew we could deliver the goods!

"Well, this was about ten days ago. And then I went after the market. I went to a man I met last year in an advertising office, and for fifty dollars we put an 'ad' in the Sunday Times. After that there was nothing to do but wait. The next day—nothing doing! I was here at seven-thirty and I went through every mail. Not a single answer to my 'ad'—and I thought I was busted! But Tuesday morning there were three, with five dollar checks inside of 'em! In the afternoon there were two more and the next day eleven! By the end of last week we'd had forty-six! Friday I put in another 'ad' and there've been over seventy more since then! That makes a hundred and twenty in all—six hundred dollars! And I'm swamped! I ain't done nothing yet—I've just kept 'em all for you to see!"

He went quickly to the table, gathered a pile of letters there and brought them over to Roger's desk. Roger glanced over a few of them, dazed. He looked around into John's shrewd face, where mingled devotion and triumph and business zeal were shining.

"Johnny," he said huskily, "you've adopted my business and no mistake." John swallowed again and scowled with joy.

"Let's figure it out!" he proposed.

"We will!"

They were at it all day, laying their plans, "adopting" the work of the office to the new conditions. They found they would need a larger force, including a French and a German translator. They placed other "ads" in the papers. They forgot to have lunch and worked steadily on, till the outer rooms were empty and still. At last they were through. Roger wearily put on his cuffs, and went and got his coat and hat.

"Say, Mr. Gale," John asked him, "how about this letter—the one you dictated this morning to that firm about your house?" Roger turned and looked at him.

"Throw it into the basket," he said. "We'll write 'em another to-morrow and tell 'em we have changed our minds." He paused for just a moment, and then he added brusquely, "If this goes through as I hope it will, I guess you'd better come into the firm."

And he left the room abruptly. Behind him there was not a sound.

At home in his study, that evening, he made some more calculations. In a few weeks he would have money enough to start Edith and her family in their new life on the farm. For the present at least, the house was safe.

"Why, father." Edith came into the room. "I didn't know you had come home. What kept you so long at the office?"

"Oh, business, my dear—"

"Have you had any supper?"

"No, and I'd like some," he replied.

"I'll see to it myself," she said. Edith was good at this sort of thing, and the supper she brought was delicious. He ate it with keen relish. Then he went back to his study and picked up a book, an old favorite. He started to read, but presently dozed. The book dropped from his hands and he fell asleep.

He awakened with a start, and saw Deborah looking down at him. For a moment he stared up, as he came to his senses, and in his daughter's clear gray eyes he thought he saw a happiness which set his heart to beating fast.

"Well?" he questioned huskily.

"We're to be married right away."

He stared a moment longer; "Oh, I'm so glad, so glad, my dear. I was afraid you—" he stopped short. Deborah bent close to him, and he felt her squeeze his arm:

"I've been over and over all you said," she told him, in a low sweet voice. "I had a good many ups and downs. But I'm all through now—I'm sure you were right." And she pressed her cheek to his. "Oh, dad, dad—it's such a relief! And I'm so happy! . . . . Thank you, dear."

"Where is Allan?" he asked presently.

"I'll get him," she said. She left the room, and in a moment Allan's tall ungainly form appeared in the doorway.

"Well, Allan, my boy," Roger cried.

"Oh, Roger Gale," said Allan softly. He was wringing Roger's hand.

"So she decided to risk you, eh," Roger said unsteadily. "Well, Baird, you look like a devilish risk for a woman like her—who has the whole world on her back as it is—"

"I know—I know—and how rash she has been! Only two years and her mind was made up!"

"But that's like her—that's our Deborah—always acting like a flash—"

"Stop acting like children!" Deborah cried. "And be sensible and listen to me! We're to be married to-morrow morning—"

"Why to-morrow?" Roger asked.

"Because," she said decidedly, "there has been enough

fuss over this affair. So we'll just be married and have it done. And when Edith and the children go up next week to the mountains, we want to move right into this house."

"This house?" exclaimed her father.

"I know—it's sold," she answered. "But we're going to get a lease. We'll see the new owner and talk him around."

"Then you'll have to talk *your father* around—"

"*You* around?" And Deborah stared. "You mean to say you're not going to sell?"

"I do," said Roger blithely. He told them the story of John's new scheme. "And if things turn out in the office as I hope they will," he ended, "we'll clear the mortgage on the house and then make it your wedding gift—from the new firm to the new family."

Deborah choked a little:

"Allan! What do you think of us now?"

"I think," he answered, in a drawl, "that we'd better try to persuade the new firm to live with the new family."

"We will, and the sooner the better!" she said.

"I'm going up to the mountains," said Roger.

"Yes, but you're coming back in the fall, and when you do you're coming here! And you're going to live here years and years!"

"You're forgetting my doctor."

"Not at all. I had a long talk with him Sunday and I know just what I'm saying."

"You don't look it, my dear," said Roger, "but of course you may be right. If you take the proper care of me here—and John keeps booming things for the firm—"

"And George makes a huge success of the farm," Deborah added quickly.

"And Deborah of teaching the world—"

"Oh, Allan, hush up!"

"Look here," he said. "You go upstairs and tell Edith all this. Your father and I want to be alone."

And when the two men were left alone, they smoked and said nothing. They smiled at each other.

"It's hard to decide," grunted Roger at last. "Which did it—my wonderful sermon or your own long waiting game? I'm inclined to think it was the game. For any other man but you—with all you've done, without any talk—no, sir, there wouldn't have been a chance. For she's modern, Baird, she's modern. And I'm going to live just as long as I can. I want to see what happens here."

The next night in his study, how quiet it was. Edith was busy packing upstairs, Deborah and Allan were gone. Thoughts drifted slowly across his mind. Well, she was married, the last of his daughters, the one whom he cared most for, the one who had taken the heaviest risks. And this was the greatest risk of all. For although she had put it happily out of her thoughts for the moment, Roger knew the old troublesome question was still there in Deborah's mind. The tenement children or her own, the big family or the small? He felt there would still be struggles ahead. And with a kind of a wistfulness he tried to see into the future here.

He gave a sudden start in his chair.

"By George!" he thought. "They forgot the ring!"

Scowling, he tried to remember. Yes, in the brief simple service that day, in which so much had been omitted—music, flowers, wedding gown—even the ring had been left out. Why? Not from any principle, he knew that they were not such fools. No, they had simply forgotten it, in the haste of getting married at once. Well, by thunder, for a girl whose father had been a collector of rings for the best part of his natural life, it was pretty shabby to say the least! Then he recollected that he, too, had forgotten it. And this quieted him immediately.

"I'll get one, though," he promised himself. "And no

plain wedding ring either. I'll make A. Baird attend to that. No, I'll get her a ring worth while."

He sank deep in his chair and took peace to his soul by thinking of the ring he would choose. And this carried his thoughts back over the years. For there had been so many rings . . . .

CHAPTER XXXVIII

It was a clear beautiful afternoon toward the end of May. And as the train puffing up the grade wound along the Connecticut River, Roger sat looking out of the window. The orchards were pink and white on the hills. Slowly the day wore away. The river narrowed, the hills reared high, and in the sloping meadows gray ribs and shoulders of granite appeared. The air had a tang of the mountains. Everywhere were signs of spring, of new vigor and fresh life. But the voices at each station sounded drowsier than at the last, the eyes appeared more stolid, and to Roger it felt like a journey far back into old ways of living, old beliefs and old ideals. He had always had this feeling, and always he had relished it, this dive into his boyhood. But it was different to-day, for this was more than a journey, it was a migration, too. Close about him in the car were Edith and her children, bound for a new home up there in the very heart and stronghold of all old things in America.

Old things dear to Edith's heart. As she sat by the window staring out, he watched her shapely little head; he noted the hardening lines on her forehead and the gray which had come in her hair. It had been no easy move for her, this, she'd shown pluck to take it so quietly. He saw her smile a little, then frown and go on with her thinking. What was she thinking about, he wondered—all she had left behind in New York, or the rest of her life which lay ahead? She had always longed for things simple and old. Well, she would have them now with a vengeance, summer and winter, the year 'round, in the battered frame house on the mountain side, the birthplace of her family. A

280

recollection came to him of a summer's dusk two years ago and a woman with a lawn mower cutting the grass on the family graves. Would Edith ever be like that, a mere custodian of the past? If she did, he thought, she would be false to the very traditions she tried to preserve. For her forefathers had never been mere guardians of things gone by. Always they had been pioneers. That house had not been old to them, but a thrilling new adventure. Their old homes they had left behind, far down in the valleys to the east. And even those valley homes had been new to the rugged men come over the sea. Would Edith ever understand? Would she see that for herself the new must emerge from her children, from the ideas, desires and plans already teeming in their minds? Would she show keen interest, sympathy? Would she be able to keep her hold?

In the seat behind her mother, Betsy was sitting with Bruce in her lap, looking over a picture book. Quietly Roger watched the girl.

"What are you going to be?" he asked. "A woman's college president, a surgeon or a senator? And what will your mother think of you then?"

They changed cars, and on a train made up of antiquated coaches they wound through a side valley, down which rushing and tumbling came the river that bore Roger's name. He went into the smoking car, and presently George joined him there. George did not yet smoke, (with his elders), but he had bought a package of gum and he was chewing absorbedly. Plainly the lad was excited over the great existence which he saw opening close ahead. Roger glanced at the boy's broad shoulders, noticed the eager lines of his jaw, looked down at his enormous hands, unformed as yet, ungainly; but in them was a hungriness that caused a glow in Roger's breast. One more of the family starting out.

"It's all going to depend on you," Roger gravely

counseled. "Your whole life will depend on the start you make. Either you're going to settle down, like so many of your neighbors up there, or you're going to hustle, plan out your day, keep on with your studies and go to college—the State Agricultural College, I mean. In short, keep up to date, my boy, and become in time a big figure in farming."

"I'm going to do it," George replied. His grandfather glanced again at his face, so scowling, so determined. And a gleam of compassion and yearning came for a moment in Roger's eyes. His heavy hand lay on George's knee.

"That's right, son," he grunted. "Make the family proud of you. I'll do all I can to help you start. My business is picking up, thank God, and I'll be able to back you now. I'll stay up here a good part of the summer. We've both of us got a lot to learn—and not only from books—we want to remember we've plenty to learn from the neighbors, too. Take old Dave Royce, for instance, who when all is said and done has worked our farm for twenty odd years and never once run me into debt."

"But, Gee!" demurred George. "He's so 'way out of date!"

"I know he is, son, but we've got to go slow." And Roger's look passed furtively along the faces in the car. "We don't want to forget," he warned, "that this is still New England. Every new idea we have we want to go easy with, snake it in."

"I've got an awful lot of 'em," the boy muttered hungrily.

At the farm, the next morning at daybreak, Roger was awakened by the sound of George's voice. It was just beneath his window:

"But cattle are only part of it, Dave," the boy declared, in earnest tones, "just part of what we can have up

here.   Think what we've got—over three hundred acres!
And we want to make every acre count! We want to get
in a whole lot more of hogs—Belted Hampshires, if we
can afford 'em—and a couple of hundred hens.   White
Leghorns ought to fill the bill.   Of course that's just a
starter.   I've got a scheme for some incubators—electric
—run by the dynamo which we'll put in down by the dam.
And we can do wondors with bees, too, Dave—I've got a
book on 'em I'd like you to read.   And besides, there's
big money in squab these days.   Rich women in New
York hotels eat thousands of 'em every night.   And
ducks, of course, and turkeys.   I'd like a white gobbler
right at the start, if we knew where we could get one
cheap."   The voice broke off and there was a pause.
"We can do an awful lot with this place."

Then Dave's deep drawl:

"That's so, George—yes, I guess that's so.   Only we
don't want to fool ourselves. That ain't Noah's Ark over
thar—it's a barn.   And just for a starter, if I was you—"
Here Dave deliberated.   "Of course it's none of my business," he said, "it's for you and your grandfather to decide—and I don't propose to interfere in what ain't any
of my affair—"

"Yes, yes, Dave, sure!   That's all right!   But go on!
What, just for a starter?"

"Cows," came the tranquil answer.   "I've been hunting around since you wrut me last month.   And I know
of three good milkers—"

"Three?   Why, Dave, I wrote we want thirty or forty!"

"Yes—you wrut," Dave answered.   "But I've druv
all around these parts—and there ain't but three that I
can find.   And I ain't so sure of that third one.   She looks
like she might—" George cut in.

"But you only had a buggy, Dave!   Gee!   I'm going to
have a Ford!"

"That so, George?"

"You bet it's so! And we'll go on a cow hunt all over the State!"

"Well—I dunno but what you're right," Dave responded cautiously. "You *might* get more cows if you had a Ford—an' got so you could run it. Yes, I guess it's a pretty good scheme. I believe in being conservative, George—but I dunno now but what a Ford—"

Their voices passed from under the window, and Roger relaxed and smiled to himself. It was a good beginning, he thought.

They bought a Ford soon afterwards and in the next few weeks of June they searched the farms for miles around, slowly adding to their herd. To Roger's surprise he found many signs of a new life stirring there —the farmers buying "autos" and improved machinery, thinking of new processes; and down in the lower valleys they found several big stock farms which were decidedly modern affairs. At one such place, the man in charge took a fancy to George and asked him to drop over often.

"You bet I'll drop over often!" George replied, as he climbed excitedly into his Ford. "I want to see more of those milking machines! We're going to have 'em some day ourselves! A dynamo too!"

And at home, down by the ruined mill he again set about rebuilding the dam.

Roger felt himself growing stronger. His sleeps were sound, and his appetite had come back to a surprising degree. The mountain air had got into his blood and George's warm vigor into his soul. One afternoon, watching the herd come home, some thirty huge animals swinging along with a slow heavy power in their limbs, he breathed the strong sweet scent of them on the mountain breeze. George came running by them and stopped a moment by Roger's side, watching closely and eagerly every animal as it passed. And Roger glanced at George's face. The herd passed on and George followed behind, his collie dog

leaping and barking beside him. And Roger looked up at
a billowy cloud resting on a mountain top and wondered
whether after all that New York doctor had been right.

He followed the herd into the barn. In two long rows,
the great heads of the cattle turned hungrily, lowing and
sniffing deep, breathing harshly, stamping, as the fodder
cart came down the lines. What a splendidly wholesome
work for a lad, growing up with his roots in the soil, in
these massive simple forces of life. What of Edith's
other children? Would they be willing to stay here long?
Each morning Roger breakfasted with Bruce the baby
by his side. "What a thing for you, little lad," he thought,
"if you could live here all your days. But will you? Will
you want to stay? Won't you, too, get the fever, as I did,
for the city?" In the joyous, shining, mysterious eyes of
the baby he found no reply. He had many long talks with
Betsy, who was eager to go away to school, and with Bob
and little Tad who were going to school in the village that
fall. And the feeling came to Roger that surely he would
see these lives, at least for many years ahead. They were
so familiar and so real, so fresh and filled with hopes and
dreams. And he felt himself so a part of them all.

But one morning, climbing the steep upper field to a
spring George wanted to show him, Roger suddenly
swayed, turned faint. He caught hold of a boulder on the
wall and held himself rigid, breathing hard. It passed,
and he looked at his grandson. But George had noticed
nothing. The boy had turned and his brown eyes were
fixed on a fallow field below. Wistfully Roger watched
his face. They both stood motionless for a long time.

As the summer drew slowly to a close, Roger spent many
quiet hours alone by the copse of birches, where the glory
of autumn was already stealing in and out among the tall
slender stems of the trees. And he thought of the silent
winter there, and of the spring which would come again, and
the long fragrant summer. And he watched the glow on

the mountains above and the rolling splendors of the clouds. At dusk he heard the voices of animals, birds and insects, murmuring up from all the broad valley, then gradually sinking to deep repose, many never to wake again. And the span of his life, from the boyhood which he could recall so vividly here among these children, seemed brief to him as a summer's day, only a part of a mighty whole made up of the innumerable lives, the many generations, of his family, his own flesh and blood, come out of a past he could never know, and going on without him now, branching, dividing, widening out to what his eyes would never see.

Vaguely he pictured them groping their way, just as he himself had done. It seemed to Roger that all his days he had been only entering life, as some rich bewildering thicket like this copse of birches here, never getting very deep, never seeing very clearly, never understanding all. And so it had been with his children, and so it was with these children of Edith's, and so it would be with those many others—always groping, blundering, starting —children, only children all. And yet what lives they were to lead, what joys and revelations and disasters would be theirs, in the strange remote world they would live in—"my flesh and blood that I never shall know."

But the stars were quiet and serene. The meadows and the forests on the broad sweep of the mountain side took on still brighter, warmer hues. And there was no gloom in these long good-byes.

On a frosty night in September, he left the farm to go to the city. From his seat in the small automobile Roger looked back at the pleasant old house with its brightly lighted windows, and then he turned to George by his side:

"We're in good shape for the winter, son."

But George did not get his full meaning.

At the little station, there were no other passengers. They walked the platform for some time. Then the train with a scream came around the curve. A quick grip on George's hand, and Roger climbed into the car. Inside, a moment later, he looked out through the window. By a trainman with a lantern, George stood watching, smiling up, and he waved his hand as the train pulled out.

CHAPTER XXXIX

THE next morning on his arrival in town, Roger went to his office. He had little cause for uneasiness there, for twice in the summer he had come down to keep an eye on the business, while John had taken brief vacations at a seaside place nearby. The boy had no color now in his cheeks; as always, they were a sallow gray with the skin drawn tight over high cheek bones; his vigor was all in his eyes. But here was a new John, nevertheless, a successful man of affairs. He had on a spruce new suit of brown, no cheap ready-made affair but one carefully fitted to conceal and soften his deformity. He was wearing a bright blue tie and a cornflower in his buttonhole, and his sandy hair was sleekly brushed. He showed Roger into his private room, a small place he had partitioned off, where over his desk was a motto in gold: "This is no place for your troubles or mine."

"Lord, but you've got yourself fixed up fine in here," said Roger. John smiled broadly. "And you're looking like a new man, Johnny."

"I had a great time at the seashore. Learned to sail a boat alone. What do you think of this chair of mine?" And John complacently displayed the ingenious contrivance in front of his desk, somewhat like a bicycle seat. It was made of steel and leather pads.

"Wonderful," said Roger. "Where'd you ever pick it up?"

"I had it made," was the grave reply. "When a fellow has got up in life enough to have a stenographer, it's high time he was sitting down."

"Let's see you do it." John sat down. "Now how is business?" Roger asked.

"Great. Since the little slump we had in August it has taken a new start—and not only war business, at that —the old people are sending in orders again. I tell you what it is, Mr. Gale, this country is right on the edge of a boom!"

And the junior member of the firm tilted triumphantly back in his chair.

With the solid comfort which comes to a man when he returns to find his affairs all going well, Roger worked on until five o'clock, and then he started for his home.

Deborah had not yet come in, and a deep silence reigned in the house. He looked through the rooms down-stairs, and with content he noticed how little had been altered. His beloved study had not been touched. On the third floor, in the large back room, he found John comfortably installed. There were gay prints upon the walls, fresh curtains at the windows, a mandolin lying on a chair. And Roger, glancing down at the keen glad face of his partner, told himself that the doctor who had said this lad would die was a fool.

"These doctors fool themselves often," he thought.

Deborah and Allan had the front room on the floor below. Roger went in, and for a moment he stood looking about him. How restful and how radiant was this large old-fashioned chamber, so softly lighted, waiting. Through a passageway lined with cupboards he went into his room at the back. Deborah had repapered it, but with a pattern so similar that Roger did not notice the change. He only felt a vague freshness here, as though even this old chamber, too, were making a new start in life. And he felt as though he were to live here for years. Slowly he unpacked his trunk and took a bath and dressed at his leisure. Then he heard Deborah's voice at the door.

"Come in, come in!" he answered.

"Why, father! Dearie!" Deborah cried. "Oh, how well you're looking, dad!" And she kissed him happily. "Oh, but I'm glad to have you back—"

"That's good," he said, and he squeezed her hand. "Here, come to the light, let me look at you." He saw her cheeks a little flushed, the gladness in her steady eyes. "Happy? Everything just right?" His daughter nodded, smiling, and he gave a whimsical frown. "No ups and down at all? That's bad."

"Oh, yes, plenty—but all so small."

"Good fellow to live with."

"Very."

" And your work?

"It's going splendidly.   I'll tell you about it this evening, after you give me the news from the farm."

They chatted on for a short while, but he saw she was barely listening.

"Can't you guess what it means," she asked him softly, "to a woman of my age—after she has been so afraid she was too old, that she'd married too late—to know at last—to be sure at last—that she's to have a baby, dad?" He drew back a little, and a lump rose in his throat.

"By George!" he huskily exclaimed. "Oh, my dear, my dear!" And he held her close in his arms for some time, till both of them grew sensible.

Soon after she had gone to her room, he heard Allan coming upstairs. He heard her low sweet cry of welcome, a silence, then their voices. He heard them laughing together and later Deborah humming a song. And still thinking of what she had told him, he felt himself so close to it all. And again the feeling came to him that surely he would live here for years.

Allan came in and they had a talk.

"Deborah says she has told you the news."

"Yes. Everything's all right, I suppose—her condition, I mean," said Roger.

"Couldn't be better."

"Just as I thought."

"Those six weeks we had up in Maine—"

"Yes, you both show it. Working hard?"

"Yes—"

"And Deborah?" Roger asked.

"You'll have to help me hold her in."

They talked a few moments longer and went down to the living room. John was there with Deborah. All four went in to dinner. And through the conversation, from time to time Roger noticed the looks that went back and forth between husband and wife; and again he caught Deborah smiling as though oblivious of them all. After dinner she went with him into his den.

"Well! Do you like the house?" she inquired.

"Better than ever," he replied.

"I wonder if you'll mind it. There'll be people coming to dinner, you know—"

"That won't bother me any," he said.

"And committee meetings now and then. But you're safe in here, it's a good thick door."

"Let 'em talk," he retorted, "as hard as they please. You're married now—they can't scare me a bit. Only at ten o'clock, by George, you've got to knock off and go to bed."

"Oh, I'll take care of myself," she said.

"If you don't, Allan will. We've had a talk."

"Scheming already."

"Yes. When will it be?"

"In April, I think."

"You'll quit work in your schools?"

"A month before."

"And in the meantime, not too hard."

"No, and not too easy. I'm so sure now that I can do both." And Deborah kissed him gently. "I'm so happy, dearie—and oh, so very glad you're here!"

There followed for Roger, after that, many quiet evenings at home, untroubled days in his office. Seldom did he notice the progress of his ailment. His attention was upon his house, as this woman who mothered thousands of children worked on for her great family, putting all in order, making ready for the crisis ahead when she would become the mother of one.

Now even more than ever before, her work came crowding into his home. The house was old, but the house was new. For from schools and libraries, cafés and tenements and streets, the mighty formless hunger which had once so thrilled her father poured into the house itself and soon became a part of it. He felt the presence of the school. He heard the daily gossip of that bewildering system of which his daughter was a part: a world in itself, with its politics, its many jarring factions, its jealousies, dissensions, its varied personalities, ambitions and conspiracies; but in spite of these confusions its more progressive elements downing all distrusts and fears and drawing steadily closer to life, fearlessly rousing everywhere the hunger in people to live and learn and to take from this amazing world all the riches that it holds: the school with its great challenge steadily increasing its demands in the name of its children, demands which went deep down into conditions in the tenements and ramified through politics to the City Hall, to Albany, and even away to Washington—while day by day and week by week, from cities, towns and villages came the vast prophetic story of the free public schools of the land.

And meanwhile, in the tenements, still groping and testing, feeling her way, keeping close watch on her great brood, their wakening desires, their widening curiosities, Deborah was bringing them, children, mothers and fathers too, together through the one big hope of brighter and more ample lives for everybody's children. Step by step this hope was spread out into the surrounding swamps and

jungles of blind driven lives, to find surprising treasures
there deep buried under dirt and din, locked in the common heart of mankind—old songs and fables, hopes and
dreams and visions of immortal light, handed down from
father to son, nurtured, guarded, breathed upon and
clothed anew by countless generations, innumerable millions of simple men and women blindly struggling toward
the sun. Over the door of one of the schools, were these
words carved in the stone:

"Humanity is still a child. Our parents are all people
who have lived upon the earth—our children, all who are
to come. And the dawn at last is breaking. The great
day has just begun."

This spirit of triumphal life poured deep into Roger's house. It was as though his daughter, in these
last months which she had left for undivided service,
were strengthening her faith in it all and pledging her devotion—as communing with herself she felt the crisis
drawing near.

CHAPTER XL

THERE came an interruption. One night when Deborah was out and Roger sat in his study alone, the maid came in highly flustered and said,

"Mr. Gale! It's Miss Laura to see you!"

He turned with a startled jerk of his head and his face slowly reddened. But when he saw the maid's eager expression and saw that she was expecting a scene, with a frown of displeasure he rose from his chair.

"Very well," he said, and he went to his daughter. He found her in the living room. No repentant Magdalene, but quite unabashed and at her ease, she came to her father quickly.

"Oh, dad, I'm so glad to see you, dear!" And she gave him a swift impetuous kiss, her rich lips for an instant pressing warmly to his cheek.

"Laura!" he said thickly. "Come into my study, will you? I'm alone this evening."

"I'm so glad you are!" she replied. She followed him in and he closed the door. He glanced at her confusedly. In her warmth, her elegance, an indefinable change in the tone and accent of her high magnetic voice, and in her ardent smiling eyes, she seemed to him more the foreigner now. And Roger's thoughts were in a whirl. What had happened? Had she married again?

"Is Edith here still?" she was asking.

"No, she's up in the mountains. She's living there," he answered.

"Edith? In the mountains?" demanded Laura, in surprise. And she asked innumerable questions. He replied to each one of them carefully, slowly, meanwhile getting control of himself.

"And Deborah married—married at last! How has it worked? Is she happy, dad?"

"Very," he said.

"And is she still keeping up her schools?"

"Yes, for the present. She'll have to stop soon." Laura leaned forward, curious:

"Tell me, dad—a baby?"

"Yes." She stared a moment.

"Deborah!" she softly exclaimed; and in a moment, "I wonder."

"What do you mean?" her father asked, but Laura evaded his question. She plied him with her inquiries for a few minutes longer, then turned to him with a challenging smile:

"Well, father, don't you think you had better ask me now about myself?" He looked away a moment, but turned resolutely back:

"I suppose so. When did you land?"

"This morning, dear, from Italy—with my husband," she replied. And Roger started slightly. "I want you to meet him soon," she said.

"Very well," he answered. At his disturbed, almost guilty expression Laura laughed a little and rose and came over and hugged him tight.

"Oh, but, father dearest—it's working out so splendidly! I want you to know him and see for yourself! We've come to live in New York for a while—he has more to do here about war supplies."

"More shrapnel, eh, machine guns. More wholesale death," her father growled. But Laura smiled good-naturedly.

"Yes, love, from America. Aren't you all ashamed of yourselves—scrambling so, to get rich quick—out of this war you disapprove of."

"*You* look a bit rich," her father retorted.

"Rather—for the moment," was her cheerful answer.

"And you still like living in Italy?"

"Tremendously! Rome is wonderful now!"

"Reborn, eh. Wings of the Eagles."

"Yes, and we're doing rather well."

"I haven't noticed it," Roger said. "Why don't you send a few of your troops to help those plucky Frenchmen?"

"Because," she replied, "we have a feeling that this is a war where we had much better help ourselves."

"High ideals," he snorted.

"Rome reborn," she remarked, unabashed. And her father scowled at her whimsically.

"You're a heathen. I give you up," he declared. Laura had risen, smiling.

"Oh, no, don't give me up," she said. "For you see," she added softly, "I'm a heathen with a great deal of love in her heart for thee, my dearest dad. May I bring him down, my husband?"

"Yes—"

"I'll telephone to Deborah to-morrow and arrange it."

When she had gone he returned to his chair and sat for a long time in a daze. He was still disturbed and bewildered. What a daughter of his! And what did it mean? Could she really go on being happy like this? Sinning? Yes, she was sinning! Laura had broken her marriage vows, she had "run off with another fellah." Those were the plain ugly facts. And now, divorced and re-married, she was careering gayly on! And her views of the war were plain heathenish! And yet there was something about her—yes, he thought, he loved her still! What for? For being so happy! And yet she was wrong to be happy, all wrong! His thoughts went 'round in circles.

And his confusion and dismay grew even deeper the

next night when Laura brought her new husband to dine. For in place of the dark polished scoundrel whom Roger had expected, here was a spruce and affable youth with thick light hair and ruddy cheeks, a brisk pleasant manner of talking and a decidedly forcible way of putting the case of his country at war. They kept the conversation to that. For despite Deborah's friendly air, she showed plainly that she wanted to keep the talk impersonal. And Laura, rather amused at this, replied by treating Deborah and Allan and her father, too, with a bantering forbearance for their old-fashioned, narrow views and Deborah's religion of brotherhood, democracy. All that to Laura was passé.

From time to time Roger glanced at her face, into her clear and luminous eyes so warm with the joy of living with this new man, her second. How his family had split apart. He wrote Edith the news of her sister, and he received but a brief reply. Nor did Deborah speak of it often. She seemed to want to forget Laura's life as the crisis in her own drew near.

CHAPTER XLI

DEBORAH had not yet stopped work. Again and again she put it off. For in her busy office so many demands both old and new kept pressing in upon her, such unexpected questions and vexing little problems kept cropping up as Deborah tried to arrange her work for the colleague who was to take her place in the spring, that day after day she lingered there—until one afternoon in March her husband went to her office, gave her an hour to finish up, and then brought her home with him. She had a fit of the blues that night. Allan was called out on a case, and a little while later Roger found his daughter alone in the living room, a book unopened in her lap, her gray eyes glistening with tears. She smiled when she caught sight of him.

"It's so silly!" she muttered unsteadily. "Just my condition, I suppose. I feel as though I had done with school for the remainder of my days! . . . Better leave me now, dearie," she added. "I'm not very proud of myself to-night—but I'll be all right in the morning."

The next day she was herself again, and went quietly on with her preparations for the coming of her child. But still the ceaseless interests of those hordes of other children followed her into the house. Not only her successor but principals and teachers came for counsel or assistance. And later, when reluctantly she refused to see such visitors, still the telephone kept ringing and letters poured in by every mail. For in her larger family there were weddings, births and deaths, and the endless savage struggle for life; and there were many climaxes of dreams and aspirations, of loves and bitter jealousies. And out

298

of all this straining and this fever of humanity, came messages to Deborah: last appeals for aid and advice, and gifts for the child who was to be born; tiny garments quaintly made by women and girls from Italy, from Russia and from Poland; baby blankets, wraps and toys and curious charms and amulets. There were so many of these gifts.

"There's enough for forty babies," Deborah told her father. "What on earth am I to do, to avoid hurting anyone's feelings? And isn't it rather awful, the way these inequalities will crop up in spite of you? I know of eight tenement babies born down there in this one week. How much fuss and feathers is made over *them*, and *their* coming into the world, poor mites?" Roger smiled at his daughter.

"You remind me of Jekyll and Hyde," he said.

"Father! What a horrible thought! What have Jekyll and Hyde to do with me?"

"Nothing, my dear," he answered. "Only it's queer and a little uncanny, something I've never seen before, this double mother life of yours."

It was only a few days later when coming home one evening he found that Deborah's doctor had put her to bed and installed a nurse. There followed a week of keen suspense when Roger stayed home from the office. She liked to have him with her, and sitting at her bedside he saw how changed his daughter was, how far in these few hours she had drawn into herself. He had suspected for some time that all was not well with Deborah, and Allan confirmed his suspicions. There was to be grave danger both for the mother and the child. It would come out all right, of course, he strove to reassure himself. Nothing else could happen now, with her life so splendidly settled at last. That Fate could be so pitiless—no, it was unthinkable!

"This is what comes of your modern woman!" Roger exclaimed to Allan one night. "This is the price she's paying for those nerve-racking years of work!"

The crisis came toward the end of the week. And while for one entire night and through the day that followed and far into the next night the doctors and nurses fought for life in the room upstairs, Roger waited, left to himself, sitting in his study or restlessly moving through the house. And still that thought was with him —the price! It was kept in his mind by the anxious demands which her big family made for news. The telephone kept ringing. Women in motors from uptown and humbler visitors young and old kept coming to make inquiries. More gifts were brought and flowers. And Roger saw these people, and as he answered their questions he fairly scowled in their faces—unconsciously, for his mind was not clear. Reporters came. Barely an hour passed without bringing a man or a woman from some one of the papers. He gave them only brief replies. Why couldn't they leave his house alone? He saw her name in headlines: "Deborah Gale at Point of Death." And he turned angrily away. Vividly, on the second night, there came to him a picture of Deborah's birth so long ago in this same house. How safe it had been, how different, how secluded and shut in. No world had clamored *then* for news. And so vivid did this picture grow, that when at last there came to his ears the shrill clear cry of a new life, it was some time before he could be sure whether this were not still his dream of that other night so long ago.

But now a nurse had led him upstairs, and he stood by a cradle looking down at a small wrinkled face almost wholly concealed by a soft woolly blanket. And presently Allan behind him said,

"It's a boy, and he's to be named after you." Roger looked up.

"How's the mother?" he asked.

"Almost out of danger," was the reply. Then Roger glanced at Allan's face and saw how drawn and gray it was. He drew a long breath and turned back to the child. Allan had gone and so had the nurse, and he was alone by the cradle. Relief and peace and happiness stole into his spirit. He felt the deep remoteness of this strange new little creature from all the clamoring world without—which he himself was soon to leave. The thought grew clearer, clearer, as with a curious steady smile Roger stood there looking down.

"Well, little brother, you're here, thank God. And nobody knows how close we'll be—for a little while," he thought. "For we're almost out of the world, you and I."

Days passed, Deborah's strength increased, and soon they let Roger come into the room. She, too, was remote from the world for a time. That great family outside was anxious no longer, it left her alone. But soon it would demand her. Never again, he told himself, would she be so close, so intimate, as here in her bed with this child of hers to whom she had given her father's name. "These hours are my real good-byes."

Two long quiet weeks of this happiness, and then in a twinkling it was gone. The child fell sick, within a few hours its small existence hung by a thread—and to Roger's startled eyes a new Deborah was revealed! Tense and silent on her bed, her sensitive lips compressed with pain, her birthmark showing a jagged line of fiery red upon her brow as her ears kept straining to catch every sound from the nursery adjoining, through hours of stern anguish she became the kind of mother that she had once so dreaded— shutting out everything else in the world: people, schools, all other children, rich or poor, well, sick or dying! Here was the crisis of Deborah's life!

One night as she lay listening, with her hand gripping

Roger's tight, frowning abruptly she said to him, in a harsh, unnatural voice:

"They don't care any longer, none of them care! *I'm* safe and they've stopped worrying, for they know they'll soon have me back at work! The work," she added fiercely, "that made my body what it is, not fit to bear a baby!" She threw a quick and tortured look toward the door of the other room. "My work for those others, all those years, will be to blame if this one dies! And if it doesn't live I'm through! I won't go on! I couldn't! I'd be too bitter after this—toward all of them—*those children!*"

These last two words were whispers so bitter they made Roger cold.

"But this child is going to live," he responded hoarsely. Its mother stared up with a quivering frown. The next moment her limbs contracted as from an electric shock. There had come a faint wail from the other room.

And this went on for three days and nights. Again Roger lived as in a dream. He saw haggard faces from time to time of doctors, nurses, servants. He saw Allan now and then, his tall ungainly figure stooped, his features gaunt, his strong wide jaw set like a vise, but his eyes kind and steady still, his low voice reassuring. And Roger noticed John at times hobbling quickly down a hall and stopping on his crutches before a closed door, listening. Then these figures would recede, and it was as though he were alone in the dark.

At last the nightmare ended. One afternoon as he sat in his study, Allan came in slowly and dropped exhausted into a chair. He turned to Roger with a smile.

"Safe now, I think," he said quietly.

Roger went to Deborah and found her asleep, her face at peace. He went to his room and fell himself into a long dreamless slumber.

In the days which followed, again he sat at her bedside and

together they watched the child in her arms. So feeble still the small creature appeared that they both spoke in whispers. But as little by little its strength returned, Deborah too became herself. And though still jealously watchful of its every movement, she had time for other thinking. She had talks with her husband, not only about their baby but about his work and hers. Slowly her old interest in all they had had in common returned, and to the messages from outside she gave again a kindlier ear.

"Allan tells me," she said one day, when she was alone with her father, "that I can have no more children. And I'm glad of that. But at least I have one," she added, "and he has already made me feel like a different woman than before. I feel sometimes as though I'd come a million miles along in life. And yet again it feels so close, all that I left back there in school. Because I'm so much closer now—to every mother and every child. At last I'm one of the family."

CHAPTER XLII

Of that greater family, one member had been in the house all through the month which had just gone by. But he had been so quiet, so carefully unobtrusive, that he had been scarcely noticed. Very early each morning, day after day, John had gone outside for his breakfast and thence to the office where he himself had handled the business as well as he could, only coming to Roger at night now and then with some matter he could not settle alone, but always stoutly declaring that he needed no other assistance.

"Don't come, Mr. Gale," he had urged. "You look worn out. You'll be sick yourself if you ain't careful. And anyhow, if you hang around you'll be here whenever she wants you."

Early in Deborah's illness, John had offered to give up his room for the use of one of the nurses.

"That's mighty thoughtful of you, Johnny," Allan had responded. "But we've got plenty of room as it is. Just you stick around. We want you here."

"All right, Doc. If there's any little thing, you know—answering the 'phone at night or anything else that I can do—"

"Thank you, son, I'll let you know. But in the meantime go to bed."

From that day on, John had taken not only his breakfast but his supper, too, outside, and no one had noticed his absence. Coming in late, he had hobbled silently up to his room, stopping to listen at Deborah's door. He had kept so completely out of the way, it was not till the baby was three weeks old, and past its second crisis, that Deborah thought to ask for John. When he came to her bed, she smiled up at him with the baby in her arms.

"I thought we'd see him together," she said. John stood on his crutches staring down. And as Deborah watched him, all at once her look grew intent. "Johnny," she said softly, "go over there, will you, and turn up the light, so we can see him better."

And when this was done, though she still talked smilingly of the child, again and again she glanced up at John's face, at the strange self-absorbed expression, stern and sad and wistful, there. When he had gone the tears came in her eyes. And Deborah sent for her husband.

The next day, at the office, John came into Roger's room. Roger had been at work several days and they had already cleared up their affairs.

"Here's something," said John gruffly, "that I wish you'd put away somewhere."

And he handed to his partner a small blue leather album, filled with the newspaper clippings dealing with Deborah's illness. On the front page was one with her picture and a long record of her service to the children of New York.

"She wouldn't want to see it now," John continued awkwardly. "But I thought maybe later on the boy would like to have it. What do you think?" he inquired. Roger gave him a kindly glance.

"I think he will. It's a fine thing to keep." And he handed it back. "But I guess you'd better put it away, and give it to her later yourself."

John shifted his weight on his crutches, so quickly that Roger looked up in alarm:

"Look here! You're not well!" He saw now that the face of the cripple was white and the sweat was glistening on his brow. John gave a harsh little nervous laugh.

"Oh, it's nothing much, partner," he replied. "That's another thing I wanted to tell you. I've had some queer pains lately—new ones!" He caught his breath.

"Why didn't you tell me, you young fool?"

"You had your own troubles, didn't you?" John spoke with difficulty. "But I'll be all right, I guess! All I need is a few days off!"

Roger had pressed a button, and his stenographer came in.

"Call a taxi," he said sharply. "And, John, you go right over there and lie down. I'm going to take you home at once!"

"I've got a better scheme," said John, setting his determined jaws. The sweat was pouring down his cheeks. "It may be a week—but there's just a chance it—may be a little worse than that! So I've got a room in a hospital! See? Be better all round!" He swayed forward.

"Johnny!" Roger caught him just in time, and the boy lay senseless in his arms.

At home, a few hours later, Allan came with another physician down from John's small bedroom. He saw his colleague to the door and then came in to Roger.

"I'm afraid Johnny has come to the end."

For a moment Roger stared at him.

"Has, eh," he answered huskily. "You're absolutely sure he has? There's nothing—nothing on earth we can do?"

"Nothing more than we're doing now."

"He has fooled you fellows before, you know—"

"Not this time."

"How long will it be?"

"Days or hours—I don't know."

"He mustn't suffer!"

"I'll see to that." Roger rose and walked the floor.

"It was the last month did it, of course—"

"Yes—"

"I blame myself for that."

"I wouldn't," said Allan gently. "You've done a good deal for Johnny Geer."

"He has done a good deal for this family! Can Deborah see him?"

"I wish she could."

"Better stretch a point for her, hadn't you? She's been a kind of a mother to John."

"I know. But she can't leave her bed."

"Then you won't tell her?"

"I think she knows. She talked to me about him last night."

"That's it, a mother!" Roger cried. "She was watching! We were blind!" He came back to his chair and dropped into it.

"Does John know this himself?" he asked.

"He suspects it, I think," said Allan.

"Then go and tell him, will you, that he's going to get well. And after you've done it I'll see him myself. I've got something in mind I want to think out."

After Allan had left the room, Roger sat thinking about John. He thought of John's birth and his drunken mother, the accident and his struggle for life, through babyhood and childhood, through ignorance and filth and pain, through din and clamor and hunger, fear; of the long fierce fight which John had made not to be "put away" in some big institution, of his battle to keep up his head, to be somebody, make a career for himself. He thought of John's becoming one of Deborah's big family, only one of thousands, but it seemed now to Roger that John had stood out from them all, as the figure best embodying that great fierce hunger for a full life, and as the link connecting, the one who slowly year by year had emerged from her greater family and come into her small one. And last of all he thought of John as his own companion, his only one, in the immense adventure on which he was so soon to embark.

A few moments later he stood by John's bed.

"Pretty hard, Johnny?" he gently asked.

"Oh, not so bad as it might be, I guess—"

"You'll soon feel better, they tell me, boy." John shut his eyes.

"Yes," he muttered.

"Can you stand my talking, just a minute?"

"Sure I can," John whispered. "I'm not suffering any now. He's given me something to put me to sleep. What is it you want to talk about? Business?"

"Not exactly, partner. It's about the family. You've got so you're almost one of us. I guess you know us pretty well."

"I guess I do, It's meant a lot to me, Mr. Gale—"

"But I'll tell you what you don't know, John," Roger went on slowly. "I had a son in the family once, and he died when he was three months old. That was a long time ago—and I never had another, you see—to take his place—till you came along." There fell a breathless silence. "And I've been thinking lately," Roger added steadily. "I haven't long to live, you know. And I've been wondering whether—you'd like to come into the family—take my name. Do you understand?"

John said nothing. His eyes were still closed. But presently, groping over the bed, he found Roger's hand and clutched it tight. After this, from time to time his throat contracted sharply. Tears welled from under his eyelids. Then gradually, as the merciful drug which Allan had given did its work, his clutch relaxed and he began breathing deep and hard. But still for some time longer Roger sat quietly by his side.

The next night he was there again. Death had come to the huddled form on the bed, but there had been no relaxing. With the head thrown rigidly far back and all the features tense and hard, it was a fighting figure still, a figure of stern protest against the world's injustice. But Roger was not thinking of this, but of the discovery he had made, that in their talk of the night before John had understood him—completely. For upon a piece of paper which Allan had given the lad that day, these words had been painfully inscribed:

"This is my last will and testament. I am in my right mind—I know what I am doing—though nobody else does—nobody is here. To my partner Roger Gale I leave my share in our business. And to my teacher Deborah Baird I leave my crutches for her school."

CHAPTER XLIII

AFTER John had gone away the house was very quiet. Only from the room upstairs there could be heard occasionally the faint clear cry of Deborah's child. And once again to Roger came a season of repose. He was far from unhappy. His disease, although progressing fast, gave him barely any pain; it rather made its presence felt by the manner in which it affected his mind. His inner life grew uneven. At times his thoughts were as in a fog, again they were amazingly clear and vistas opened far ahead. He could not control his thinking.

This bothered him at the office, in the work he still had to do. For some months he had been considering an offer from one of his rivals, a modern concern which wished to buy out his business together with that of three other firms and consolidate them all into one corporation. And Roger was selling, and it was hard; for the whole idea of bargaining was more distasteful than ever now. He had to keep reminding himself of Edith and her children.

At last it was over, his books were closed, and there was nothing left to be done. Nor did he care to linger. These rooms had meant but little to him; they had been but a place of transition from the old office far downtown, so full of memories of his youth, to the big corporation looming ahead, the huge impersonal clipping mill into which his business was to merge. And it came to his mind that New York was like that—no settled calm abiding place cherishing its memories, but only a town of transition, a great turbulent city of change, restlessly shaking off its past, tearing down and building anew, building higher, higher, higher, rearing to the very stars, and shouting,

310

"Can you see me now?" What was the goal of this mad career? What dazzling city would be here? For a time he stared out of his window as into a promised land. Slowly at last he rose from his desk. Clippings, clippings, clippings. He looked at those long rows of girls gleaning in items large and small the public reputations of all kinds of men and women, new kinds in a new nation seething with activities, sweeping on like some wide river swollen at flood season to a new America, a world which Roger would not know. And yet it would be his world still, for in it he would play a part.

"In their lives, too, we shall be there—the dim strong figures of the past."

From his desk he gathered a few belongings. Then he looked into John's small room, with the big gold motto over the desk: "This is no place for your troubles or mine." On the desk lay that small album, John's parting gift to Deborah's boy. Roger picked it up and walked out of the office. He had never liked good-byes.

In the elevator he noticed that his shoes needed shining, and when he reached the street below he stopped at the stand on the corner. The stocky Greek with bushy black hair, who had run the stand for many years, gave him a cheery greeting; for Roger had stopped there frequently —not that he cared about his shoes, but he had always liked to watch the crowds of people passing.

"No hurry, boss?"

"None," said Roger.

"Then I give a fine shine! Polish, too?"

"Yes, polish, too." And Roger settled back to watch. "And put in new shoe strings," he added, with a whimsical smile.

Men and women, girls and boys by thousands passed him, pushing, hurrying, shuffling by. Girls tittering and nudging and darting quick side glances. Bobbing heads and figures, vigorous steps and dancing eyes. **Life**

bubbling over everywhere, in laughter, in sharp angry
tones, in glad expectant chatter. Deborah's big family.
Across the street was a movie between two lurid posters,
and there was a dance hall overhead. The windows were
all open, and faintly above the roar of the street he could
hear the piano, drum, fiddle and horn. The thoroughfare
each moment grew more tumultuous to his ears, with
trolley cars and taxis, motor busses, trucks and drays. A
small red motor dashed uptown with piles of evening
papers; a great black motor hearse rushed by. In a taxi
which had stopped in a jam, a man was kissing a girl in his
arms, and both of them were laughing. The smart little
toque of blue satin she wore was crushed to one side.
How red were her lips as she threw back her head. . . .

"Silk or cotton, boss? Which you like?" Roger glanced
at the shoe strings and pondered.

"Silk," he grunted in reply. Idly for a moment he
watched this busy little man. From whence had he come
in far away Greece? What existence had he here, and
what kind of life would he still have through those many
years to come? A feeling half of sadness crept into
Roger's heavy eyes as he looked at the man, at his smiling
face and then at other faces in the multitudes sweeping
past. The moment he tried to single them out, how
doubly chaotic it became. What an ocean of warm
desires, passions, vivid hopes and worries. Vaguely he
could feel them pass. Often in the midst of his life, his
active and self-centered life, Roger had looked at these
crowds on the street and had thought these faces commonplace. But now at the end it was not so.

A woman with a baby carriage stopped directly in front
of him and stood there anxiously watching for a chance
to cross the street. And Roger thought of Deborah.
Heavily he climbed down from his seat, paid the man and
bade him good-night, and went home to see Deborah's
baby.

For a long time he sat by the cradle. Presently Deborah joined him, and soon they were laughing heartily at the astonishing jerks and kicks and grimaces of the tiny boy. He was having his bath and he hated it. But safe at last on his mother's lap, wrapped to his ears in a big soft towel, he grew very gay and contented and looked waggishly about.

There followed long lazy days of spring, as April drifted into May. Early in the morning Roger could hear through his window the cries of the vendors of flowers and fruits. And he listened drowsily. He rose late and spent most of the day in the house; but occasionally he went out for a stroll. And one balmy evening when groups of youths came trooping by, singing in close harmony, Roger called a taxi and went far down through the tenement streets to a favorite haunt of his, a little Syrian pawnshop, where after long delving he purchased a ring to put in the new collection that he had been making lately. He had nearly a dozen now.

Days passed. The house was still so quiet, Deborah was still upstairs. At last, one night upon leaving his study, he stopped uncertainly in the hall. He took more time than was his wont in closing up the house for the night, in trying all the windows, in turning out the various lights. Room after room he left in the dark. Then he went slowly up the stairs, his hand gratefully feeling those guiding points grown so familiar to his touch through many thousand evenings. His hand lingered on the banister and he stopped again to listen there.

He did not come downstairs again.

He was able to sleep but little at night. Turning restlessly on his bed, he would glance out of the window up at the beetling wall close by, tier on tier of apartments from which faint voices dropped out of the dark. Gradually as the night wore on, these voices would all die away into long mysterious silences—for to him at least such silences had grown to be very mysterious. Alone in the hours that followed, even these modern neighbors and this strange new eager town pressing down upon his house seemed no longer strange to him nor so appallingly immense, seemed even familiar and small to him, as the eyes of his mind looked out ahead.

From his bed he could see on the opposite wall the picture Judith had given him, always so fresh and cool and dim with its deep restful tones of blue, of the herdsmen and the cattle on the dark mountain rim at dawn. And vaguely he wondered whether it was because he saw more clearly, or whether his mind in this curious haze could no longer see so well, that as he looked before him he felt no fear nor any more uncertainty. All his doubts had lifted, he was so sure of Judith now. As though she were coming to meet him, her image grew more vivid, with memories emerging out of all the years gone by. What memories, what vivid scenes! What intimate conversations they had, her voice so natural, close in his ear, as together they planned for their children. . . . Wistfully he would search the years for what he should soon tell his wife—until the drowsiness returned, and then again came visions.

But by day it was not so, for the life of the house would rouse him and at intervals hold his attention.

One evening a slight rustle, a faint fragrance in the room, made Roger suddenly open his eyes. And he saw Laura by his bed, her slender figure clad in blue silk, something white at her full bosom. He noticed her shapely shoulders, her glossy hair and moist red lips. She was smiling down at him.

"See what I've brought you, dear," she said. And she turned to a chair where, one on the other, tray after tray, was piled his whole collection of rings. At sight of them his eyes grew fixed; he could feel his pulse beat faster.

"How did you ever find them?" he asked his daughter huskily.

"Oh, I had a long hunt all by myself. But I found them at last and I've brought them home. Shall we look them over a little while?"

"Yes," he said. She turned up the light, and came and sat down at the bedside with a tray of rings in her lap. One by one she held them up to his gaze, still smiling and talking softly on in that rich melodious voice of hers, of which he heard but snatches. How good it felt to be so gay. No solemn thoughts nor questionings, just these dusky glittering beauties here, deep soft gleams of color, each with its suggestion of memories for Roger, a procession of adventures reaching back into his life. He smiled and lay in silence watching, until at last she bent over him, kissed him softly, breathed a good-night and went out of the room. Roger followed her with his glance. He knew he would never see her again. How graceful of her to go like that.

He lay there thinking about her. In her large blue limousine he saw his gay young daughter speeding up the Avenue, the purple gleaming pavement reflecting studded lines of lights. And he thought he could see her smiling still. He recalled scattered fragments of her life—the first luxurious little ménage, and the second. How many more would there be? She was only in her twenties still. Uneasily he tried to see into the years ahead for her, and he thought he saw a lonely old age, childless, loveless, cynical, hard. But this fear soon fell from his mind. No, whatever happened, she would do it gracefully, an artist always, to the end. He sighed and gave up the effort. For he could not think of Laura as old, nor could he think of her any more as being a part of his family.

Edith came to him several times, and there was something in her face which gave him sharp forebodings. Making a great effort he tried to talk to her clearly.

"It's hard to keep up with your children," he said. "It means keeping up with everything new. And you stay in your rut and then it's too late. Before you know it you are old."

But his words subsided in mutterings, and Roger wearily closed his eyes. For a glance up into Edith's face had shown him only pity there and no heed to his warning. He saw that she looked upon him as old and still upon herself as young, though he noticed the threads of gray in her hair. . . . Then he realized she had gone and that his chamber had grown dark. He must have been dreaming. Of what, he asked. He tried to remember. And suddenly out of the darkness, so harsh and clear it startled him, a picture rose in Roger's mind of a stark lonely figure, a woman in a graveyard cutting the grass on family graves. Where had he seen it? He could not recall. What had it to do with Edith? Was she not living in New York? . . . What had so startled him just now? Some thought, some vivid picture, some nightmare he could not recall.

His last talks were with Deborah. All through those days and the long nights, too, he kept fancying she was in the room, and it brought deep balm to his restless soul. He asked her to tell him about the schools, and Deborah talked to him quietly. She was going back to her work in the fall. She felt very humble about it— she told him she felt older now and she saw that her work was barely begun. But she was even happier than before. Her hand lay in his, and it tightened there. He opened his eyes and looked up into hers.

"All so strange," he muttered, "life." There was a sharp contracting of her wide and sensitive mouth.

"Yes, dearie, strange!" she whispered.

"But I'm so glad you're going on." He frowned as he tried to be simple and clear, and make her feel he understood what she had set herself to do. "All people," he said slowly, "never counted so much as now. And never so hungry—all—as now—for all of life—like children—children who should go to school. Your work will grow—I can see ahead. Never a time when every man and woman and child could grow so much—and hand it on—and hand it on—as you will do to your small son."

He felt her hand on his forehead, and for some moments nothing was said. Vaguely in glimpses Roger saw his small grandson growing up; and he pictured other children here, not her own but of her greater family, as the two merged into one. He felt that she would not grow old. Children, lives of children; work, dreams and aspirations. How bright it seemed as he stared ahead. Then he heard the cry of her baby.

"Shall I nurse him here?" he heard her ask. He pressed her hand in answer. And when again he opened his eyes she was by his side with the child at her breast. Its large round eyes, so pure and clear, gazed into his own for a long, long time.

"Now he's so sleepy," she whispered. "Would you like him beside you a moment?"

"Please."

He felt the faint scent of the tiny boy, and still those eyes looked into his. He forgot his daughter standing there; and as he watched, a sweet fresh sense of the mystery of this life so new stole deep into his spirit. All at once the baby fell asleep.

"Good-night, little brother," he whispered. "God grant the world be very kind." He could feel the mother lift it up, and he heard the door close softly.

Smiling he, too, fell asleep. And after that there were only dreams.

CHAPTER XLIV

AND his dreams were of children. Their faces passed before him. Now they were young again in the house. They were eating their suppers, three small girls, chattering like magpies. From her end of the table their mother smiled quietly across at him. "Come children," she was saying, "that will do for a little while." But Roger said, "Oh, let them talk." . . . Then he saw new-comers. Bruce came in with Edith, and George and young Elizabeth, and Allan came with Deborah who had a baby in her arms, and Laura stood beside them. Here were his three daughters, grown, but still in some uncanny way they looked to him like children still; and behind them he detected figures long forgotten, of boys and girls whom he had known far back in his own childhood. John, too, had come into the house. Strangely now the walls were gone, had lifted, and a clamorous throng, laughing, shouting, pummeling, hedged him in on every hand—Deborah's big family!

Soon the uproar wearied him, and Roger tried to shut them out, to bring back again the walls to his house. And sometimes he succeeded, and he was left for a while in peace with Judith and his three small girls. But despite his efforts to keep them there, new faces kept intruding. Swiftly his small family grew, split into other families, and these were merged with other figures pressing in from every side. Again he felt the presence of countless families all around, dividing, reuniting, with ceaseless changes and fresh life—a never ending multitude. Here they were singing and dancing, and Laura gaily waved to him. At another place were only men, and they were struggling savagely to clutch things from each other's hands. A sea of scowling visages, angry shouts, fists clinched in air. And he thought he saw Bruce for an instant. Behind them lay wide valleys obscured by heavy clouds of smoke, and he could hear the roar of guns. But they vanished suddenly, and he saw women mourning now, and Edith with her children turned to him her anxious eyes. He tried to reach and help her, but already she had gone. And behind her came huge bending forms, men heaving at great burdens, jaws set in scowls of fierce revolt. And John was there on his crutches, and near him was a figure bound into a chair of steel, with terror in the straining limbs, while in desperation Deborah tried to wrench him free. Abruptly Roger turned away.

And in a twinkling all was gone, the tumult and the clamor, and he was in a silent place high up on a mountain side. It was dusk. A herd of cattle passed, and George came close behind them. And around him Roger saw, emerging from the semi-dark, faces turning like his own to the summits of the mountains and the billowy splendors there. It grew so dark he could see no more. There fell a deep silence, not a sound but the occasional chirp of a bird or the faint whirr of an insect. Even the glow on the peaks was gone. Darkness, only darkness.

"Surely this is death," he thought. After that he was alone. And presently from far away he heard the booming of a bell, deep and slow, sepulchral, as it measured off his life. Another silence followed, and this time it was more profound; and with a breathless awe he knew that all the people who had ever lived on earth were before him in the void to which he himself was drifting: people of all nations, of countless generations reaching back and back and back to the beginnings of mankind: the mightiest family of all, that had stumbled up through the ages, had slaved and starved and dreamed and died, had blindly hated, blindly killed, had raised up gods and idols and yearned for everlasting life, had laughed and played and danced along, had loved and mated, given birth, had endlessly renewed itself and handed on its heritage, had striven hungrily to learn, had groped its way in darkness, and after all its struggles had come now barely to the dawn. And then a voice within him cried,

"What is humanity but a child? In the name of the dead I salute the unborn!"

Slowly a glow appeared in his dream, and once again the scene had changed. The light was coming from long rows of houses rising tall and steep out of a teeming city street. And from these lighted houses children now came pouring forth. They filled the street from wall to wall with a torrent of warm vivid hues, they joined in mad tempestuous games, they shouted and they danced with glee, they whirled each other 'round and 'round. The very air seemed quivering. Then was heard the crash of a band, and he saw them marching into school. In and in and in they pressed, till the school seemed fairly bursting. Out they came by another way, and went off marching down the street with the big flag waving at their head. He followed and saw the street divide into narrower streets and bye-ways, into roads and country lanes. And all were filled with children. In endless multitudes they came—marching, marching, spreading, spreading, like wide bobbing fields of flowers rolling out across the land, toward a great round flashing sun above a distant rim of hills.

The sun rose strangely dazzling. It filled the heavens with blinding light. He felt himself drawn up and up—while from somewhere far behind he heard the cry of Deborah's child. A clear sweet thrill of happiness came. And after that—we do not know.

For he had left his family.

Printed in the United States of America

THE following pages contain advertisements of books by the same author and new fiction.

The Harbor

New Edition, $1.50

"This first book of his is by all odds the best American novel that has appeared in many a long day. It is earnest, sincere, broad in scope and purpose, well balanced, combining intellect and emotion . . . the characters are ably drawn, strikingly contrasted, essentially American. . . . Mr. Poole may be congratulated upon having written an absorbingly interesting and very significant novel."— *New York Times.*

"A novel of unrest, . . . a dramatization of labor under present conditions. The story of a strike is told with graphic power, and the treatment of the men and women who share the tidal movement of antagonism has a kind of epical breadth and energy. . . . THE HARBOR will awaken protest, cause irritation, and will be regarded as an essentially revolutionary story; but its underlying motive is constructive."—*Outlook.*

"A fine, new American story, in the spirit of the hour. . . . A work which must be placed at once among the rare books that count. . . . The New York it presents is no limited city, but a vast world centre of ideas, ideals, hopes, passions, and struggles."—*New York World.*

"THE HARBOR is the first really notable novel produced by the New Democracy."—*New York Tribune.*

THE MACMILLAN COMPANY

Publishers   64–66 Fifth Avenue   New York

Changing Winds

BY ST. JOHN G. ERVINE

$1.60

Wells has pictured the tragedy of war as it falls upon people looking as it were the other way. Mr. Ervine in this novel "Changing Winds," shows the same tragic force falling upon four young men as sparkling and vehemently alive as ever were, looking directly and intently at life in all its aspects; and accepting war (all but one of them) almost blithely when it comes. The title is from the famous sonnet, The Dead, by Rupert Brooke, to whose memory the book is dedicated, by whose spirit it is filled. And, to use the words of the sonnet, these four lives are pictured as "blown by changing winds to laughter" winds of all sorts of interest, the Irish situation (which is frankly and freshly treated), industrialism, society—"lit by the rich skies all day." Split, so blown that when the frost of war does settle upon them there is left for all the pathos (is it by reason of art or the truth of life?) "a white unbroken glory," "a shifting peace under the night." The book is the longest and most ambitious Mr. Ervine has yet written; it will rank high among the very best novels written about the war.

THE MACMILLAN COMPANY

Publishers   64–66 Fifth Avenue   New York

Jerry

BY JACK LONDON

There cannot be many more new Jack London books, a fact which will not only be a source of deep regret to the lover of truly American literature, but which also gives a very deep significance to the announcement of Jerry. It is not at all improbable that in this novel Mr. London has achieved again the wide-sweeping success that was his in the case of "The Call of the Wild." For Jerry is a dog story; a story which in its big essentials recalls the earlier masterpiece, and yet one which is in no way an echo of that work, but quite as original in its theme and quite as satisfying in the way in which that theme is treated.

Louisburg Square

BY ROBERT CUTLER

In Louisburg Square Mr. Robert Cutler gives a general picture of contemporary Boston—intimate, kindly, shrewd —through which plays the theme of a romance as delightful as it is natural and credible. Louisburg Square with its moribund aristocrat, is as real as the very real (that is, occasionally perverse) heroine who pauses so long at the door of dramatic self-sacrifice as to allow for a genuine gasp of satisfaction when she finds it closed to her and the door opening to "happiness ever-after."

THE MACMILLAN COMPANY

Publishers 64–66 Fifth Avenue New York

Regiment of Women

BY CLEMENCE DANE

$1.50

This is a story of a clash of wills. How Alwynne Durrand, a sweet-natured, optimistic young girl, comes under the sway of Clare Hartill, clever, attractive, unprincipled, wholly selfish, and how in the end the spell is broken by a man,—this is the author's theme and as she handles it, it is a tremendous theme. Seldom has there been so outstanding a character in fiction as is Miss Hartill. She dominates the entire story, and though the reader cannot like her, nevertheless he will be fascinated by her, much as Alwynne is. And in addition to Miss Hartill there are other clearly drawn people in the book; Alwynne, who is all that a heroine should be; Roger, who saves Alwynne from the unhappiness towards which she seems to be moving, and Elsbeth, Alwynne's aunt, who more than once crosses swords with Clare. The tale is full of incident and variety and cannot but be welcomed by the reader who appreciates a story in which real people move and act.

Lost Endeavour

$1.50

Another of John Masefield's earlier works is now reprinted. "Lost Endeavour" is a stirring story of adventure, dealing with pirates and buccaneers, and life on the seas in a day when an ocean trip was beset with all kinds of dangers and excitements. Those who have enjoyed "Captain Margaret" and "Multitude and Solitude" will find this tale equally exhilarating.

THE MACMILLAN COMPANY

Publishers   64–66 Fifth Avenue   New York

A Soldier of Life

BY HUGH DE SELINCOURT

$1.50

An altogether unusual piece of work is this story of a man who returns from the war crippled, and who must readjust himself with life. The strength of the story lies in its character drawing and in its vivid presentation of war, particularly its after effects. The hero, James Wood, is portrayed with astonishing reality; the reader sees his vain endeavors to get hold of himself, to keep in line his overwrought nerves and the hallucinations which they induce. The effect of Wood's somewhat unbalanced state of mind upon his love affairs, his gradual restoration to health and the problem which this creates in the various human relationships involved complete a novel valuable not only from the psychological standpoint, but one in which the " story interest " itself never lags.

Benoit Castain

BY MARCEL PREVOST

This story deals with an episode that took place in a little corner of northern France just after the outbreak of the war. It is as well written as the author's reputation would lead one to expect and has been splendidly rendered into English. The theme is handled in a direct and simple way and shows special knowledge of the section of the country where it is laid. It is altogether a most interesting human document in novel form.

THE MACMILLAN COMPANY

Publishers   64–66 Fifth Avenue   New York

Gold Must be Tried by Fire

BY RICHARD AUMERLE MAHER

There are a great many people who regard Mr. Maher's "The Shepherd of the North" as one of the finest stories published last year, a fact which taken in connection with the praise which critics bestowed upon the author for that book makes the announcement of a new story by the same author of distinct importance. "Gold Must be Tried by Fire" is a vivid and powerful piece of writing, with a central character quite as satisfactory as was the Bishop of the first tale. This character, Daidie Grattan, is a mill hand, who revolts at the monotonous drudgery of her existence. Something closely akin to tragedy touches her and she acquires a new vision. Fortified with this she sets out to alleviate the industrial injustices with which she is familiar from her own personal experience, aiming in the end to uplift and encourage her people. The love story which is woven into this is one of engaging proportions and the happy solution of the problem which has kept the lovers apart brings the volume to a satisfactory close.

THE MACMILLAN COMPANY

Publishers   64–66 Fifth Avenue   New York